Visual Basic

Developer's Toolkit

Visual Basic

Developer's Toolkit

2nd Edition

John Robert Onda

Eric Engelmann

ADVICE Press
366 Cambridge Avenue
Palo Alto, CA 94306

Visual Basic Developer's Toolkit
by John Robert Onda & Eric Engelmann

Copyright © 1997 ADVICE Press. All Rights reserved.
Printed in the United States of America.

Published by ADVICE Press, 366 Cambridge Avenue, Palo Alto, CA 94306.

Editor David Fickes

Printing History:

November 1996	CD-ROM Edition (1st edition) 1-889871-00-2	
July 1997:	Book Edition (2nd edition) 1-889671-02-9	
	CD-ROM edition (2nd edition) 1-889671-01-0	
	significant updates	

This book is printed on acid-free paper with 85% recycled content, 15% post-consumer waste. ADVICE Press is committed to using and selecting paper, printers and other suppliers in a fashion consistent with a sustainable environment.

ISBN: 1-889671-02-9   [8/97]

TABLE OF CONTENTS

INTRODUCTION

This book and software collection is designed to deliver the largest possible single group of code, pre-built systems and information on building applications using the Microsoft Visual Basic language.

The book and companion CD-ROM provides the latest "web enabled" HTML file listings, an advanced Windows based search engine, and even a traditional DOS search engine to help you locate specific tools from among the over 1998 packages on the CD-ROM.

Visual Basic and Community Building

What has Visual Basic and this toolkit have to do with a community? All of the materials provided on this CD-ROM have been created by programmers who have specifically decided to share their work with other programmers. ADVICE Press plays a small role in collecting and documenting these materials. The idea is to simply try to eliminate constant programming repetition of the same features and instead sharing our work so people can spend their time on developing new materials.

We encourage both individuals and companies to consider the code that they create as potentially useful to other programmers. There are many ways of making this material usable by others. The packages on the CD-ROM cover almost the entire gamut of these possibilities. If you are considering releasing Visual Basic code or related information, please feel free to contact us as we are happy to help.

Freeware, Shareware and Other Licensing

It seems that everyone understands the various terms associated with freeware, shareware and the many variants. The large majority of the packages we've included are freeware which means you are able to use the code without restriction on the assumption that you will provide this code as it was originally given to anyone who requests.

Shareware authors generally insist that you send them some nominal amount of money if you are going to keep using their code.

Terms for each package are included in the zip file and should be examined. We've classed each of the products and these designations appear in all of the indices. To assist in this task we have listed all of the authors of the packages in this book and in the index. We no longer have valid contact information for a small number of these individuals. In addition, a few have asked that we not publish their contact information.

Registration of the Product

We would appreciate you taking a few moments to register yourself as a user of this product. There is a form available on the CD-ROM as well as a form on our website: *www.advice.com*

If you just want to send us email, please send us the product name and your name along with any other information you're willing to let us know to *register@advice.com* For the curious, we don't rent out our mailing list.

Using This Product

There are three basic methods to find a specific set of code or information. In general we refer to all of the materials packed on the CD-ROM as packages and they are packaged in a ZIP format for convenience.

These methods include looking up code in this printed book, using the HTML trees provided, using a Windows or DOS based browser.

Organization

All of the packages are grouped into categories and correspond to chapters. Please note that **the categories are not perfect** and many times you will discover a package that can be used for your particular purpose even if it isn't in the most obvious place. For example, the "Business" packages in the first section can also be used as example code to be modified for very different purposes.

Another example are the many text facilities. These can be found in the text area as well as the many programming and DLL sections. There are in fact several different approaches to handling text for spell checking which we have put in the Spellcheck section but there are other facilities in the Program Utility area which focus on spell checking of Visual Basic code itself. In addition, the Help section has entries that describe how to access API spell check functions.

In addition, there are quite a few packages that actually are toolsets within themselves that cross over many of our categories. Unfortunately, it is almost impossible to envision all of the uses of a particular code set. Our best suggestion is to start working with some of the packages that seem most appropriate to your application and then continue to examine others on a regular basis.

The Printed Entries

A printed entry follows the form:

Package Name — Description of the package is here and usually goes on for at least a line or two.

      FILENAME   filesize   Cost   *Package Author / Company*

The listing in the book correspond to the HTML and Search Engine listings. There are a small number of changes from the CD-ROM organization. The two most notable are that the CD-ROM categories of Games and Entertainment have been merged. In addition, there are two different Sound areas on the CD-ROM one for DLLs and the other for other applications. To save space in the book these all appear in the Sound chapter.

HTML Access to Packages

A web enabled set of listings for the CD-ROM is in the \HTML directory, but may be started by loading the \README.HTM file in the root directory. Pages were designed for Netscape 2.0 or later, but should work well with any modern web browser. The actual tools, in ZIP format, are in the \VBASIC directory and its subdirectories, sorted alphabetically by ZIP file name. If you don't have an UNZIP program already, you can use the UNZIP.EXE in the CD-ROM's root directory.

The materials on the CD-ROM in HTML format correspond to this book edition but may be easier to use in some respects. Notably, all of the links to authors are accessible from each package name and you can email them directly from this listing.

Also, most browsers including Netscape will prompt you for a save location whenever you double-click on any of the package filenames.

Windows Search Engine

The Windows search engine is named VBASIC.EXE and can be found in the \EXE directory. Most parts of this program will run directly from the CD-ROM, but will run even better if you move the files in the \EXE directory to your local hard disk drive.

If, for some reason, you prefer a DOS based program, VBASICD.EXE is also available in the \EXE directory. Some parts of this program require the ability to write to the current drive, so we recommend copying the \EXE directory to your hard disk to use it. You must also make the directory of VBASICD.EXE your current directory before executing it. Note also that the DOS program assumes a different file structure than this CD-ROM, and some advanced features will not work.

The Windows and DOS search engines are copyrighted by Eric Engelmann, of EMS Professional Shareware, and Steffan Surdek.

Errors & Omissions

We've tried to do a respectable job of getting all of this code together and indexing and documenting it accurately. However, we are mortal and have undoubtedly made some errors in this process. If you find something that is an error or is something that you simply don't understand, please contact us and let us know. We will fix it in the next release and inform others as well. Contact for this sort of information is: *bugs@advice.com* or call us. Please try to detail the problem and mention which product you are using.

Legalities

Like most publishers, this software is provided "as is" and without any express or implied warranties, including without limitation, the implied warranties of merchantability and fitness for a particular purpose.

Trademarks published herein are the property of the respective trademark holders. When you examine many of the packages, you will discover specific instructions on copyright notices and other conditions of use. We have attempted to comply with these; go thou and do likewise. Portions of this distribution are Copyright © 1996-1997; ADVICE Press, Palo Alto, CA.

Now that we've handled the lawyers, we will note the following few items. Portions of this distribution are copyright ADVICE Press. However, we make **no claims whatsoever,** either singly or collectively regarding the packages themselves. Our single restriction on the use of those portions of the product produced by ADVICE are simple, don't use them to create a competitive product. For the packages, you should consider yourself bound by the conditions of the authors.

Submissions

We encourage programmers to make their efforts available to others to reduce the vast amount of "reinvention" in the industry and for instructional purposes. If you wish to include a package on our next CD-ROM or wish to suggest materials to be included, please contact us.

Individuals or groups interested in creating, editing a new collections are also encouraged to contact us.

Updates

This collection is continuously updated and published on a regular basis. Updates and a subscription plan are available from the publisher. We would also encourage you to contact your local bookstore or software outlet and ask them to notify you of new editions. If you care to register the product, we'll be happy to let you know as well.

Contacting ADVICE Press

For information on this CD-ROM and other products from ADVICE Press:

ADVICE Press
366 Cambridge Avenue
Palo Alto, CA 94306

Voice: +1(650)321-2197
Fax: +1(650)321-2199

info@advice.com
http://www.advice.com

1

BUSINESS

Auto Maintenance — A quick way to keep track of auto maintenance. Includes a "Next Service Due" option based on a user entered service interval. Also includes a "Remind" program for DOS which checks the status of the datafile kept by the Windows program.

AUTOV10   51 *K* $1.00SW   *Schoeffel, Dave*

Journal Program — Daily information manager. Information can be copied from the Clipboard or imported from disk files.

JNAL10   151 *K* $25 SW   *Smith, Gordon*

Peer Evaluation System — Questionnaire for employees to evaluate fellow workers in several personality areas. Choices are made from pick lists. (This is one of the earliest Visual Basic programs. Author Steve Gibson wrote about this program in Infoworld before VB was released.)

PES   22 *K*   *Gibson, Steve*

Time And Billing For Windows — Time usage tracker and billing program for professionals. Good layout and design.

TIMEB2   91 *K* $65 SW   *Leaning Birch Computer Cons.*

VB Project Manager — VB 4.0 Add-In that allows viewing program statistics and printing source code from VB. Shows an expandable tree listing all the code files in the project and the functions, subroutines, and properties in each file.

VBPROJ   538 *K* $25   *Galaxy Software*

2
BUTTONS

3-D How To — Source code for VB 2.0 shows how to draw 3-D button controls with no add-on tools.

    3DHOWTO   *4 K*   Free   *Wisecarver, Mike*

3D-Spin-Demo 1.0 — Application demonstrating a 3D spinbutton. Uses no third party VBX or DLL. Avoid using the 22K spin.vbx that comes with VB. Requires only a few lines of VB code. Easily customized.

    SPINDEMO   *4 K*   SW   *Behling, Jutta*

Animated Xerox Copy Button — CCB file for the animated buttons control. The button is an animated Xerox type copier which moves a green light back and forth when pressed.

    ANICPY   *2 K*   Free

Another Button Bar — Simple "button bar" program launcher. Takes a Windows program group and turns it into a grid of icon buttons that resides on the Windows desktop. Full VB source code included.

    TKBAR   *69 K*   Free   *Koffley, Tim*

BtnTools 3.0 — Two VB 3.0/4.0 controls to create a toolbar and an alternative to the standard command button.

    BTNTOOLS   *27 K*   15PST SW   *Activ Software*

Butt(N)Meister — Creates and maintains efficient rectangular (vertical or horizontal) Button Bars and Floating Tool Palettes for VB applications. Requires no VBX. Replaces the PICCLIP control and compiles all buttons to a single bitmap.

    BUTNMSTR   *1081 K* $35   *Perkins, Brad*

Button Custom Control — Simplifies button control programming and adds additional button styles and features.

    SCENTBNS   *135 K* $15SW   *SRC Enterprises*

Button Picture 1.75 — Allows you to incorporate picture buttons, with optional text, into VB projects. Separate UP and DOWN pictures, or a single picture will be shifted and shaded when depressed. Can be used in designing toolbars. Supports ICO and BMP buttons. Demo source.

    BTTNPI   233 *K* $10 SW   *Digital PowerTOOLS*

Buttonmaker VB — Utility generates buttons for use in toolbars. Just load an icon into Buttonmaker and press the <Make> button to generate two BMP files, one "up" and one "down". VB samples and source code included.

    BM12   37 *K* $12   *Naumann, Christian*

Buttons By Freel — Buttons for use with ToolButton (TOOLBT).

    BUTNUP   27 *K*   Free   *Freel, Fred*

Cancel Button For Long Process — VB project demonstrates how to provide the user with a CANCEL button option on a long running process. The modeless cancel dialog uses SetWindowWord API to create a child form that remains above the parent but is automatically minimized if the parent is.

    CANDEM   3 *K*   Free

Easy ToolTips — Source code shows how to implement "ToolTips" help in pure Visual Basic code.

    EZTIPS   6 *K*   Free   *Clark, Paul*

Edit Button For Database — How to implement read-only controls, both bound and unbound. Editing of data fields is allowed only when the user clicks on an Edit button. Full documentation and source code.

    EDITBT   18 *K*   Free   *Riley, Barth*

Multipic — An example of how to apply pictures to buttons without having to load from disk during runtime. Gives a nice 3-D effect. Includes source, BMPs, ICOs, and docs.

    MULTIPIC   8 *K*   Free   *Gamber, Mark*

Multiple Selection File List — Multiple selection file list control button. C source included.

    FILELI   77 *K*   Free   *Guardalben, Giovanni*

My Spin — Demo of a Spin button written in VB. Source code is included, encrypted before registration.

    YMYSPIN   14 *K* $13   *Trova, Marco*

Resize And Move Controls — Full source code demonstrates how to resize and move controls. Uses Multiple Document Interface.
    SLYDED   9 K   Free

Richter's Spin Button (CK) — Spin Button control in VB source code. Adapted from the book "Windows 3: A Developer's Guide" by Jeffrey Richter.
    SPINCK   5 K   Free   *Kitsos, Costas*

SuperSpin — Enhanced Spin button in pure VB source code. Adds/subtracts values automatically in a linked control, supports numbers, date and time values and custom value-lists, get minimum and maximum values with one click of the mouse.
    SPRSPIN   51 K   Free   *Slagman, Herman*

VBSpin DEMO — Simple demo of how to create a spin button without the use of a VBX. Source code with registration.
    VBSPIN   5 K $5   *Abujain, Tony*

3
CALCULATOR

Access Jet Expression Evaluato — Small VB project shows how to use the Access JET engine as an expression evaluator by passing the expression as an SQL select statement. Can call internal Access functions such as log(), cos(), and abs() and string functions.

   ACCEVL   16 *K* Free

Algebraic Expression Eval. VB4 — Algebraic expression evaluator written in Visual Basic 4.0 with full source code. (Will not work in previous VB versions.) From Jonathan Wood's Programming Techniques column in the 12/1995 issue of Visual Basic Programmer's Journal.

   EVAL   7 *K* Free   *SoftCircuits Programming*

Average — Simple program finds the average of a list of numbers. Source code included in a text file.

   AVERAGE   3 *K* Free   *Woolfe, Jeremy*

Calculator — Graphical improvement on the sample CALC application included with Visual Basic. Full source code included.

   CALC   9 *K* Free

Calculator - Bercik — The Visual Basic 3.0 Calculator with modified graphics. Source code included.

   CALCBERC   34 *K* Free   *Bercik, Bill*

Calculator In 3D — Calculator with 3-D effects. Allows for keystroke entry as well as mouse-push-button. A demonstration of SetFocus, SendKeys, and using indexing with push buttons. Full source code.

   CALC3D   8 *K* Free   *Main, Mark*

Credit Card Check — Source code and full example program (without source) for a credit card number checking program.

   CCCHECK   7 *K* Free   *Sparks, Ron*

Factorial! — Factorial calculation.

    FACTOR   4 K   *Williams, Charles*

GSScalc — Full featured calculator custom control useful for forms requiring numeric calculations and input. Supports drag and drop operations for placing totals in text boxes in your forms. Source code available.

    GSSCALC   16 K $10+   *Guttilia, Brad*

Italian Codice Fiscale Calcula — VB source code to find the check-code for Italian Codice Fiscale and Partitia IVA.

    CODICI   6 K Free   *Sorrentino, Silvio*

NCALC Keyboard Handling — Modification of the CALC sample that comes with Visual Basic. Keyboard entry is activated, and the screen keys depress as if they were mouse-clicked.

    NCALC   7 K Free   *Smaby, Marcus*

Parser - Evaluate Formulas — Source code allows entering formulas, which are evaluated. As many functions and variables as needed.

    PARSER   26 K Free   *Tricaud, Christophe*

RPN Calculator — Reverse Polish Notation Calculator. Full source code.

    RPNCAL   17 K PD

Round Function — Converts multiplace decimal numbers rounded to a certain number of decimal places.

    ROUND   1 K Free   *Grabe, Marcus O. M.*

Set Operations — Source code to illustrate the following set operations: Union (A or B), Intersection (A and B), Difference (A and not B). The operations are performed on long integer arrays.

    SETOPS   4 K Free   *Pastel Programming*

Suite Of Calculators Demo — Calculator including listbox memory, trace functions, scientific functions, cut and paste functions. "Tape" calculator with memory, RPN version calculator. Source code with registration.

    VBTOL2   97 K $15   *Owens, Mike*

Test For Calculator Bug — This program (includes source code) uses SendKeys to test the Windows Calculator, and compares it to results calculated with Visual Basic. Unique technique used to read the result from the Windows Calculator.

    CALCTE   12 K Free   *Holland, Sarah*

VB Calc — Invisible custom control that evaluates complex arithmetic expressions at runtime. Useful in any application that lets users perform runtime calculations, such as calculators or spreadsheets. Help and demo application included.
    VBCALC   48 *K* $15+   *Wogan, David*

Wind Chill — Calculates the wind chill factor from formulas from the National Weather Service. Source code included.
    WINCHIL2   12 *K* Free   *Huss, Dennis L.*

WindChill — Windchill factor computation program. Visual Basic source code only.
    WINDCH   7 *K* Free   *Trunck, James P.*

CALENDAR

3D Perpetual Calendar — 3D calendar created with VB and TIME2WIN.DLL. Displays a perpetual 3D calendar in multi languages with the week number, the day number. Source code included.

    T2WCALEN   9 *K*   Free   *Renard, Michael*

CalVBX 2.0 (Winter) — Calendar custom control. The date is initially set to current date and appears on a fixed size 3D calendar. Clicking on the dates will change the displayed date and the value of NewDate (type string). Clicking on arrows advances or reduces the month.

    CALVBXW   35 *K* $35   *Winter, G. M.*

CalVBX12 — Calendar custom control. Source code for the control available at extra cost.

    CALVBX12   15 *K* $10+SW   *Guttilla, Brad*

Calendar — Small popup calendar modeled after the PowerBuilder calendar. Source code included.

    CAL   7 *K*   Free

Calendar — Simple VB source code for displaying a calendar.

    CALZIP   7 *K*   Free   *Meadows, Al*

Calendar 3-D — Calendar has 3-D look without using VBXs. Full source code.

    CALENDAR   4 *K*   Free

Calendar Control — Calendar custom control for VB, Delphi, VC++, etc.

    CALEND2   41 *K* $50SW   *Software FX Inc.*

Calendar Demo — Pure VB source code calendar that can be placed on forms and customized.

    CALDR   6 *K*   Free   *Silverman, Glenn*

Calendar Input Form — Form allows you to create a point and click calendar without using a third party control. Full source code included.

    CALENDEI   7 K   Free   *Eisenberg, David F.*

Calendar OCX — OLE Control which lets you place a calendar into VB-applications.

    CALCTL   23 K   SW   *Theobald Soft Design*

Calendar Object Source 1.0.01 — Calendar object for VB4 16/32 looks and feels just like the one in MS-Schedule+ 7.0. Just add a small form and module to your project. Attach this pop-up to any combo box, text box, grid cell, etc. Output the date in any format.

    AHCAL10   20 K   *Hohl, Alfred*

Calendar Pro Demo — Add a calendar to your VB application without having to use a VBX. One function call. Use Calendar Pro like a combo box with only a few more lines of code.

    CALPRO   22 K $10+   *Moon, Brian*

Calendar Program/Add-In — Replacement calendar source code. Does not use GRID.VBX.

    VBCALN   17 K $10 SW   *Integration Ware, Inc.*

Calender [Sic] — Source code for a simple calendar, where the user can pick a date, which is passed back to a global variable.

    VBCAL   57 K   Free   *Mower, Chris*

Code Calendar Demo — DEMO executable of a calendar using any control that uses graphic methods. The calendar can be programmed to expand with your forms. Source code provided with registration.

    CDCAL1   11 K $15SW   *Hocker, Paul*

Date Tracker — Provides a popup calendar facility, wherever you need to enter or select a date. Full source code included.

    DT01   11 K   Free   *Barrett, David*

Date/Time Entry Form — Demo source code shows how to allow complete date and time entry using only a mouse. Minimizes clicks needed while shielding the programmer from idiot checking user input.

    DTENTRY   73 K   Free   *Rogers, Kerry*

DateComp Function — Function shows how to compare two dates. Returns <0 if Date1<Date2, 0 if Date1=Date2, >0 if Date1>Date2.

    DTCMP   2 K   Free   *Wray, Richard*

DateTime — Unsupported. Configurable date and time display. Source code included.

    DATETIME   23 *K* PD   *Michna, Hans-Georg*

Drag And Drop Calculator Demo — Drag'n'drop calculator with several functions including a listbox memory, trace functions, and some scientific functions, and cut and paste functions. Visual Basic source available with registration.

    VBTOL1   26 *K* $15   *Owens, Mike*

Easter Calculator — Full source code for calculating the date of Easter. Program uses the German language exclusively.

    EASTER   4 *K* Free

Graphical Calendar — Form and function call combination displays a graphical calendar and then returns either the date or FALSE, depending on whether OK or CANCEL was clicked. Full source code.

    CALENDJM   6 *K* Free   *Marlow, James*

Graphical Calendar Variation — Form and function call combination displays a graphical calendar and then returns either the date or FALSE, depending on whether OK or CANCEL was clicked. Full source code. Modified from CALENDJM; does not require THREED.VBX.

    CALENDEK   6 *K* Free   *Eka*

Holiday Calendar Demo — Displays a calendar and, if desired, maintains a "Holiday Schedule" in an Access database. Can be used standalone or embedded in another application via DDE. Sample Visual Basic source code included.

    HOLCAL   231 *K* $20SW   *Bridge, Inc.*

Holiday.Bas — Source code function to calculate the day of a holiday for holidays which do not fall on specific days of the year.

    HOLIDAY   3 *K* Free

Popup Calendar 3 — Pop-up calendar form module written in VB3. Returns/Updates current date field. Full source available. Supports drag 'n' drop and keyboard events.

    CALEND   28 *K* $10   *Wessex Systems*

Popup Lunar Calendar Demo 3/95 — Popup Lunar Calendar demo. Source code, no DLLs or VBXs. One line subroutine brings up the Popup Calendar and sets the output placement. Full source code is contained the the Help file, which requires a key which will be sent upon registration.

    LUNCAL   205 *K* $15SW   *Crazy Rides*

VB TrueCal 2.2 — Demo of a sizable 3-D calendar that can be plugged into a VB application royalty free. Registered users receive the full native VB source code (not a VBX) that can be customized.

    TRUEC   13 *K* $12SW   *IntuiTech Systems, Inc.*

VBCalendar 1.4 DEMO — DEMO of a calendar control for Visual Basic. Encrypted source code included, password supplied with registration. Many graphic options. VB3 and VB4.

    VBCALNDR   41 *K* $10   *Wolfebyte Ltd.*

5
CLIENT/SERVER

Choreo 1.1 DEMO — Client/server development extension providing automated data access and synchronization. Local SQL database. Support for SQL Server, Oracle6 and Oracle7, Gupta SQLBase 5.2, and ODBC. Third-party control support.
     CHOREO11   1810 *K* $595   *CenterView Software*

Developing AS/400 Client/Serve — Sample VB AS/400 client/server programs. Full source code and documentation for creating client/server applications.
     COMMONVB   494 *K*   Free   *Genesis Software*

ODBC Logon Form — Source code form. Enter a Username/Password, either from the command line or from the form itself, and it creates an ODBC connect string which can be used in your application, or can pass you to another application.
     OPENDB   3 *K*   Free   *Lee, Michael*

SQL Programmer 1.8507 Demo — Complete development environment to edit, debug, and test your SQL Server code and much more. Provides virtual editing of stored procedures, triggers, batch objects, views, rules, and more. DEMO copy limited to 5 objects and 20 object changes.
     SQLPR185   3333 *K*   *Sylvain Faust Inc.*

6
CLOCK

All The Time 3.4 — Versatile clock. Show time/date in any format. MOnitor memory/ resources. Display tree/moon graphics showing seasons, moon phases, night/day. Play WAV files. Full source code.

    ATTALL   395 *K*   Free   *Smith, Wilson, And C.Rogers*

Atomic Clock Set VB4 — VB4 source code sets the computer's internal clock using the National Institute of Standards and Technology's atomic clock located in Boulder, Colorado, USA.

    ATOMIC   15 *K*   Free   *Bergmann-Terrell, Eric*

ClocVBX — Clock custom control for VB3 that adds normal or 3D system clock to forms. Clock refresh rate can be adjusted by milliseconds. Clock face can be changed to a resettable elapsed timer.

    CLOCVB   17 *K* $10+SW   *Guttilla, Brad*

NAlarm32 — 32 bit OCX control that lets VB Programmers set alarms to go off at various times of the day (similar to an alarm clock). It's easy to use - just drop it on a form and set the alarm times needed. It then fires events at the correct times.

    NALARM32   970 *K* $20   *Nanoware*

Scary Time — A simple clock for Halloween. It uses a special ATM Type 1 font (provided), although that font is not necessary. Source code and font included.

    SCARY   46 *K*   Free   *Zeitman, Dan*

The Time 2.5 — Graphical, customizable replacement for the Clock application supplied with Windows. Includes source code to a free subclass custom control, and several bitmap icons and textures. Shows how to add/remove a title bar at runtime, and much more.

    TTCODE   86 *K*   Free   *Visual Bits*

VB Button Clock — Simple time/date display with VB source.

    BTNCLO   5 *K*   Free

VBClock 1.2 DEMO — DEMO of a clock control for Visual Basic. Encrypted source code included, password supplied with registration. Many graphic options. VB3 and VB4.

VBCLOCKW	38 *K*	$10	*Wolfebyte Ltd.*

VBClock 2.1 — Another VB clock. Also shows date and percent of free resources. Source code included.

VBCLK2	26 *K*	$15 SW	*Holland, Sarah*

X World Clock — World clock with extended setup for all time displays, time zones, and alarms to any city or country in the world.

XCLOCK	42 *K*	Free	*Kienemund, Wilfried*

7

COMMUNICATIONS

AS/400 File Transfer API Fix — DLL replaces IBM's EHNTFW.DLL for use with VB 4.

    EHNTFWVB   5 *K*   Free   *Jones, Ron C.*

ActiveX SDK — ActiveX SDK Beta.

    ACTIVEX   5460 *K*   Free   *Microsoft*

Alpha-Pager VBX 2.0 — Custom control allows developers to provide automated communications from Windows based applications to anyone carrying a modern alpha-numeric pager. VBX and sample source code included.

    APAGER   304 *K* $50 SW   *Significa Software*

Comm — Source code that provides an example of how to use Windows API calls to manipulate a modem.

    COMM   9 *K*   Free

Communications Control — A control which gives access to the communications ports. Controls the port, baud rate, parity, data and stop bits. Includes COMTEST, sample source code.

    VBCOMM   9 *K*   Free   *Gamber, Mark*

Communications Control 2.0 — A control which gives access to the communications ports. Controls the port, baud rate, parity, data and stop bits. Includes COMTEST, sample source code.

    VBCOMM20   18 *K*   Free   *Gamber, Mark*

Communications Demo — Not available from MicroHelp. A limited but functional terminal program which demonstrates the advanced functions of the MicroHelp communications library. Partial source code is included.

    COMDEM   46 *K*   Free   *MicroHelp, Inc.*

Communications Tool Kit INFO — DLL - Multilanguage communication library. The kit's high-level dialog box functions allow you to prompt users for COM port selection, UART settings, auto dialer, modem defaults, and file transfer options. Windows Help file only.

    SWCTB1   161 *K* $299   *SilverWare, Inc.*

Creting Multiuser Environment — Three major components: 1) messaging system for communicating with other users 2) error handler 3) event logger that is used by the error handler, the login code, and any other time the developer would like events recorded.

    MSGSYS   23 *K* Free   *Cornish, Randy*

DAO Registry Local Settings — Utility with VB4 source code. Makes server based DAO files local again. Stops the Setup Wizard failing on client machines.

    DAOLOCAL   6 *K* Free   *Numatic International Ltd.*

DDE Control Centre — Utilize built-in DDE features of Windows applications. Supports simple command language and script files to automate tasks.

    DDECC   92 *K* $45   *O'Neill Software*

DDESHR — Not supported. Visual Basic implementation of the Windows for Workgroups DDEShare application. VB source code demonstrates how to create DDEShare entries from any application. Custom DLL is provided to act as a filter between VB and the WfWG API.

    DDESHR   23 *K* Free   *Garrison, Gary P.*

Dynamic Data Exchange Monger — Utility to test programs attempting to use DDE. Just type in the server name, the topic, and the item, and you can send the link to an execution string or request some text or a picture.

    DDEMNG   60 *K* $10   *Averbuch, Michael*

FSSocket Custom Control 1.4 — Communications custom control for transmission and reception of data through the Winsock DLL. Provides properties and events to configure and control a network connection. Help file and sample source code included.

    FSSOCKET   48 *K* $75   *Fenestra Software L.L.C.*

Fax Resource Print-2-Image 4.1 — DEMO of fax and e-mail products produced by Resource Partners. DLLs add fax support to any Visual Basic program. Various versions of the program allow network, client/server, or single-user uses.

    P2I   480 *K*   *Resource Partners North*

Forecast — Program retrieves and parses weather information from the Weather Underground Web site. All URLs are within the code. It will display an updated forecast every 5 minutes or on demand. Full VB source code.

FORECAST 10 *K* Free *Feller, Bob*

GCP++ TCP/IP Custom C. Eval. — Lets you incorporate TCP/IP networking into your application with no coding. Supports TELNET, TCP, UDP, TFTP, FTP, SMTP, and VT-200 emulation controls. Handles any TCP/IP networking task using familiar VB properties and events. Evaluation edition.

GCP24 904 *K* $298 *Dart Communications*

Generic DDE In Visual Basic — Source code demonstrates how to do DDE in a generic fashion. Prompts for application name, pathname, topic, item, execute string, window mode and attempts to conduct the DDE link. Useful for testing which DDE commands will work with an application.

DDEUTI 5 *K* Free

IMEX OLE Server — OLE Server that offers import/export properties and methods. A reusable solution for database management. Rapidly implement import, export, update and delete functionality in the background. Touchy installation-copy DLLs to path,HLPs to IMEX sub.

IMEX 3480 *K* $40 *Solugistics Ltd.*

IPPort Control — The IPPort custom control facilitates TCP/IP communications by providing an easy interface to Winsock functions. It allows a client application to communicate with a server using stream sockets.

IPPORT 39 *K* $25 *DevSoft Inc.*

Internet — Internet code for Visual Basic.

INTER 160 *K*

Lcl4B V 4.2(1) — Lite (Personal) Communications Library for Basic. Asynchronous communications library for software developers using Visual Basic for DOS. 30 communications and support functions. Interrupt driven receiver. 300 - 115K baud. Com1-4 support. More.

LCL4B42 45 *K* $65 SW *MarshallSoft Computing, Inc.*

Log Window — MDI OLE 2.0 automation component that provides window login services for your applications. Useful for displaying status information and can be used to display variable values and other program information while debugging. VB and Access samples included

LWPACKAG 2013 *K* $30+ *Solution Studios Inc.*

MicroHelp Demo Communications — Not available from MicroHelp. A well polished terminal program which includes protocols such as ZModem, YModem-G, and CIS B. Transfer rates of up to 19,200 bps are supported.

    MHCOMM   86 *K*   Free   *MicroHelp, Inc.*

Modem Configuration Example — Two source code projects. MDMCFG contains a database of suggested modem initialization strings for about 175 modems. COMMMSG is a simple program that shows how to use event processing to send and receive data.

    MODEMX   29 *K*   Free   *Grier, Dick*

Multiple Server Example — Program designed to work on Novell 3.0 networks (required). Examples of attaching to and detaching from network servers. Full source code.

    NVLEXP   33 *K*   Free   *Johnson, L. J.*

NetVBX — VBX designed to provide Visual Basic programmers an easy way to access Windows for Workgroups network functions. Full source code available for $200.

    NETVBX   25 *K* $35SW   *Huon, Benoit*

Netuser - Obtain User ID — Source code and DLL to obtain the login name of the person using the system. If the user cannot be identified the string "UnknownUser" is returned.

    NETUSER   23 *K* $10   *Hegerty, Chad*

Netware Bindery Browser — Browse the NetWare bindary in Windows. Source code and executable. This is a sample program to demonstrate the use of some NetWare function calls from VB.

    NWBIND2   12 *K*   Free   *Johnston, Scott*

OLE Destination Example — Cleans up the OLE example that comes with Visual Basic 3.0 and provides fully commented code. Also shows a working Standard Edit menu for OLE 2.0 Container applications.

    OLE   28 *K*   Free   *Febish, George J.*

OLE Server Sorter — OLEGridSort effectively subclasses the VB MSGRid control and adds new properties and methods, giving it full sorting by column capability. Contains VB 4 16 and 32 bit versions.

    SGOLE10   156 *K* $30+   *Carter, Ian*

Ogmess Network Lan Messaging — Used for sending quick messages to users in a work group on a network.

    OGMESS   25 *K* $5   *Chavez, Steven R.*

Personal Communications Lib — Async comm library supporting COM1-COM20 to 115,200 baud, 4+ ports concurrently, many dumb multiport boards, 16550 UART, interrupt driven, RTS/CTS flow control, any UART address using IRQ2 thru IRQ1.

    PCLVBW11   65 *K* $75   *MarshallSoft Computing*

Position For WordBasic — A listing of WordBasic (Microsoft Word for Windows 6.0) functions, which can be accessed from Visual Basic using OLE automation.

    POSIWORD   32 *K*   Free   *Microsoft*

PostIt Messaging System 32-Bit — Simple messaging system to send a message to a single user, the entire department for a user, or the whole network. Keeps a log of all messages in an Access database. Full source code.

    POSTIT   52 *K*   Free   *Numatic International Ltd.*

Power Page 1.13 — DLL allows sending alpha-numeric (full text) messages to pagers. INtegrate the power of paging with a single function call from virtually any language supporting DLLs. Example source code contained in documentation. Unreg version limited to 40 characters

    POWERP   40 *K* $25SW   *Tanner, Ron*

Power Page 32-Bit 1.0 — DLL allows sending alpha-numeric (full text) messages to pagers. INtegrate the power of paging with a single function call from virtually any language supporting DLLs. Example source code contained in documentation. 32-bit VB4 only.

    PAGE32   46 *K* $35   *Tanner, Ron*

PowerTCP Demo — Lets you incorporate TCP/IP networking into your application with no coding. Supports TELNET, TCP, UDP, TFTP, FTP, SMTP, and VT-200 emulation controls. Handles any TCP/IP networking task using familiar VB properties and events. DEMO version.

    PWRTCP   753 *K* $598   *Dart Communications*

Public Lists In Cc:Mail — Demonstrates how to manage public lists in Lotus cc:Mail. DLLs and sample VB source code included.

    PUBLICCC   115 *K*   Free   *Radium Software*

RAS (WFW) Declarations — VB source code module contains the declarations needed to control the RAS interface (Remote Access Service, part of Windows for Workgroups). Also has VB functions which encapsulate the the DLL calls, making it a bit easier to work with.

    VBRASA   7 *K*   Free   *Zieglar, Adam*

RASCall 1.0 — Allows applications to control the Windows Remote Access Service (Windows for Workgroups) via DDE, input files, or the Windows command line. Useful for testing and for the automation of RAS operations from applications that cannot access RASAPI16.DLL.

RASCAL	46 K	Free	*Zieglar, Adam*

Simple Network Control — Simple control allows VB applications to talk to each other over a network. Support Windows for Workgroups, Windows NT and Windows 95. Sample source code included.

LEESNET2	11 K	Free	*Hedtke, Lee*

Simplfax - Link Winfax Pro — Sample program for sending short fax messages from Visual Basic to the commercial program Winfax Pro from Delrina. Source code included, sets the default printer (to Fax); retrieves Winfax settings from WIN.INI; sends parameters to Winfax using DDE; et.

SFAXV1	7 K	Free	*De Bruijn, Michiel*

Sliding Windows — VB implementation of a "sliding windows" data transfer protocol, which delivers data with the greatest efficiency. Intended for the user who needs simple point-to-point communication between two applications, without the need to know complex protocols.

SW	171 K	Free	*AeroData*

SocketWrench Custom Control — Custom control uses the standard Windows Sockets library to provide network communications services for VB applications. Supports both stream and datagram protocols, a buffered text mode, and client/server functionality.

CSWSK10A	197 K	Free	*Catalyst Software*

Standard Communications Lib — Serial communications DLL based on the Windows API. Includes 25 functions plus modem control and four example programs.

WSC4VB10	66 K	$40+	*MarshallSoft Computing, Inc.*

Stock Index — STINDEX - application from Dan Appleman's "Design True Event-Driven Code" article from Aug/Sept 1994 issue of Visual Basic Programmer's Journal. Requires MS Excel as OLE object.

DANVBP	76 K	Free	*Visual Basic Programmer's Jrnl*

Trace Plus 1.1 For Windows — Windows 3.1 API trace/debugger. Shows you the interaction between your application and the Windows 3.1 API with no modifications to your existing program. 12 classes of API functions are available. Displays all file accesses by application.

TPLUS	366 K	$110	*Systems Software Technology*

Trace Plus ODBC 2.0 — Shows the interaction between your application and the ODBC API with no modifications to your existing program. Shows the following information: Parameters before and after the call, return value, pointer validation and more.

      XRAYODBC   329 *K* $110   *Systems Software Technology*

Undocumented Quicken DDE — Quicken for Windows Dynamic Data Exchange Development Kit. Everything needed to use Quicken's DDE interface to extend Quicken's functionality by making it interoperable with other DDE applications.

      QWDDEDK   147 *K* Free   *Wild Rose Software*

Using DDE With Access Basic — A method of using Access Basic functions when Access is operating as a DDE server to Visual Basic. Complete Visual Basic source code included.

      DDE   4 *K* Free   *Tissington, Mike*

Using MCISendString — Source code demonstrates using the Windows API to play WAV and MID files.

      MMAPIEX   14 *K* Free   *Hipp, Frank*

VB WNet* Functions And Example — Collection of wrapper and utility functions for Windows WNet* API calls. Functions include mounting and dismounting network services, getting the name of a service connected to a drive, getting the drive being used for a particular service, etc.

      VBNETS   9 *K* Free   *Computer Technologies, Inc.*

VBTerm — A simple VT100 Terminal emulation program in Visual Basic, with source code files included.

      VBTERM2   39 *K* Free   *McGuiness, Charles*

WinFTP Developer's Kit — WINFTP.DLL/WINFTP32.DLL is a Windows File Transfer Protocol (FTP) Application Programming Interface (API) for client applications using Windows Sockets (WINSOCK.DLL/WSOCK32.DLL).

      WINFTP   199 *K* $79+   *Lee, Tony*

WinSend 1.5 — Control center for sending and receiving Network Broadcast Messages from NetWare 3 under Windows. Send messages using Windows front end; handles any messages sent to you with the ability to reply; stores the last 5 message you've sent; etc.

      WINSEN   17 *K* Free   *Larcombe, Andrew*

8
CUSTOM CONTROL

3-D Gauge Bar — A gauge type control written in pure Visual Basic source code, which is included. A 3-d bar to show the status of any activity.

    BAR   3 *K*   Free   *Polowood, Felipe*

3D Picture Button — A picture button with up/down pictures, caption display under picture, hotkey support, automatic 3-D shading.

    VBPIC3D   16 *K*   Free   *Gamber, Mark*

3D Widgets DEMO — Demonstrates some capabilities of Sheridan's "3D Widgets" series of custom controls. Includes Listbox, Combobox, File Listbox, Directory Listbox and Drive Listbox. Multiselect and multiple column select modes.

    MENULBOX   74 *K*   *Sheridan Software Systems*

3D Widgets Demo Diskette — Demo of Sheridan's 3D Widgets. (See listings.)

    SHERIDAN   184 *K*   Free   *Sheridan Software Systems*

3D-VB Input 3.0d — Emulates the standard VB TextBox control which allows the user to enter text. 3D-VB can give the text a 3D look. Text formatting, 3D look, fonts, alignment, default property settings and other properties can be changed with the right mouse button.

    INPUT3   47 *K* $22 SW   *Opaque Software*

5 Pak Custom Controls 3.6 — Five custom controls: Balloon Help, Dynamic menu Help; Enumerate Desktop Windows; Popup windows; Soundex word search. Version 3.6 despite the filename 5PAK20.

    5PAK20   135 *K* $45 SW   *Weimar Software*

AAVBSORT.Dll - Sorts VB Arrays — Sorts VB arrays fast by providing a set of simple to use routines. Faster than VB sorts. Two types of sort: in-place and sort via index. Shareware version sorts all types of arrays. Registered users can sort user-defined. Sample source code included.

    AASORT   97 *K* $35SW   *AA-Software International*

ALARM Custom Control 1.4 — This control lets you set an alarm, or multiple alarms, to go off at particular time(s). An event id fired at the appropriate time. You can easily specify times such as: 10:45pm, every hour on the hour, every ten minutes, etc. Source code available.

ALARM14   36 K $10 SW   *Mabry Software*

About Magic 1.0 — Custom control that lets developers see Windows information in an "About" box. Includes a drive information function that gives info on drives, free space, total space, etc.

ABOUTM   17 K $15SW   *Bits & Bytes Solutions*

Advanced Control Library VBX — Custom control provides VB with System Disk functions. Format disk, copy disk, system reboot, Windows restart, file search, Sample source code included.

ADVCTRL   81 K $35 SW   *Advanced Applications*

Aircraft Instrument Cont. 2.5 — This control displays a variety of small airplane flight instruments, including compass, heading indicator, altimeter, vertical speed indicator, horizontal situation indicator, artificial horizon, and turn coordinator. Source code avail. at extra cost.

AIR25   272 K $40+SW   *Global Majik Software*

Angular Gauge VBX 2.5 — Generic Gauge control is a highly customizable gauge or meter control. Properties are provided to modify gauge's scales, tics, needles, annulars, captions, borders, and background.

AGAUGE25   354 K $30+SW   *Global Majik Software*

Assoc Custom Control — Custom control implementing in-memory associative arrays. Items are automatically sorted into key order. An element can be retrieved using the key or the whole array can be scanned using a custom event. Object code only.

ASSOC1   17 K   Free   *Axiomatic Software*

BLFX 1.0 — Customizable task wide 3D custom control. PicButton, Toolbar, Panel, FormBrush, FormEx, FormMsg, Tabbed dialogs, etc. No need for CTL3D.DLL.

BLFX10   63 K   *Bytes & Letters*

Browse Bound Control VB3/Acc. — Bound CC for browsing any RecordSet using the VB3 data control. On-the-spot editing with data pre-and post-validation. Mouse resizable columns, freeze columns to the left, etc. Online help.

BROWA   80 K $20   *Delta Soft Inc.*

Browse Custom Control — CC for browsing and DBF file using vxBase.DLL as an engine. fast index scope/filter. Editing with data pre- and post-validation. Display fields/expressions including VB variables. Mouse resizable columns, freeze columns, etc., online help.

      BROWSE   118 *K* $20   *Delta Soft Inc.*

Bystrom VBXs — Four custom controls: DBPush emulates the 3D command button supplied with VB; DBTtip creates small popup windows for balloon help or toolips; DBAppMon notifies a VB program each time an app or DLL starts or exits; DBHots creates invisible hot spots.

      DBSTUF   140 *K*   Free   *Bystrom, Dan*

CBoxList — Custom Control to create groups of checkboxes or radio buttons in a single Control. Evaluation/demo version works only within the Visual Basic environment.

      CBLIST   29 *K*   Free   *OPen Software*

CTGauge — Gauge custom control allows the user to define all needle properties (place, size, color), the minimum and maximum values, and the starting angle for the minimum and maximum values. Part of the Component Toolbox set (see CTDEMO).

      CTGAUG   19 *K* $25   *Gamesman Inc.*

CUA Controls Demonstration — 22 custom controls including sample source code and full demo program. Included are Label, TextBox, Frame, Command, CheckBox, RadioButton, Combobox, ListBox, Thermometer, IconText, ToolTips, Toolbar, Statusbar, Spin button, Meter Slider, etc.

      CUACTLS   257 *K* $45   *Stingsoft*

Canimate Animation VBX — Custom control supports sprite and cel animation, concurrent or separate. High speed animation without multimedia extensions. Includes transparency, collision detection, custom animated cursors, buttons, and target controls. Large demo source file.

      CANIMATE   111 *K* $39   *Componere Software*

Car Gauge Control 2.5 — This control creates various automobile gauge including tachometer, speedometer, fuel level, oil pressure, amps, and temperature. The mouse can be used for input. Source code available at extra cost.

      CAR25   254 *K* $20+SW   *Global Majik Software*

CdSelect 1.01 — Custom control emulates the behavior of the Windows Dialog Box. When you get focus with the Tab or Alt key, all text is selected. Sample source code included.

    CDSELE   19 *K*   Free   *Serpoul, Jean Jacques*

Cleanup VBX Clears Screen — Custom control automatically minimizes the windows of any non-VB application running. Appends a "Cleanup" menu item to VB's main menu. "A VB programmer's dream come true."

    CLEAN11   32 *K* $15   *Syncom, Inc.*

Code Browser Using VBAWK — Sample project parses your MAK and FRM files and allows you to select routines to cut and paste through the Clipboard. Source code included.

    CODEB   54 *K* $45   *VideoSoft*

Component Toolbox 32-Bit Demo — Demo version of the 32-bit Component Toolbox. Contains 25 32-bit OCX controls, including tabs, calendars, sliders, gauges, etc. Sample VB4 source code included.

    CT_OCX   523 *K* $159   *Gamesman Inc.*

Component Toolbox Demo 2.5 — Demo of a set of general VBX controls. Includes tab controls, sliders, meters, animated push buttons, etc., eleven total. Sample source code for each control. Full version and documentation with registration.

    CTOOLS   386 *K* $99   *Gamesman Inc.*

Component Toolbox Sampler — Five VBXs from the Component Toolbox series. ctCheck-check box; ctFrame-frame control; ctPush-push button control; ctRadio-radio button control. Replacements for the standard Visual Basic controls. Sample VB source code included.

    CTCTRL   59 *K* $30   *Gamesman Inc.*

Control Probe 1.1 — Custom control to examine and modify other controls' properties at run-time. Gives a list of properties in a control. Can display a dialog box that lets you modify other controls' properties interactively or at run-time. Source code available.

    PROBE11   40 *K* $15   *Mabry Software*

Control95 1.1 — Library of source code allows the programmer to use Windows95 look-alike tabs, gauages, sliders, and toolbars in VB3, VB4/16, and VB4/32 projects without any DLL, VBX, or OCX.

    CTRL95   32 *K* $50   *Inlog*

CtDATE Custom Control — Calendar custom control. From the Component Toolbox (see CTDEMO). Sample source code included, no documentation.

  CTDATE   68 *K* $35SW   *Gamesman Inc.*

CtFOLD Custom Control — Tabbed folder custom control. See CTDEMO. Sample source code included, no documentation.

  CTFOLD   81 *K* $35SW   *Gamesman Inc.*

CtSplit Split Window VBX — Custom control that divides a window into two regions. Has no elastic properties of its own, so sizing and moving controls is the responsibility of the programmer. Part of the Component Toolbox set (see CTDEMO). Sample source code included.

  CTSPLIT   12 *K* $25   *Gamesman Inc.*

CtTips Help Tips VBX — Custom control is used to supply a popup help window to any control form with a valid handle. Part of the Component Toolbox set (see CTDEMO). Sample source code included.

  CTTIPS   19 *K* $25   *Gamesman Inc.*

CtTree Outliner / Tree VBX — Outliner custom control. Stores up to 32000 items. Virtual mode to save global memory. Each node can have different foreground and background colors and different bitmap images. Word wrap.

  CTTREE   88 *K* $65   *Gamesman Inc.*

Cursor Libraries Manipulations — Libraries of cursor animations. Include animated cursors in your programs or create your own library. Over 25 cursors included. Source code included to load library and use cursors.

  CURLIBM   25 *K* $15 SW   *Fillion, Pierre*

Cursor Manipulation Control — How to control the cursor in VB. How to move to specific position, how to retrieve the position of the cursor, how to hide and restrict the cursor to a specific part of the screen. Demo and source.

  CURSMAN   9 *K* $15 SW   *Fillion, Pierre*

Custom 3-D Buttons — Custom 3-D buttons. C source and VBX included.

  VBRDOBTN   18 *K* Free   *Gamber, Mark*

Custom Control Code Example — Source (C) and compiled result for a simple custom control. An example of VBX coding with custom events and properties. It is a customized multiple select list box with unique selection properties. No support from the author, this is a learning tool file

  LEARNV   37 *K* Free   *Big Dog Software*

Custom Group Box — New groupbox control. Provide 3-D shading, text justification, text shadowing. VBX and demo source files included.

VBGP	20 *K*	Free	*Gamber, Mark*

DBEngine Custom Control — Custom control interface to Borland's Paradox engine. See file DB3V.ZIP for sample VB source code.

DBENG3	143 *K*	$75 SW	*DB Technologies*

DBEngine Custom Control Source — Custom control interface to Borland's Paradox engine. Sample VB source code files for use with file DBENG3.ZIP.

DB3V	28 *K*	$75 SW	*DB Technologies*

DBTTip 1.21 — Tool tip Window creation VBX supporting custom shapes. No programming needed.

DBTTIP12	30 *K*	Free	*Skoog, Bengt-Arne*

DataBar 1.33 DEMO — Data-aware toolbar which aids in the development of large scale database applications by centrally locating database access and control code. Sample source code included.

DATABAR	555 *K*	$60	*PowerTools Software*

Date/Time Custom Control — Custom control designed to speed up processing whenever you need the current date or time in your program. The property is always a formatted string, formatted in one of thirteen choices. DEMO version will expire on Feb 28, 1995.

MIDAT500	103 *K*	*Mitromar, Inc.*

Date/Time Edit Control — Custom control with a number of custom properties that let you specify the format of the date/time to be displayed. A single custom event is supplied that is fired whenever the date/time is changed.

DATEEDIT	29 *K*	*Jeffery, John*

DayTip.ocx — Tip of the Day OCX custom control. Opens modal dialog displaying a tip from a parameter specified tip file.

DAYTIP	1414 *K*	$SW	*Advanced Applications*

Dialog Builder Cc — DEMO of Dialog Builder Custom Control for dynamic control creation.

DLGBLD	17 *K*	Free	*Beekes, Bernd*

Diamond Arrow Pad — An arrow control consisting of up, down, left and right combined into four sub-buttons in a diamond shaped pad. DLL and sample source code.

VBDIA	7 *K*	Free	*Gamber, Mark*

Disk And File Info CC 2.3 — Disk information gets amount of free disk space and volume name. File information finds size, attributes, date, time, and allows changing attributes and the size of the file. Source code available for $35.

| DFINFO23 | 44 K | $15 SW | *Mabry Software* |

Drag 'n Drop Using TList — Source code illustrates a method of using drag & drop within a TLIST control (a commercial VBX product from Bennet-Tec).

| TLDD | 40 K | Free | *Bennet-Tec Information Serv.* |

EZ-Tab Tabbed Dialogs DEMO — Custom control gives an easy way to implement tabbed dialogs in Visual Basic. Used like the VB standard Frame control; each pane of the dialog is in a separate control. Built-in Focus tracking. DEMO version can be used in design mode only.

| EZTABD | 32 K | $28SW | *Beekes, Bernd* |

Easybar VBX — Custom control for creating barcodes. Invisible at runtime. Supports rotation and various drawing styles. All barcode parameters are adjustable. 20 barcode types are included; 12 basic types and 8 add-ins.

| EASYBA | 52 K | $25 | *Bokai Corporation* |

Easynet Custom Control 1.82 — Control allows user to draw net graphs interactively in forms, which means to draw nodes and link them. An Easynet control contains links or nodes. You can associate data text, picture, integer, reference) to each item. Demo version for use within VB.

| EASYNE | 170 K | $125SW | *Lassalle, Patrick* |

EditTool Demo — Source code as a demo of EditTool, which creates custom controls.

| ETDEMO | 2 K | Free | *BitRider Inc.* |

Elastic Control / Splitter Bar — CtSIZE control will resize and or reposition controls placed inside it (including text size) and can be aligned to all or part of its parent form. CtSPLIT control can be used to divide a work area into parts.

| CTSIZE | 36 K | $99 | *Gamesman Inc.* |

FieldPack 1.2 — Three data management add-ons. SuperString Tools - pack mixed data formats into any database. Delimited SubString Tools - hierarchical data management with variable-length fields. Utility String Tools - justification, filters, and more.

| FLDPAK12 | 125 K | $39 | *Software Source* |

File Mgr Drag And Drop CC 1.2 — Custom control notifies program when a file has been dragged and dropped from the Windows File Manager. Source code available at extra cost.

    FMDROP12   29 *K* $15 SW   *Mabry Software*

File Wizard VBX — Custom control allows Drag'n'drop to your VB application. File Wizard returns the path and filename of every file dropped, for further processing. Documentation and sample source code included in a Windows Help File.

    FILEWI   12 *K* $10SW   *Jantzi, Steve*

Finger VBX — Custom control implements the "Finger" protocol. It assumes the presence of a Winsock compliant DLL. Demo source code included.

    FINGER   8 *K* Free   *Bridges, Steve*

Folder Custom Control — Custom control provides a file-folder tabs metaphor. Tabs can be placed upwards or downwards; tabs can have a perspective effect where tabs in "back" appear smaller; tabs can have straight or rounded corners.

    FOLDERCC   31 *K* $30   *Mullins, Robert*

Form Scroller — Custom control provides scroll bar support with TotalHeight and TotalWidth properties. Will scroll all types of forms in design or run mode.

    FRMSCROL   57 *K* $50   *DataObjects Inc.*

Formatted Edit Custom Control — Designed as a superclass of the VB EDIT control, provides the developer with all facilities needed to ensure the data received by the program is correct.

    FEDIT30   105 *K* $159   *Computer Mindware Corp.*

Formatted Label Custom Control — Label control that lets you format the text within it. You can have different fonts, different colors, multiple paragraphs, paragraph formatting, etc. Using properties, you can print your text. All this, and it's bound, too.

    FLABEL10   40 *K* $20   *Mabry Software*

GS Help Files — Help files for GSVBX.ZIP - Demo version of 3 custom controls: TabFrame provides tabbed dialogs; ToolTip provides MS style tooltips and other features; Toolbar provides dockable toolbars similar to Word, Excel, etc.

    GSHLP   93 *K* $85   *GC Consulting Services Ltd.*

GSS Tools Custom Controls — Four custom controls. CLOC embeds a 12 or 24 hour timer or elapsed timer. CAL is a full featured calendar. GSSCALC is a full featured calculator. GSSGRAD fills any form with a gradient color. Sample source code included. Source code for VBXs available.

GSSTOOLS	55 *K*	$35+	*Guttilia, Brad*

GSS Wallpaper VBX — Custom control will tile any BMP onto the client area of a form creating an interesting background. The control can also stretch the BMP to cover the entire form. Source code for VBX available.

GSSWALL	11 *K*	$12+	*Guttilia, Brad*

GSSgrad Gradient VBX — A gradient custom control that fills any VB form in increasing color values from top-bottom, bottom-top, left-right and right-left. Use any Windows colors and change and runtime.

GSSGRAD	8 *K*	$10+	*Guttilia, Brad*

GT Tabbed List Box CC 2.0 — Custom control similar to the standard Listbox control with additional properties: DisNoScroll, ItemForeColor, TabStops, ItemImage, and Transparent Bitmap. Sample Visual Basic source code included.

TLSTVBX2	23 *K*	$15 SW	*Torralba, George R.*

GT Toolbar Kit 1.0 — Custom control helps the VB programmer implement a toolbar. Contains two custom controls: GTTBAR and GTPANEL. Can also be used as a status bar container.

GTTBAR01	26 *K*	$15 SW	*Torralba, George R.*

Gadgets For Windows 1.1 Demo — DEMO. Gives apps a unique, professional look with these 3D custom controls. You control the size, the scaling, and the number of tic marks displayed. Choose smooth movement of faders and knobs or incremental movements based on a scale you set.

GADGETS	205 *K*	$40	*Universal Dynamics Inc.*

Gantt/VBX 1.16 DEMO — Visually interactive Gantt control. Lets users directly modify their data with mouse drag and drop technology. Change any of over 100 properties to change look and feel. Adds project scheduling with the click of a button.

GANTTV	743 *K*	$249	*AddSoft Inc.*

Grid 3 — Grid Custom Control. C source code included.

VBGRID	37 *K*	Free

Grid VBX With SQL Querybuilder — One VBX from a suite of nine "Advanced Database Environment" ODBC compliant database management custom controls. ADEGrid is a powerful grid control which allows the user to reposition to any record in a table and make modifications as desired.

    ADEVBX   932 K   ROYALTY *Marasco Newton Group Ltd.*

Hardware Control VBX — Helps with project development requiring a Windows front-end for PC hardware control - anything from a stage lighting system to an industrial control application. Hardware may be designed with positive or negative logic, maskable I/O, polled or event.

    EVIO   209 K $45   *Vermont Peripherals*

Hierarchy Listbox 1.1 — Custom control allows Visual Basic developers to display pictures and/or text in a hierarchical format (as in a directory tree).

    HIERLB   32 K $55+SW   *Krausse, Ralph*

HotMap Custom Control 1.5 — VBX allows you to define regions on selected bitmap and get events with region info when user clicks on any part of the selected region. When control is resized, all region's sizes rescale automatically. Regions may be saved to file and restored any time

    HOTMAP   100 K $60   *SoftLand Inc.*

Hotkey VBX — Custom control lets you define a Hotkey, and the control will fire its event whenever the hotkey is pressed from anywhere in Windows. The Hotkey can be any normal key or key combination.

    HOTKEYPP   27 K $20   *Pagett, Paul*

IList Custom Control — Enhanced listbox control. It can accept and process multiple selections, and it can accept another data item which is linked to a textbox entry. Source code available on registration.

    ILIST   12 K $25   *Taylor, Ian*

INI Custom Control — Custom control provides easy access to the initialization file features of Windows 3.1. No more fooling with API declarations or C strings. You can create INI files or modify existing INI files.

    INI2   25 K $12   *Stubbs, Scott*

INI File Custom Control 3.2 — IniCon makes it easy to read and write INI files. Sample source code is included. Source code for the VBX is available for $25.

    INICON32   29 K $5+   *Mabry Software*

INI.VBX Custom Control — Custom control provides method for accessing INI files from Visual Basic without using Win31 API calls. Full C source code is included for compilation with Borland C++ 3.1.

INIVX1   23 K   Free   *Dexter, Walter F.*

InFocus Status Line CC — Custom control provides true context-sensitive status lines. Generates events: when any control receives the input focus; when any menu item is highlighted; when the mouse moves over any control.

INFOC   33 K $20SW   *Hanson, Mark*

IndexTab And Ruler CC Demo — DEMO of Custom Controls: IndexTab displays tabs similar to those in a looseleaf notebook; Ruler controls allow creating 3D look horizontal and vertical rulers without writing code.

MANAGE   21 K   *VideoSoft*

InfoSoft VBTables — Custom control lets you organize, sort, search, and save various "tables" of data and information. Data is stored in a table using rows and columns. Table can be stored and accessed from a DOS program. Table can be used to pass info between forms.

VBT100E   76 K $32   *InfoSoft*

Inimagic 2.2 — Replaces unnecessary API calls. Properties such as accessmode, encryption, encryptionkey, inifilename with a file dialog for easy selection, inisection, inikey, and inistring. Includes full Windows help file and demo source code.

INIMGC   49 K $30SW   *Bits & Bytes Solutions*

Joystick Custom Control 1.3 — JoyStk CC gives joystick information (movement, buttons) for your programs. Supports two joysticks, one 4-button joystick, or one 3-D joystick.

JOYSTK13   50 K $15 SW   *Mabry Software*

Kalendar Custom Control — Calendar custom control. Lets you affect the way each "day-box" is drawn, and draw anything within each day box. You can print the calendar with any custom drawing, either full page or anywhere and any size on the page. DEMO version.

KALEND   69 K $25 SW   *Parachute Software*

Knob Control 2.5 — Highly customizable knob or dial control. Properties are provided to modify knob style, mark, scale, tics, annulars, captions, border, and background. Includes "snap" and "multiturn" functions.

KNOB25   332 K $20+SW   *Global Majik Software*

LED Custom Control — Custom control that behaves like an LED. 3D effects and colors are all user definable.

    LED11   *36 K* $15 SW   *Mabry Software*

LED Custom Control 2.5 — This control displays a variety of LED shapes such as rectangular and circular. User supplied bitmaps may also be used to define an LED's appearance. The mouse can be used for input. Source code available at extra cost.

    LED25   *232 K* $15+SW   *Global Majik Software*

LED Display Control 1.2 — Custom control simulates a multi-digit seven segment LED display. Colors, number of digits and other attributes are all user definable. Integrated design-time help file included. Sample source code included.

    LEDDSP12   *49 K* $22SW   *Syncom, Inc.*

LFStatus Custom Control — Status bar VBX patterned after status bars found in many Microsoft products. Adds a professional touch to your programs. Includes Align, FloodColor, FloodPercent, Font Info, ShowDate, ShowTime, etc.

    LFS13S   *22 K* $14SW   *Lake Forest Software*

LFStatus Custom Control 32-Bit — Status bar 32-bit OCX patterned after status bars found in many Microsoft products. Adds a professional touch to your programs. Includes Align, FloodColor, FloodPercent, Font Info, ShowDate, ShowTime, etc.

    LFDEMO   *358 K* $15   *Lake Forest Software*

Label Turn Text Rotation — Similar to the standard Label control, LBTURN.VBX allows you to define the degrees of rotation of the text. Captions are automatically centered and have transparent backgrounds. Demonstration source code and HLP file explain how to use LBTURN.

    LBTURN   *189 K* $10 SW   *Digital PowerTOOLS*

Leong Profile CCs 1.02 — VBX makes it easy to use INI files with your programs. Also lets you save Captions and Tags in INI files to help with help prompts and translations to other languages. Contains Color Control, Font Control, String Control, and Expose Control.

    LEONGI   *114 K* $25SW   *Leong, Mabel*

Linear Gauge Custom Ctrl 2.5 — Versatile linear gauge custom control useful as a level or meter indicator. The pointer can be configured to display a value or a value range. Multiple scales or pointers can be incorporated in a single instrument. Mouse may be used for input.

    LGAUGE25   *285 K* $30+SW   *Global Majik Software*

MCursor 2.0 — VBX customizes mouse cursor and lets you use it with any control. Assign any icon or BMP to the mouse pointer. Use "JumpIn" feature to jump cursor to the center of the specified control. Set HotSpot of the cursor.

    MCUR   *40 K* $30   *SoftLand Inc.*

MPopup 1.0 — Popup menu custom control for VB 3.0. Lets you add context sensitive popup menus to your applications with ease and simplicity of VB. You define your menu with the common menu editor, and set the menu location and attributes in code or interactively.

    MPOPUP   *14 K* $15+SW   *McKean Consulting*

MS Mega Pack 1.1 — One dozen of Mabry Software's most popular custom controls. Alarm, BarCod, BmpLst, DFInfo, FMDrop, IniCon, JoyStk, MenuEv, PerCnt, RoText, SoundX, ZipInf. One registration fee covers all these controls.

    MSMEGA11   *361 K* $90 SW   *Mabry Software*

MSLOT - W4WG Mailslot CC 1.2 — Custom control provides simple interprocess communication between programs running on the same or different computers running Windows for Workgroups. Enables you to create and use a W4WG Mailslot, and application-defined buffer that holds messages.

    MSLOT12   *42 K* $30SW   *Mabry Software*

Mailslot.Vbx — W4WG Mailslot Control (VBX). Custom control that makes Mailslot use simple. Requires Windows for Workgroups.

    MAILSLOT   *15 K* $25   *Mabry Software*

Menu Event Custom Control 3.2 — MenuEv makes it easy to get menu item events. Place MenuEv on your form, events start coming in at run time. Source coed available for $25.

    MENUEV32   *36 K* $10 SW   *Mabry Software*

MenuWatch Custom Control — Adds full-featured help status bar to your application. Displays help snippets in a help status bar at the bottom of the window as the user highlights menu items.

    MNUWAT   *58 K* $15 SW   *Lathrop, Steve*

Menudemo Custom Control — Custom control provides the capability to determine when someone has selected a menu item before it is clicked. Can be used to display a message in a status bar while the user scrolls through menu choices. Shareware version limited to 10 menu items.

    MENU320D   *31 K* $15   *Becker, Jeff*

Message Spy Custom Control 2.1 — Custom control used to "spy" on Windows and Visual Basic messages received by VB forms and controls. It fires an event when a message is received, passing the message details and the actual control the message is intended for.

    MSGSPY   44 K $20 SW   *Anton Software Limited*

Meter Bar Control — Meter Bar custom control for VB 3.0, simulates a gas gauge or progress indicator. It allows you to "fill up" the control in any direction and at any rate.

    MBAR   59 K $12   *Stubbs, Scott*

Metrix — No longer supported. Custom Control provides an analog meter. Programmer can alter the details of the meter elements, or replace any elements with a picture. Sample source code and graphics files provided.

    METRIX   51 K   Free   *Wilkinson, Robert*

MouseKeeper 1.0b — Custom control which triggers MouseDown, MouseMove and MouseUp events when the mouse is over any control in any application. Lets you maintain centralized code, such as displaying a status line or giving context sensitive help.

    MKEEPR   22 K $30+SW   *JOSWare, Inc.*

MsgBox3D - 3D Message Box 3.0 — The MsgBox statement and function provided with VB lacks a 3 dimensional look. MsgBox3D adds a 3 dimensional effect to VB's MsgBox. Exactly duplicates VB MsgBox functions. Uses 3D effect found in newer application. Source code with registration.

    MSGB3D   283 K $19SW   *Bridge, Inc.*

MsgHook Subclassing Control — Custom control lets 16-bit VB programs intercept Windows messages. File also includes 8 example programs from the September 1995 issue of Visual Basic Programmer's Journal, along with 4 additional examples from the same authors.

    SUBCLS   45 K   Free   *SoftCircuits Programming*

Multi-Button Control — The Multi-Button is a single control which divides itself into multiple sub-buttons, each acting as an independent button. A single control may act as up to 256 different controls. Includes source code sample.

    VBMBTTN2   14 K   Free   *Gamber, Mark*

Multilingual Messages Manag2.0 — Custom control by PTAHSoft provides a consistent method for managing the messages that appear in an application. Allows the development of applications which can show one of several (international) languages at runtime.

PSMMM	640 K $50	*PTAHSoft*

Multimedia Button VBX 1.6b — Transparent bitmaps, transparent button, WAV sound clicks, custom mouse pointers, custom font and border settings and more. Works with VB, VC++, Delphi, etc.

MMBUTTON	25 K $38	*Stedy Software*

Multimedia VBX Button Demo — Enhance version of the Visual Basic button control. Creates custom buttons with "depressed" or "raised" bevels and font shading, and other 3D effects. Has the ability to display odd shaped bitmaps, can display background image thru button face.

MMBUTT	92 K $38SW	*Stedy Software*

NUMWIN HWND Finder CC 3.8 — Makes it easy to add DDE and OLE and other custom features which require hWNDs of other applications windows. Can also be used to find the hWnd of all VB hWnds of the current application to send message or manipulate windows.

NUMW20	21 K $18 SW	*Weimar Software*

NavButton Custom Control — Custom control provides a set of buttons to replace the buttons attached to the Data Control. The buttons are separate from the control so they can be placed and sized anywhere on your form, and are enabled/disabled based on whether records exist.

NAVBTN	16 K $5	*Theis, H. Eric., Jr.*

NetCode Control 1.30 — Custom control to encode or decode files or strings. UUEncode, Base64 and Quoted-Printable formats are supported. Sample source code included.

NETCODE	40 K $30	*DevSoft Inc.*

Network Control VBX — VBX enables all Visual Basic applications to be network aware with the drop of one control. Performs almost all Windows network functions (connect, disconnect, get next available network drive, etc.).

NETCTR	11 K $35SW	*Wright Futures, Inc.*

NiftoMeter Custom Control — Custom control gives special user feedback during lengthy operations.

NIFTOM	18 K $7 SW	*Noonan, Timothy D.*

OLE Control Support File — OLE custom control support DLL that comes with the OLE Control Development Kit. Needed for many controls developed after October 1994. May be redistributed.

    OC25   245 *K*   Free   *Yukish, Gary*

OXButton 2.2d — 3D picture and text command button. Allows for different alignment of text and picture. A moving drop-shadow is created when the button is pressed. Includes PropertyMenus and ControlWiz.

    OXBTN1   166 *K* $19SW   *Opaque Software*

Odometer Custom Control 2.5 — This control is a numeric display similar to an automobile's odometer or tripometer. The font, number of digits, number of decimal and reset button are definable. Sample source code included; source code for VBX available at extra cost.

    ODOM25   190 *K* $40SW   *Global Majik Software*

OutReach For Windows DEMO — DEMO of OutReach for Windows, which allows using VBX custom controls in other applications. For the Excel or FoxPro examples, you must have those programs installed. Examples use certain MicroHelp controls (provided).

    OUTRCH   983 *K*   *InterGroup Technologies*

PSPNum Arithmatic VBX — Custom control for exact number arithmetic. Edit-style box with user-defined number attributes and masking. Much better than floating-point or VB currency type. For serious VB finance apps. Sample source code included.

    PSPNUM   215 *K* $75   *Prospero Software Products*

Percent Bar Custom Control — Percentage bar custom control useful as level or progress meter. Properties provided to select orientation, direction, style (linear or pie), colors, bitmaps, fonts and bevels. Percent level can be set directly by percent property or by calculation.

    PERCNT   195 *K* $15+SW   *Global Majik Software*

Percent Bar Custom Control 2.5 — Percentage bar custom control useful as level or progress meter. Properties provided to select orientation, direction, style (linear or pie), colors, bitmaps, fonts and bevels. Percent level can be set directly by percent property or by calculation.

    PRCNT25   341 *K* $15+SW   *Global Majik Software*

Percentage Bar Control 2.6 — PerCnt paints a percentage (status) bar on your form. Makes status reporting simple. 3-D effects, fonts, colors all user definable. Source code available for $25.

PERCNT26	*37 K* $10 SW	*Mabry Software*

Picture Button CC — Custom control - a command button that has both text and a picture on it. The picture can be scaled and placed above, below, to the right, or to the left of the text. The text may be multi-line. Sample source code included.

PICBTN	*202 K* $15	*Mabry Software*

Pizazz 1.55 Custom Control — Custom control that can emulate labels, panels, buttons, tabs, polygons, or any combination. Shadowed text, bevel and borders for 3D effects, tiled/stretched background bitmaps, icons, etc. Shareware version limited to one form save per VB session.

PZDEMO	*81 K* $30	*Visual Bits*

Popup Menu Custom Control — Custom control allows the creation of popup menus within a Visual Basic program. the Popup can be activated in response to an event on the parent form or another control. The control can emulate items within the main menu. Source avail. at extra cost.

POPUP	*20 K* $30SW	*Mullins, Robert*

Port I/O For Visual Basic — Port I/O custom control. Two properties: PortAddress set I/O address; PortData reads data from port or sets the I/O port.

IOVBX	*26 K* Free

Professional Toolkit Control C — Professional Toolkit Control Center provides an efficient way of adding Professional Toolkit Custom Controls to Visual Basic applications.

PROADD	*154 K* $10	*Obeda, Ed*

Prompt Control — This .VBX allows users to enter command-line style input similar to VB debug window or the dot prompt of xBase products. The Prompt Control automatically parses user input commands and provides a command line history mechanism.

PROMPT12	*25 K* $15 SW	*Dean, Andrew S.*

Pushbutton Control — A pushbutton for Visual Basic. Use a different bitmap or icon for the raised button and the pressed button.

VBPICBTN	*12 K* Free	*Gamber, Mark*

Quickhelp Tooltip VBX — Tooltip custom control adds tooltip help to any custom or standard control on the form. Source code from Borland Pascal is included.

PASVBX   26 K   Free   *Steingraeber Fachverlag*

RASVBX RemoteAccessServer 1.34 — Custom control allows you to programatically call a Remote Access Server. You set the user name, password, and phone number, and RASVBX establishes the network connection. Information dialog appears keeping the user notified of the status.

RASVBX   31 K $45   *Cutting Edge Consulting Inc.*

RDB Clipboard Tool — Allows you to display, print, save and load text and graphics from the clipboard. Complete VB source code. Includes use of INI file access, Windows open/save common dialog, tool button and sound.

CLPTL   175 K $5 SW   *Thomas, Zane*

ReSize Custom Control 3.5 — DEMO Custom control resizes all other controls on a form proportionally as the form is resized. An invisible control that works with the other controls on your forms, and does not need to contain them as children. Resizes fonts as they change positions.

RESIZE   41 K $34   *Larcom And Young*

Recorder Control — Recorder custom control to access Windows journaling. Applications include macro recording and playback abilities within an application, building CBT apps, and recording scripts for app testing and performing demonstrations.

VBHOOK   19 K $30SW   *Mullins, Robert*

Resource Monitor VBX 1.1 — Custom control enables the developer to report on and monitor three types of system resources: system memory, the User heap and the GDI heap. Can be used as a simple reporting tool for an About box, or to check system resources during runtime.

FSRMON   86 K   Free   *Stefanik, Michael J.*

Rotated Label CC — Label control that can be rotated to any angle. Data aware and will bind to a data control. Source code available at extra cost.

ROTEXT   180 K $15   *Mabry Software*

SIZ Form Sizer Custom Control — Adds controls to a Visual Basic form that the user can use to resize at run time by dragging corner handles, or move by dragging. Source code sample programs included.

SIZ_CC   34 K $15 SW   *Raike, William*

SPush VBX Demo — Custom control provides a button which can have unique graphics for UP (normal appearance), DOWN, FOCUS (focused but not clicked) and DS (disabled). Sample source code included.

JWSP	16 K	Free	*Jwpc, Inc.*

ScaKey Custom Control — Custom Control has one event: EnvKeyDown. Detects special keys (ALT, CTRL, etc.) and returns the value.

SCAKEY	19 K	Free

Scale Custom Control — VBX custom control provides a ruler which can be placed on any form. Useful for writing a screen painter or similar tool. Requires VB 3.0.

SCALE	11 K	Free	*Venugopalan, Vivek*

Scraper VBX 1.1 — Allows you to extract data from another application. Useful for integrating applications that cannot be integrated via OLE, DDE, or other means. Operates by allowing the user to select a window in another application, then extracting and formatting data

VBSCRA	25 K	$55SW	*Northeast Data Corp.*

Selector/Knob VBX 2.5 — An alternative to option buttons which uses a knob/pointer to select options. Properties are included to modify options, colors, knob style, alignment, border, background, etc. Sample VB code is included. VBX Source code available.

SELECT25	318 K	$20+SW	*Global Majik Software*

Shadowbox Popup Window CC 3.8 — Popup text display feature similar to Windows Help. Allows you to provide an advisory or "hotspot" context sensitive text for your VB app. Mouse click or keypress removes the window and continues program.

SHAD20	25 K	$18 SW	*Weimar Software*

Show - VBX Demos — Independently written demonstration of custom controls from MicroHelp. Includes tab, command, option, check, calendar, picture, normal and 3D versions. (Installs 2 Megs of VBXs into WINDOWSSYSTEM, so be careful.)

SHOW	564 K	Free	*PDA, Inc.*

Simple 3D VBX — Simple VBX to give forms a 3D look. Does not subclass all forms automatically.

SIMPLE	22 K	$18SW	*Liedtke, Brian*

Size Handle — VBX which makes sizeable borders or drag boxes on forms or on any other type of control. The size handle can be made transparent, giving mouse behavior and sizing events when placed over other controls. Can be used to trap/block built-in mouse sizing.

| SZHAND11 | 17 *K* | $18SW | *Objective Technologies Ltd.* |

Skeleton VBX Source Code — Skeleton VBX custom control source code in C++, and a VBX custom control to be used in designing new custom controls. Requires Visual C++ or other C++ compiler compatible with VBX custom controls.

| SKELET | 36 *K* | $50SW | *Anton Software Limited* |

Sleepless Nights Fx CCs — Label custom control with special effects; button custom control with special effects; enhanced spin button; FXDEMO.EXE sample program to show the properties of these controls; help file documentation.

| SNFXVB | 43 *K* | $35 SW | *Page, Preston* |

Slider Control DEMO — VBSlider control module can be used in VB3 or VB4, in full VB source code, not VBX or OCX. More than 20 properties allow you to create the slider control needed. Encrypted source code included, unlocked with registration.

| VBSLIDER | 27 *K* | $10 | *Wolfebyte Ltd.* |

Slider Controls — Alternative to using the standard Windows scroll bar control for numeric value control. Slider control appearance is completely defined with face and knob bitmaps.

| SCENTSLS | 127 *K* | $15SW | *SRC Enterprises* |

Slider VBX Control 2.2 — Custom control appears to user like a slider similar to those used on audio/video equipment such as stereo tuners and amplifiers. Includes 3-d effects, and is database enabled.

| SLIDER22 | 39 *K* | $55SW | *Northeast Data Corp.* |

Slider/Meter VBX 2.5 — Slider or linear meter control that you can customize. Properties are included to modify the On/Off characteristics of the sliding bar, background, tic marks, etc. Sample VB code is included. VBX Source Code available.

| SLIDER25 | 329 *K* | $20+SW | *Global Majik Software* |

Solution Studio OCX Catalog — Windows Help File catalog of Solution Studio's OCXs. Includes descriptions of LogWindow OCX, Initialize OCX, and License OCX.

| SFCATLOG | 19 *K* | Free | *Solution Studios Inc.* |

SoundEX/Metaphone VBX — Custom control to create SoundEx and Metaphone codes as used in database applications to give easy name lookup routines. Sample source code included. C source code for VBX available.

    SNDXSW   16 K   Free+   *Porter, Todd*

Soundex Word Matching CC 3.8 — Custom control for doing soundex "sounds like" word matching. Especially applicable to database applications where soundex is typically used to search for names which might be misspelled.

    SNDX20   23 K $18 SW   *Weimar Software*

Splitter Window Custom Control — Custom control implements a splitter bar in VB. Virtually no code required. Simply place the splitter control on a form. Add the two other controls you wish to split, and you are done. Choice of 3D or plain appearance. Sample source code included.

    SPLITTER   10 K $25   *Wogan, David*

Statbar Status Bar VBX — Status bar sits on a Parent form and provides information to the user. Displays the current date and time, keystates of NumLock and CapsLock, and custom messages and information panels from your program.

    STAT21   35 K $10   *WingedAxe Software, Inc.*

Status Bar Custom Control — Status bar VBX. This control displays a multi-element status bar on the bottom of your form. It automatically handles the NumLock, CapsLock, ScrollLock, and Insert key indicators. It also displays dates/times in international and programmer defined form.

    MSSTAT   52 K $20   *Mabry Software*

StatusBar Control — Custom control properties: DrawMode - gives a 3-D or flat look to the corresponding status line section; Indicator: makes a section of status bar indicate Num, Caps, Scroll, or Ins key; LinkedTo: links that section to another StBar instance.

    STBA2   18 K   Free   *Beekes, Bernd*

StatusFX V2.5 Standard Edition — Full Blown status bar features 6 caption/gauges each able to display keystates, date/time and more in a single control. Over 150 properties and 16 events, menu connectivity, built in popup menu, two timers and more.

    STATUS25   44 K $35   *Megabyte Services*

StatusFX V3.0 Itn'l. Edition — Everything the standard edition can do plus the added ability to meet a a Country's needs. This version can also read the WIN.INI section and automatically adjust itself.

    STATUS30   47 K $45   *Megabyte Services*

SuperButton — DEMO - Multipurpose Custom Control to create 'all kinds of buttons'. Demo runs within Visual Basic environment only.

    SBUTTO   37 K $58   *Manfred Walmeyer*

TX Text Control (DEMO) — Adds true WYSIWYG text processing to your application. Multiple font and paragraph attributes; inserts graphics; four different tabulator types for table editing; zoom in/out from 20% to 255%; ruler, status bar, and button bar.

    TX4VB   1117 K $249   *European Software Connection*

Tab/VBX Demo — DEMO of Tab/VBX. Offers a unique tab interface to your application, as well as as an Imprint control. Gives the ability to place any number of tabs on a form. Customizable properties include: 3-D effects, framing, bordering, adding colors or lines.

    FPTDEM   88 K   CONTACT *FarPoint Technologies, Inc.*

TabFrame, ToolTip, Toolbar Dem — Demo version of 3 custom controls: TabFrame provides tabbed dialogs; ToolTip provides MS style tooltips and other features; Toolbar provides dockable toolbars similar to Word, Excel, etc. See file GSHLP.ZIP for help files.

    GSVBX   109 K $85   *GC Consulting Services Ltd.*

Thunder Bars Bar Codes DEMO — Thunder Bars program generates bar codes, patch codes, and postal codes that can be copied to the Clipboard. Full Visual Basic source code is provided with the full product.

    TRUBAR   140 K   *Thunder Island Software, Inc.*

TipButton 2.0 — Custom control lets you create a Microsoft style toolbar, including Tooltips, with absolute minimum VB code. Just place a button on a form, give it a picture (bitmap), set the Tip text, and that's it. Help file and sample source included.

    TIPBTN2   28 K $30   *Wogan, David*

Tips - Tool Tips VBX — Custom control provides Microsoft style tool tips. Small bits of info popup when the user parses the mouse over your controls. Source code available for $50.

    TIPS11   34 K $15SW   *Mabry Software*

TitleSpy 5.0 — Custom control lets you change the size and orientation of the Title (Caption) Bar. Make it as large or small as needed. Also allows modifying the System Menu. Make your form always be on top of all the other windows. Includes sample source code.

    TTLSPY   60 K $40   *SoftLand Inc.*

Toggle Switch Control 2.50 — A TRUE/FALSE, YES/NO, or ON/OFF indicator. The control displays captions or pictures to represent the toggle state depending on the control's value. Capable of playing WAV files to indicate the switch turning on or off. Source code avail. at extra cost.

TOGGLE25   *239 K* $15+SW   *Global Majik Software*

ToolButton 2.0 — Custom control that supports command and attribute buttons in toolbars. Sample button images are supplied, or can be created. Generates up to six button images from one button bitmap, as needed for the button function.

TOOL20   *36 K*   Free   *Foster, Brett*

ToolTip Demo 1.4 — ToolTip custom control allows you to add Microsoft style tool tips and context sensitive hints to your VB applications. Includes mouse tracking, menu tracking, and focus tracking. Demo version.

TOOLTI   *59 K* $40   *GC Consulting Services Ltd.*

Toolbar Button & Statusbar CCs — Control allows you to set up toolbar buttons using only a single image which the control will automatically convert into a down and disabled image when required. Source code demo supplied. C source for VBXs supplied with registration.

STATUSB   *66 K* $60   *Westacott, Andrew*

Toolbar Custom Control 1.1 — Custom control which adds tiny captions and control menus to container objects. Creates floating toolbars from ordinary VB forms and picture boxes. Forms containing a TBar control can be moved or closed using the tiny caption and control menus.

TBARWW   *41 K* $20SW   *Washington, Winefred*

Toolbar Custom Control 2.5 — Custom control for implementing industry standard toolbars. TBAR uses one bitmap, created by the developer, to display all buttons, in all button states. You can design, define, and implement the behavior of your toolbar without writing a line of code.

TBAR25   *58 K* $20 SW   *Klasman Quality Consulting*

Toolbar Custom Control 3.0 — Custom control allows the VB developer to place true "buttons" on a toolbar. no longer will you have to write code to swap out pictures when the mouse button is pressed or released. Focus is NOT transferred to the TBTN control when it is selected.

TBTN   *8 K* $7   *McKean Consulting*

TurboPack 1.0 — Contains five custom controls: HotMap, Titlespy, MCursor, PopHelp, PopHelp.

TURBOPAC   *578 K* $120   *SoftLand Inc.*

UDPPort Control 1.01 — UDPPort custom control used to facilitate datagram communications. It can act both as client and server. Can communicate with any number of hosts simultaneously as well as generate broadcast packets.

    UDPPORT   30 *K* $30   *DevSoft Inc.*

Updated MSCOMM.VBX 2.1.0.1 — Updated MSCOMM.VBX control from Microsoft fixes 14.4 baud bug.

    MSCOMM   14 *K*   Free   *Microsoft*

VB Controls — Set of custom controls. Included: 3 listboxes, 2 file listboxes, File drag-and-drop, Common dialog control, 3-D radio button, 3-D checkbox, Wave file playback, 3-D label, 3-D groupbox, Multi-button. VBX and sample source code files included.

    VBCTRL10   105 *K*   Free   *Gamber, Mark*

VB Drag-Drop 1.0 — Drag and drop custom control. C source included.

    VBDD   14 *K*   Free   *Gamber, Mark*

VB File Listboxes 1.0 — Provides a multi-selection File Directory listbox and a multicolumn, multi-selection File Directory listbox. Full VBX file and sample source codes included.

    VBMFILE   15 *K*   Free   *Gamber, Mark*

VB Label 1.0 — Custom control allows the creation of 3D labelboxes. C source included.

    VBLABEL   19 *K*   Free   *Gamber, Mark*

VB Listbox Controls 1.1 — Provides a multi-selection, multicolumn and combination listbox. VBX and demo files included.

    VBLISTBX   16 *K*   Free   *Gamber, Mark*

VB Messenger - Subclassing CC — VB Messenger Subclass Custom Control can be placed in any VB application to subclass windows and/or controls. Virtually allows you to create custom events in VB by intercepting messages sent to windows. Demo source code included. See VBMSG20 for new vers

    VBMSG   67 *K*   See Memo

VB Messenger Subclassing CC 2. — Four custom controls. VB Messenger Subclass Custom Control, Mouse Hook Control, Keyboard Hook Control and Callback Control. Can be placed in any VB application to subclass windows and/or controls. Fills the gaps between Visual Basic and C++.

    VBMSG20   289 *K* $129   *GreenTree Technologies*

VB Wizard 3.13 — Includes 3 wizards and 3 utilities. Procedure Wizard creates standardized documented routines; Comment Wizard formats and inserts ad hoc comments; Picture Wizard set control picture property by viewing pictures; Toggle VB Toolbar and Project window.

| VBWIZ | 247 K | $35 SW | *Pocket Change Software* |

VBBACKUP.VBX — Custom control for saving and restoring data from your VB application. Built in data compression and error checking. Just add to your project file, place it on a form, and make two simple calls.

| VBBACKUP | 151 K | | *RUW-Computer* |

VBCtl3D 2.10 — Simple-to-use custom control gives a 3-D look and feel to VB's built-in controls and to the complete Visual Basic environment.

| VBCTL3D | 133 K | $29 SW | *Simms, Jeff* |

VBForm Custom Control — Custom control provides a 3D look to all the forms in your project if you add the control to the first form in your project. Source code provided.

| VB3DFR | 9 K | Free | *Venugopalan, Vivek* |

VBMoreControl For Mouse 0.9 — Custom control provides information about the user's mouse, and provides an easy way to control mouse pointer movements, mouse pointer locations, and mouse clicks from VB. Fully functional, but beta test version which may not be released to end users.

| VBMMOU | 59 K | Free | *Brown, Tim* |

VBWsk - Winsock Custom Control — Winsock custom control provides access to the Windows Sockets network programming API for TCP/IP. Sample VB source code included. ALPHA TEST version.

| VBWSK01A | 23 K | Free | *Syme, Brian* |

VBX Generator 2 — Utility for use with Visual Basic. A source code generator provides full C source code to compile your VBX from Visual Basic source code. Shareware version restricts user defined event parameters. Requires C compiler capable of generating VBX files.

| VBXG2M | 52 K | $50SW | *Pagett, Paul* |

VBX Interface To Intel 8255PPI — Custom control interface to Intel's 8255 Programmable Peripheral Interface. VBX can directly manipulate up to 24 digital input/output lines on the 8255 chip.

| V8255 | 9 K | $15 | *DB Technologies* |

VBX Studio 1.2 — 15 custom controls. Bitmapped listboxes, comboboxes, spins, tabbed dialogs, formatted edit controls, gauges, animated picture buttons and more.

 VBXSTD   750 K $55+SW   *Chevron, Denis*

VBXgen 3.0 — VBX custom control building tool. Creates all the C code framework for creating your own custom controls for use in Visual Basic. Point and click to select standard properties and events, or build your own on screen. Limited demo version.

 VBXG3   496 K $80   *J&K Software Productions*

VBXpress Custom Controls Demo — Sample custom controls created with VBXpress (a commercial product). Includes a sample Visual Basic source code program and a German help file describing the included sample custom controls.

 VBXPRS   385 K   *AJS Publishing*

VSVBX Library 4.01 — Indextab: creates notebook tabs horizontal, vertical, or scrollable. Elastic: never align controls by hand again, splitter bar, and flood. Makes any control inside 3D. AWKsome: general parsing control for VB.

 VSVBX401   118 K $45 SW   *VideoSoft*

VideoSoft Custom Controls Libr — Elastic auto-resize all the controls on a form; Splitter bars, add 3D perspective to any control. Replace labels in form with one elastic, makes forms screen res independent. IndexTab organizes forms with notebook style tabs. More.

 3CTRLS   118 K $45 SW   *VideoSoft*

WSIHLP Custom Controls — Eight custom controls: Balloon help popup windows; Clacker - hooks for dynamic menu help; Numwin - enumerates and returns hWnds for all windows; Rtmouse - popup help from right mouse button; Shadbx - popup shadowed text message; Snddex - soundex; etc.c

 WSIHLP   315 K $75 SW   *Weimar Software*

Wapix Custom Controls — Set of VBX custom controls provide an easy and safe way to use Windows API functions without the need for declarations or DLL calls. Includes: reading/writing INI files, getting memory and resource info, set wallpaper and other system parameters, etc.

 WAPIX   62 K $29   *Huntington Software*

Wave Maker 1.5 Demo — Utility to create two kinds of VBXs containing up to 64 WAV files you select. No programming is required. Eliminates the need to use cumbersome API calls and external WAV files.

 WAVMAK   432 K $20SW   *Washington, Winefred*

WinMsg — Custom control gives the programmer the ability to receive messages being passed by Windows. You can change the way programs function by changing the parameters being passed to a program.

| WINMSG | 13 K | $25 SW | SoftBit Enterprises |

XFile Custom Controls 2.5 DEMO — DEMO of custom controls allow you to do fast application prototyping with access to Dataflex and Powerflex database files and any databases supported by Visual Basic. Includes a comprehensive Database API. Sample VB source code.

| XFILE2 | 597 K | $399 | BC Soft AB |

ZZHot.Vbx — VBX to create arbitrary, polygonal hot spot regions in VB programs. Very small resource usage.

| ZZHOT | 334 K | | Solid Software Inc. |

9
DDE

Code Master Macro Pack #1 — Macro examples for using Access as a DDE server.
  MACRO1   56 *K*   Free   *Teletech Systems*

DDE In Visual Basic — Using Dynamic Data exchange in Visual Basic. Source code included. From the article "Link, Then Leap" in the May 1992 issue of Windows Tech Journal.
  DDEVB   32 *K*   Free   *Pleas, Keith R.*

ODBC Encapsulation — Source code of encapsulated ODBC routines. Functions include the ability to build paremeter-marker queries and stored procedure calls, datatype conversion and formatting, automatically disconnecting and reconnecting to your client/server datasource, etc.
  ODBCNCAP   16 *K* $10   *Lowrey, Richard*

Small Database OLE Server — Small Database OLE Server can be used with Access, Excel, VB3, VB4 (16 or 32 bit) and any other application that can utilize Ole Server technology. Redistributable engine adds less than 50K to your project size. VB and Excel sample source code included.
  SMDBFULL   1960 *K* $30   *Burgess, Mike*

StoreIt OLE Custom Control — 32-bit custom control provides access to OLE structured storage. Through its classes and properties, you can create and open storages, get/set the Summary properties of a storage, edit storage elements, etc.
  STOREIT   1238 *K* Free   *Gouge, David W.*

VB To Excel — Demonstration of Dynamic Data Exchange using Microsoft Excel.
  VBXLDEMO   8 *K*   Free

X-Ray/WINSOCK 1.2 — X-Ray/WINSOCK shows the interaction between your application and the Winsock API with no modifications to your existing program. Shows the following info: Parameters (before and after the call); return value in native format; pointer validation, etc.
  XRAYWI12   225 *K* $80 SW   *Systems Software Technology*

10
DLL - COMMUNICATION

Locker API DLL 1.0 Demo — Controls the number of concurrent users that may access a program. When the maximum number of users is reached, the program is notified for further handling.

    LKAPI1   8 *K* $245+   *Hampshire Software*

PDQComm For Windows Demo — DEMO of Crescent's PDQComm for Windows.

    PDQCOM   76 *K* $149   *Crescent Software Inc.*

Winsock RCMD.DLL — DLL provides a function similar to the Berkeley Sockets "rcmd" function. Provides the ability to initiate Unix commands from within your Windows program and process any output from that command. Example programs provided for C and Visual Basic.

    WRCMDD   52 *K* $35SW   *Denicomp Systems*

Winsock RCP.DLL — DLL provides a function similar to the Berkeley Sockets "rcp" function. Provides the ability to copy files to and from remote hosts, and to on-the-fly text file conversions. Example programs provided for C and Visual Basic.

    WRCPDL   68 *K* $35SW   *Denicomp Systems*

11
DLL - DATABASE

Dataworks — Dictionary based XBase file management. Complements VXBASE (see VXBASE and VXBDOC).

    DWORKS   204 *K* $50   *VXBase Systems*

Updated XBS110.DLL — Updated XBS110.DLL from Microsoft fixes several bugs in the original file shipped with VB 3.0 and Access 1.0.

    XBS110   138 *K*   Free   *Microsoft*

VXBase 1.07 — Database programming library for Visual Basic providing the usual xBase functions. A demonstration program using Clipper compatible data and index files is included.

    VXBASE   345 *K* $59.95SW   *VXBase Systems*

VXBase Documentation — Documentation files for VXBase.

    VXBDOC   180 *K*   *VXBase Systems*

12
DLL - General

3-D 1.1 — Gives all Windows applications the 3-D look of Excel and Access, etc.
    3D11   11 *K* Free   *Biggins, Aidan*

3D CTL3DV2.DLL Sample — Sample application shows 3D effect message box. Source code included.
    3DVB   15 *K* Free   *McGregor, Rob*

3DfxPlus — Automatically adds 3D effects to VB forms, system dialog boxes, and message boxes. Numerous configuration options.
    3DFXPLUS   59 *K* $10 SW   *Digital PowerTOOLS*

AA-ARRAY.DLL Extended Arrays — DLL for extended arrays in VB. Manages the creation, accessing, saving to and restoring from disk of arrays with up to 4 Gigs elements and >64K of VB strings. No VB imposed limits. Arrays can be Integer, Long, Single, Double, Currency or String.
    AAARRAY   92 *K* $30   *AA-Software International*

About! and Errors! — Demo provides examples of About! and Errors! DLLs. About! provides a customized About box which can include system information and a password. Errors! contains every error code from VB and Access and generates an error message the user can understand.
    DEMOS   222 *K* $75   *White, Wayne*

Advanced Disk Library 3.11 — DLL provides Disk Total and Free Space; Drive Checking; DriveTypes; Move and Copy Files; Search List; Split path into one of four segments; Create/Delete up to nine directories at one time; File Exist; Format Disk; etc. Sample source code included.
    ADL311   215 *K* $35 SW   *Advanced Applications*

BITS.DLL — DLL supplies bit operations.
    BITS_DLL   11 *K* Free   *Peters, Constantine*

Big Disk Array Demo Of TIME2WI — Demo shows features of the TIME2WIN library. (see file TIMxxxxx). Full Visual Basic source code is included.

    BIGARR   129 *K*   Free   *Renard, Michael*

CX Data Compression Library — Data compression library with sample Visual Basic source code. Full C source available for the compression DLL.

    CXE103   38 *K* $45   *Nelson, Eugene*

Call InterruptX In VBWin — DLL for the implementation of DOS interrupts and functions. Generates interrupts and evaluates the results. Includes demo VB source code and full documentation.

    VBINT10   45 *K*   Free   *Esterling, Rick*

CsrPlus — Adds nearly 100 new cursors for VB in several categories. Easy programmer interface. Also adds instant form backdrop patterns. Sample source code included.

    CSRPLUS   210 *K* $10 SW   *Digital PowerTOOLS*

Custom Cursors Over Buttons — DLL and sample source code demonstrates how to have custom cursors over button controls. DLL contains several sample cursors.

    CURSOR   8 *K*   Free   *Swift, W*

DameWare Cal32 OCX — Calendaring routine OCX. Graphical depiction of a calendar for the user to select a date and/or time for any given occasion or event. Many different formats for the program to retrieve the data from the calendar routine.

    CAL32   61 *K*   *Dameware Development*

DameWare Calendar DLL — Calendaring routine DLL. Graphical depiction of a calendar for the user to select a date and/or time for any given occasion or event. Many different formats for the program to retrieve the data from the calendar routine.

    CAL10   180 *K* $18   *Dameware Development*

Data To DLL Example — An example VB program and DLL with source code. Demonstrates one way to pass data to a DLL and return it to VB.

    VBDLLCOM   28 *K*   Free   *Weidinger, Andreas*

Drive Type DLL — 16-bit DLL contains an exported procedure "pbGetDriveType" which returns the type of drive specified. If Windows 95 or Windows NT is detected the 32-bit API call is made, otherwise the 16-bit call is made.

    DRVTYPE   6 *K*   Free

DrvPlus — Adds dozens of new commands for disk/drive control and information. Easily determines if a file exists, obtains drive size, drive used size, renames volumes, etc. Much more.

DRVPLUS   67 K $10 SW   *Digital PowerTOOLS*

End Task DLL — DLL corrects the problem of Windows "End Task" selected from the Task List passing a message to a hidden VB form, which does not pass the information on. ENCASE.DLL hooks into the form to receive the message.

ENTASK   5 K   Free   *Simms, Jeff*

Extending VB With Windows DLLs — Technical article, with sample source code for linking to a DLL function from Visual Basic, Visual Basic data types as parameters, how to debug a DLL called from Visual Basic, and VBFILEIO sample DLL giving VB apps access to C runtime I/O.

VBDLL   36 K   *Microsoft*

GBLIB 1.1c — DLL contains 86 functions. Loads Waves, Icons, Cursors, Bitmaps, and Text from a resource DLL file. Has extensive sound functions, pause function, animated hourglass and more.

GBLIB1C   215 K   Free   *Bamber, Gordon*

GetIdleTime — DLL provides a call that returns the last time stamp of the last time the user moved the mouse or pressed a key anywhere in Windows. Useful for detecting how long the user has been idle. Sample source code included.

GETIDL   12 K   Free   *Malik Information Services*

How To Call A DLL From VB — Sample C and VB source code shows how to make a DLL and call it from VB. Borland C++, Symantec C++, and MS Visual C++ source code files included.

VBDLLCAL   42 K   Free   *Kligman, Rick*

MC Bundle — Bundle of Renard's "Time to Win", "VB/Error Handler" and "VB/Tracer Profiler".

MCBUNDLE   586 K $99   *Renard, Michael*

Magical 1.0 — Calendar in a DLL. Creates an on-screen calendar and reports the user-selected date to the program. Sample source code provided.

MAGICAL1   37 K   Free   *Karkada, Sudarshan*

Outline Control 1.3 — No longer supported. Outline control can be used as a numerically numbered outline or, with numbering and editing turned off, as an editable listbox. Demo version with full capabilities. Sample source code is included.

    OLVBX13   40 *K* $75 SW   *Abel, Todd J.*

Outport DLL Demo — DLL which allows output to a port using the command OUT in Visual Basic. It is used in the same manner as the statement OUT is used in BASIC.

    OUTPORT   7 *K* $10+   *Coggin, Daniel*

PBClone Windows Library 2.0 — General purpose DLL with 78 VB/Windows routines most requested by users of Hanlin's QuickBasic (DOS) libraries.

    PBCWIN20   49 *K* $12SW   *Hanlin III, Thomas G.*

PCDone.DLL Status Bar — DLL to display a percentage progress bar window while a task is working. Use during long printing procedures, large calculations, scanning through long databases, etc.

    PCDONE   9 *K* $18 SW   *Abri Technologies Inc.*

PPRTR 4.7 — DLL providing higher-level language access via functions to retrieve and change all printer attributes available via ExtDeviceMode in DEVMODE structures (orientation, pagesize, etc.). Also get list of available printers, get/change default printer, etc.

    PPRTR4   55 *K* $10 SW   *Poellinger, Paul F.*

StrPlus.DLL — Adds several string functions to VB. GetToken easily parses strings, build command interpreters, parse Command$, separate comma-delimited strings for database conversions, etc. ReadDate simulates old Read/Data statements. Much more.

    STRPLUS   59 *K* $10 SW   *Digital PowerTOOLS*

String.DLL String Manipulation — Fast string manipulations not found in VB. DLL source available with $20 registration. Includes Sort, ReverseString, FindRightChar, FindFirstNIS (not in substring).

    STRNGD   21 *K*   Free   *INside*

T2WIN-16 — Collection of over 642 routines for use by the VB 4.0 (16-Bit) Developer under Windows.

    T2WIN_16   334 *K* $43   *Renard, Michael*

T2WIN-32 (v2.52) — Collection of over 642 routines for use by the VB 4.0 (32-Bit) Developer under Windows 95/Windows NT 3.51, in DLL.

    T2WIN_32   388 K $52   *Renard, Michael*

Time 2 Win - 16 bit for VB3 — VB 3.0 DLL with 685 functions for 2D/3D geometry, array, binary, bitmap, compression, CRC32, date/time, encrypt/decrypt, file, file I/O from C, huge memory array, huge string, IEEEnum, interest rate, language control, matrix, network, object, etc.

    T2WIN910   457 K $43SW   *Renard, Michael*

Time 2 Win Hints — Windows Help file contains hints for using the TIME2WIN.DLL library.

    T2WHINTS   10 K   Free   *Renard, Michael*

Time To Win 7.00 — DLL contains 640+ routines for VB 3.0. Array routines, Big numbers, Bitstring manipulation, Date/Hour/Time routines, Disk Array routines, IEEE conversion routines, String manipulation routines, Timer functions, Type functions, etc. See BIGARR.

    TIME2WIN   344 K $61   *Renard, Michael*

Time To Win Light 4.0 — DLL contains 400+ routines for VB 3.0. Array routines, big numbers, bitstring manipulation, date/hour/time routines, disk array routines, IEEE conversion routines, string manipulation routines, timer functions, type functions, etc.

    T2WLIGHT   168 K $43   *Renard, Michael*

UFLHTS String Formatting — DLL contains three functions; fmpth(string) formats a string of numbers in a special fixed way for phone numbers; fmtzip(string) formats a string of numbers as a Zip code; bAND(integer,integer) returns a boolean value indicating bitwise AND result.

    HTS   11 K   Free   *Heritage Technology Solutions*

VB Array Manipulation DLL — DLL contains a function that can delete an entry in a Visual Basic array. Operates on the array regardless of the array type. Much faster than manually coding a routine to move entries in an array. Sample source included.

    ARRAYCB   11 K   Free   *Benedict, Chuck*

VB Error Handler 3.0 — Utility to add or remove error handling in a Visual Basic program. Full source code and DLL can easily be added to any program. Error messages are contained in an external file.

    VBERRHND   116 K $34   *Renard, Michael*

VB Error Handler 4.0 (VB4) — Utility to add or remove error handling in a Visual Basic program. Full source code and DLL can easily be added to any program. Error messages are contained in an external file. 16-bit version of VB 4 only.

> VBERR16   124 *K* $34   *Renard, Michael*

VB-ASM 1.3 — DLL provides services that are difficult or impossible to do in VB alone. Includes: vbInterrupt, vbRealModeX, vbInp, vbOutp, vbPtr, vbSeg, vbLoWord, vbHiWord, and more. Includes sample VB source code.

> VBASM   35 *K*   Free   *SoftCircuits Programming*

VBossAPI Function Lib 2.11 — Library of functions help the VB programmer develop script-parsing applications. Functions offer both Word-related and Keyword/Token related operations required to implement text parsing and script processing applications. Sample source code included.

> VBOSSAPI   122 *K* $21SW   *Truesdale, Greg*

VBstrAPI Huge String Array — VB String Object Library DLL. Buffers medium to huge amounts of string data (>64K). Demo version includes full sample source code.

> VBSTRA   131 *K* $20SW   *Truesdale, Greg*

Virtual Desktop — Virtual Desktop is a DLL which lets you expand the Windows desktop into "virtual screens". Provides functions to divide up the screen into as many "virtual" screens as you wish, both horizontally and vertically, switch from screen to screen, etc.

> VIRTDESK   12 *K* $17 SW   *Rathwick, Zane / Addsoft*

WGLIB 1.01 — A DLL library of general purpose routines. This file is a development (demo) library only and will work only within the Visual Basic programming environment. See docs for use restrictions; contact vendor for price of current release.

> WGLIB101   112 *K*   *InfoSoft*

WinfoXL System Control API — DLL provides system information and system control API functions not found in the Windows API or the VB command structure. Disk functions, bit functions, system functions, string functions, color functions. Full demo source code.

> WINFOX   491 *K* $20   *Digital PowerTOOLS*

13
DLL - GRAPHICS

256 Colors Control — Demonstrates how to load 256 colors in a Visual basic picture box control. Includes full VB source code plus full C source code for the supplied DLL.

      256PB2   *25 K*   Free   *Rpb*

Access 3DCTL.DLL From VB — Shows use of CTL3D.DLL to give dialogs and message boxes a 3-D appearance. [CTL3D.DLL is contained in file 3D11.ZIP.] EXE and source code included.

      3DCTL   *12 K*   Free   *Bonner, Paul*

Axtel Tools DEMO — Demonstrates Axtels' engines for processing scanned bitonal images. Includes compress, scale to view, noise removal, skew correction, line removal, barcode recognition and insertion. Install from a subdirectory named DISK1.

      AXDEMO   *741 K*   *Axtel, Inc.*

DLL - Load Bitmaps And Strings — Visual Basic source code and a DLL to load bitmaps and strings into an application.

      FROMDL   *13 K*   Free   *Lyk, Edward*

DXF-IN For VB DEMO — DEMO of DLL to create and view AutoCAD DXF format files. Adds DXF support to the standard Visual Basic picture control.

      DXFSUITE   *205 K* $200+   *Ideal Engineering Software*

GIF To BMP DLL — DLL converts and 8-bit GIF to BMP. Includes sample source code.

      GIFBMP   *6 K*   Free   *Cramp, Stephen*

GTIcon - DLL For Icons — DLL contains two functions: AssignDragIcon - assigns an icon to a control's DragIcon property; GetDragIcon - copies an icon and assigns it a handle. Sample Visual Basic source code included.

      GTICON   *10 K*   Free   *Torralba, George R.*

Geometry DLL — DLL of Geometry functions. Sample source code included, minimal documentation.

    GEO   14 K   Free   *Sirabella, John*

Graphics Viewer DLL — DLL for viewing and printing graphics. Reads BMP, CUT, DIB, GEM, GIF, IFF, IMG, LBM, MAC, MSP, PCX, PIC, RLE, TGA, WMF, and WPG formats. Based on the bitmapped graphics books by Steve Rimmer. Full source code for viewer is included.

    GVJO   46 K   Free   *Oliphant, Joe*

HALO Visual Image DEMO — Three custom controls. Image performs general image processing and conversion. Acquisition acquires images from scanners, video camera, etc. Gallery manages collections of image thumbnails. Supports TIFF, JPEG, BMP, CUT, PICT, EPS, GIF and more.

    HVIDEMO   1301 K $399   *Lifeboat Publishing*

LDRSUtil Graphics DLL Demo — DEMO of DLL library featuring special graphics effects, string compression, file archiving, encryption, CRCs, disk functions, multimedia functions.

    LDRU2016   265 K $40   *LDR Systems*

Spinlist Demo — DLL that allows you to lay out reports in your word processor of choice: Word for Windows, Ami Pro, Wordperfect for Windows, and Ventura Publisher, and any program accepting the RTF format. Demonstration program only, with sample source code.

    SPINVB   129 K   *OSoft Development Corporation*

Turbo DXF — DLL to create AutoCAD DXF format files. Sample source code included. Demo version limited to 25 graphic elements.

    DXFDLL   51 K $50 SW   *Ideal Engineering Software*

14
DLL INTERFACE

Access 16-Bit DLL From VB4 — Demo source code shows how to use OLE automation to wrap a 16-bit DLL so its functions are accessible from 32-bit VB4. Full source for all parts of the demo (the DLL, go-between file, and VB4/32 end-code file).

      VB16TO32   29 *K*   Free   *Trupin, Joshua*

Access 2 Error Msg DLL — DLL displays the reserved error messages associated with the Access 2.0 Jet engine.

      A20DLL   15 *K*   CR   *Lynn F. Solon Foundation*

Fortran DLL To VB Demo — Sample files demonstrate how a DLL written in Fortran can use Windows 3.1 API calls to send status messages to a Visual Basic program while the DLL is executing. Pertains to Visual Basic 3.0 and Fortran 5.1.

      F2VB2   28 *K*   Free   *Lewis, Tony*

NTG Interface I/O DLL — This is a DLL for Windows (16 & 32bit) to manipulate bits, bytes, integers, longs, and Hardware Port I/O or to call CPU interrupts. For C/C++, Visual Basic.

      NT86IO10   62 *K*   Free   *NTG*

Paradox Engine Interface — A DLL interface between Visual Basic and the commercial Paradox Engine DLL (required; not supplied).

      VBPXEN   20 *K*   Free   *Dooley, Sharon F.*

Power.DLL — DLL uses certain characteristics of 30+ Windows API functions to allow them to appear as native VB functions. The difference in code and speed is dramatic.

      VBABK   58 *K* $20 SW   *BKMA Inc.*

Using BWCC.DLL Message Box — Example of using Visual Basic to access the dialog box function of BWCC.DLL (required, not included).

      VBBWCC   2 *K*   Free   *Duhamel, Guy*

15
DATA ACCESS

AFD Postcode 3.0 DEMO — Provides a simple way to speed the entry of address information. Type in the postcode, and the Street, Locality, Town, County, and STD or ZIP code are provided. DDE and DLL versions and sample source code provided.

    PCEVAL   541 *K* $200+   *AFD Computers*

AFD Postcode Plus 1.1 DEMO — Simple way to speed the entry of address information. Type in the postcode and the street, locality, town, county, and STD or ZIP code are provided. Organization and property data, grid references, ward codes, NHS codes for UK points.

    PCPEVAL   1201 *K* $1000+   *AFD Computers*

Applications Data Server DEMO — Extremely fast database server engine for use in a client/server environment. Automatic data conversions for Windows display. Supports a proprietary application data exchange protocol easier than DDE or OLE, and a SPY utility for modifying data.

    ADSC15   502 *K* $99   *International Technology Devel*

Btrieve ISAM Driver Update — Update driver for Btrieve access with VB 3.0.

    BTR110   56 *K* Free   *Microsoft*

Charlie Data Dictionary Manage — Program to add/delete/change/list/edit the tables, fields, indexes, relations and query definitions for a VB Access database. You can measure performance and print the dictionary of your database.

    CHAR27   191 *K* $20   *Monte Carlo Software*

ContACT - Access DBase In ACT! — Small application uses Q+E/VB to access dBase files in ACT!Q for Windows. Requires (commercial programs) Q+E and ACT!. Full source code.

    CONTAC   34 *K* Free   *Barlow, Chris*

Creating DDF Files — Instructions and examples for creating DDF files for your Btrieve file using VB3 or Access.

    DDFDOC   20 K   Free

Crystal Reports/MS Access Time — Crystal Reports 2.0 (supplied with VB 3) cannot handle time formatting for MS Access fields defined as "date/time"; Crystal Reports Pro can handle it only through ODBC. These Crystal Reports formulas will format the time from Access databases.

    CRWTIM   4 K   Free   *Becker, Thomas*

DBT Grid Working Model — Provides an editable GRID control for your applications. Properties include: About, CellStyle, ColumnHeading, ColumnLabels, ColumnWidth, DataModel, DragIcon, DragMode, EditMode, EventMask, etc. This working model disables certain properties.

    DBGRID   326 K $40   *DB Technologies*

DDL Manager 1.1 — Obsolete, see VB Data Companion. Program to ease creating of Access format databases from VB. Create, repair and compact, copy, delete databases; list, add, change tables; list, add change fields ion a table; list, add change indexes in a table.

    DDLMGR   439 K $30 SW   *MM Technology*

Data Manager Source Code — Microsoft's source code for the Visual Basic Data Manager.

    DATMGR   24 K   Free   *Microsoft*

DataPRO Enhanced Data Control — Complete replacement for the Visual Basic Data Control. Pure VB source code (supplied, unlocked with registration). Offers a colorful interface with features such as Add, Save/Update, Delete, Search, Delete, and QBE buttons.

    DATAPRO   42 K $20   *Anno Domini, Inc.*

Datafile Controls Demo FoxPro — Simple demo of the use of data controls to view and modify a FoxPro 2.5 file. Demos fields bound to the data control in addition to the recordsets operations for AddNew, Edit, Update, Delete, etc.

    APPRAI   5 K   Free   *Tucker, Barry G.*

Diamond Report Writer 1.14 — Fast and easy report generator. Supports Access, dBase and Foxpro formats. VB developer's edition available, $199. Full VB source code available, $799.

    DIAMOND   320 K $149   *XDev Inc.*

Edit Batch Files — A technique for changing File Manager to allow easy editing of batch files. Visual Basic source code is included to make the changes automatic.

    EDITBATS   19 *K*   Free   *Davis, Mike*

FieldPack Demo (Gregg Irwin) — Sample of the Delimited SubString functions available in FieldPack (FLDPAK.ZIP). Full source included. Manipulate a delimited substring, clear list, load list, word count, parse string, etc.

    FPDEMO   15 *K*   Free   *Irwin, Gregg*

Get Network Login — How to get the network login without shelling or using environment variables. Short, simple source code.

    NETID   2 *K*   Free   *Healy, Joe*

How To Correct ISAM Error — This document describes how to fix the 'Can't find installable ISAM' error. It covers several steps you can take to fix this problem and prevent it in applications you distribute.

    ISAMER   3 *K*   Free   *Carr, J. Frank*

IPX And SPX Custom Control 2.0 — Custom controls to create applications that can communicate as clients and/or servers on Novell NetWare networks. Partial demo version; IPX control is fully functional; SPX control will not load in the design environment.

    IPXSPX   67 *K* $30 SW   *Wiltbank, Lee*

Linked List Demo — Demonstration of how to implement a linked list and linked list processing in VB without using VBXs or DLLs. Data is stored in an array. Pointers point to array elements instead of memory addresses.

    LL   3 *K*   Free   *Weiss, Thomas R.*

NetWare API Test For VB — Example program illustrates how to use the NetWare Interface for Visual Basic (NIVB).

    NIVBSRC   92 *K*   Free   *Novell Inc.*

NetWare Interface For VB — NetWare interface to Visual Basic.

    NIVB   28 *K*   Free   *Novell Inc.*

ODBC Sniffer For Windows 1.1 — Utility finds and reports the most common used ODBC functions to quickly find programming errors. This demo version has limited functions, but the complete help file of the full version is included.

    ODBC   149 *K* $295   *Blue Lagoon Software*

OLE-Obj <-> Database Tables — Small VB source code module with two functions to copy the contents of embedded OLE objects from a VB-OLE2.0 control into a database field and vice versa. Also includes a function to copy the contents from one OLE control to another.

OLETOO   2 *K*   Free   *Schloter, Martin*

OpenExchange Guided Tour — Guided tour of OpenExchange.

OETOUR   608 *K*   *Innovative Solutions & Techn.*

Reformat Utility — Visual Basic program, source code, that constructs and output file from an input file based on control statements. The program has the ability to unpack data fields in files that were downloaded from a host.

REFORM   15 *K*   Free

SQL Data Administrator 1.3 DEM — Front-end database for ODBC users. Automatically collects and stores critical data sources, catalog and ODBC setup information in an MDB database for off-line reference and backup. DEMO version, fully functional, limited to 30 days use.

SQLDTA   2508 *K*   *DataTools*

SQL Sniffer For Windows — Utility finds and reports the most common used dbLib functions to quickly find programming errors. This demo version has limited functions, but the complete help file of the full version is included.

SQLSNI   139 *K* $295   *Blue Lagoon Software*

SQL Test — Simple program to perform interactive SQL statements on an Access database. Useful for learning SQL or verifying Visual Basic's handling of SQL.

SQLTST   9 *K*   SEE DOC   *Weaver, Peter R.*

SQL-Sombrero/VBX 32-Bit Demo — Complete VBX DB-library for SQL Server. Direct interface to use DB-library functions without using C or C++. Direct access to the Sybase/Microsoft DB-library functions from Visual Basic. 32-bit demo only, 16-bit library included with registration.

OCXDBDEM   1149 *K*   *Sylvain Faust Inc.*

VBA Array Sorter — Excel 5.0 spreadsheet uses Visual Basic for Applications to sort arrays created in VBA in ascending or descending order.

SORTAR   5 *K*   Free   *Hamilton, Peter*

VBench Data Access Benchmark — The source, executable, and MDB file described in the August 1994 issue of Visual Basic Programmer's Journal. Compares five different methods of data access using the JET engine to aid in optimizing database operations.

    VBENCH   12 *K*   *Fawcette Technical Publication*

WinBrowse 2.5 — Multiple access program for databases. Allows browsing, editing, and reporting using dBase, FoxPro, Paradox, and Access files. Convert data from one format to another quickly. Can also sort and filter.

    WINBRS   1560 *K* $34   *Q&D Software Development*

ZIP File Into CC 1.2 — Custom control finds the contents of ZIP files using VB properties. Source code available at extra cost.

    ZIPINF12   41 *K* $15   *Mabry Software*

16
DATABASE

ASC2MDB Ascii To MDB Utility — A VB3 framework (full source code) for loading MDB files from various format ASCII sequential files. Designed to get each application running with minimum effort, and keep the framework reusable.

     AS2DB1   *34 K*   Free   *Curzon, Richard*

About DDF Files — Discussion and examples of creating DDF Btrieve files for use with Visual Basic or Access.

     DDF   *7 K*   Free   *Sunil*

Access 2.0/VB 3.0 Compat.Layer — Compatibility Layer contains all the files necessary to use an Access 2.0 format database from Visual Basic 3.0. Requires Access 2.0 and the Jet 2.0 engine supplied there.

     COMLYR   *727 K*   Free   *Microsoft*

Access Import Spec Converter — Access MDB file contains routines to turn an Access Import Specification into a series of Access Basic or Visual Basic code statements. The generated code can be used to read a a flat ASCII text file, break the records into fields, write records to table

     IMPSPC   *20 K*   Free   *Ferguson, Jim*

Access Jet 2.0 Reserved Errors — Reserved error numbers from the Access Jet 2.0 engine in an Access format MDB file. Reformatted from the Microsoft Knowledgebase.

     ACCREN   *23 K*   Free

Access-Style Adding To Tables — Workaround for adding a new record to related tables. Visual Basic source code and Access database included.

     ADDNEWJS   *19 K*   Free   *Snyder, James Wj*

AddNew - Multiple Relationship — An example of how to add new records to the master database, then secondary tables and keep the relationships. Access 2.0 format database and Visual Basic source code.

ADDNEW 19 *K* Free *Snyder, James Wj*

Address Application For FoxPro — Simple address book for VB 3. Demonstrates how to access, update, and maintain a dBase/FoxPro table, including a routine to Pack the table.

FOXADR 19 *K* Free *Anderson, Tim*

Address Database — Example code for a simple database.

ADDRES 29 *K* Free *Murphy, Michael J.*

Area Codes And Zip Codes — Access database containing tables of United States Zip Codes and telephone area codes.

AREAZIP 1874 *K* $10 *Marks, Paul*

Attach Docs To Records DEMO — Attach documents to database records like MS Mail. Documents appear as icons in Program Manager. Documents can be opened, edited, updated, removed, and labeled right from their records. DEMO program with encrypted VB source code.

ATTACH 53 *K* $17 *Lee, Joseph*

Binary Large Object Demo — Example of storing large binary objects (BLOBs) in an Access database using GetChunk and AppendChunk functions with a data control.

BLOBTE 15 *K* Free *Rohn, Gary W.*

Btrieve Create — Example of Btrieve Create. Simple id/name/address/city/state/zip that create Btrieve file first then allows entering data. Requires Btrieve for Windows DLL.

BTCREA 16 *K* Free *Highsmith, J*

Btrieve For Windows Test Prog — Source code example of using Visual Basic to access Btrieve files.

BTRTES 46 *K* Free *Meyer, David*

BtrieveWiz 1.6 DEMO — VB4 add-in gives the ability to work with Btrieve data files and Btrieve File, Field and Index definitions (DDF files) from within the VB4 design environment. Demo version.

BTRWIZ16 174 *K* $99 *WinCorp Consulting Company*

Build MDB Create Code 1.1 — Utility program to read an Access MDB database file and build Visual Basic source code to create a database in the same format.

MAKEDB 5 *K* Free *JB & Associates*

Call Btrieve — Sample source code demonstrates accessing Btrieve files using a VB function called CallBtrv.

    CALLBT   22 K   Free   *Kubelka, Bob*

Clip Calendar — Utility for entering dates. Several date formats are supported. Copies dates to the Clipboard. Use included macros to automatically paste selected dates into Word, Excel, Access, or Visual Basic programs.

    CLIPCA   395 K   Free   *Opalko, John*

Copy Database Structure — Reads a database and translates its structure into VB code. The VB code is placed on the clipboard to pasted into your program. The VB code generated is a SUB called "Build". When this sub is called the database structure is recreated on disk.

    DB2BAS   6 K   Free   *Hernandez, J. M.*

Create DBF — DLL and sample source code to allow you to create empty dBase III DBF and DBT files. Non-registered version will create tables with 5 fields.

    Z1DBF   12 K $20   *Jones, Peter D.*

DBDocumentor 1.1 — Will print the field and index definitions for any Microsoft Access database.

    DBDC11   10 K $8   *Dilley, John J., CCP*

DBase III File And Index Read — Demo source code showing access to dBase II DBF and NDX files.

    DBASE   6 K   Free   *Schulze, Peter*

DRemake — Rebuilds VBISAM datasets by copying the data to another file. Some dataset damage can be repaired in the process and the group size can be changed if necessary for expansion.

    DREM207   202 K   Free   *Altwies, Tony*

Data Demo — Commented source code shows how to create a database, how to add tables and indexes, how to add data, and how to set up the data control. Requires Vb 3.0 Professional.

    DTADMO   14 K   Free   *Fulton, Bruce*

Data Widgets Demo — Custom data controls that let you design without code. DataGrid-bound data grid with in-place editing. DataCombo - bound to the VB 3 data control. Edit and drop down portions can be linked to separate data controls. Four more controls.

    DWDEMO   243 K $129   *Sheridan Software Systems*

DataAwareCollection — Plug-compatible replacement of the VB4 Collection object. Adds object persistence through database tables; automatic implementation of the object containment hierarchy; automatic instantiation of contained objects; encapsulated SQL; etc.

DBAWARCO   66 K $29   *MitranoSoft*

DataInformatter — Access/VB table structure browser. Pick from a list, view field and index information in an outline control. VB source code, requires MSOUTLIN.VBX and THREED.VBX.

DBINF   29 K   Free   *Roussos, D.*

DataTable Custom Control — Discontinued. Custom control (working model) designed to provide VB programmers access to the Borland Paradox Engine (included). Build sophisticated, multiuser network compatible database applications. Registered version has additional functions.

DTBL11   155 K $50   *DB Technologies*

Database Maintenance — Tool for anyone needing to maintain Access databases. Compacts, repairs, compacts & repairs Access databases. Full VB source code available with registration.

PMUTIL   104 K $15 SW   *Moss, Kevin*

Database Table Structure Print — Source code to choose and open a database and add its tables to a listbox.

DBPRN   10 K   Free   *Gallo, Charles*

Db2db — Utility program allows for quick and easy transformations of database record information from one database to another. Any field of one database can be linked to another field in a second database for the purposes of data transfer.

DB2DB   45 K   Free   *BillT121*

Determining Access DB Versions — VB 3.0 Professional code to determine the version of an Access database. Tested on Access 1.1 and 2.0.

AV   5 K   *Martin, Wayne*

EOF/BOF — Sample code demonstrates how to prevent "No Current Record" from occurring. Useful after adding some records, using MoveFirst, then trying MovePrevious. This code prevents moving beyond the end of the database.

EOFBOF   21 K   Free   *Willits, Don*

EZAccess 2.5c For VB — VB programming tool that creates subroutines you can call from your program to access Access MDB files. Created routines run in the background so you don't have to see or debug them.

    EZACCE   91 K $10SW   *Robichaux, Roy J.*

Field Pack Parse for VB3 & VB4 — Field manipulation tool now available in a VB4 16 & 32-Bit version. The VB4 versions are included with the VB3 version. Read, write, insert, and remove variable-length fields delimited by any sequence of characters.

    FLDPAK   125 K   *Altwies, Tony*

GBSZipCode DLL — DLL to access data files containing all US Postal Service Zip Codes, including all USPS approved city mailing names.

    GBSZIPCO   1014 K $59   *Group Benefits Shoppers*

Gentypes — Generates two files, one listing the structure of the MDB file including tables and querydefs, and another with TYPE definitions for all tables/querydefs.

    GENTYP   17 K   Free

ISAM Emulation For VB — Beta version of ISAM emulation for Visual Basic. Follows the same conventions as MS Basic 7.1. Requires the Btrieve DLL for Windows.

    ISAM   8 K   Free   *Eibl, Gunter*

Info Recall 1.1 — Database application created in Visual Basic. Full use of graphical interface, icons, and database access techniques. Can be used as an engine for many types of help files or other unstructured information.

    INFO11   491 K $70 SW   *Curtram Consulting*

JET Inspector Test Drive — Application designed to assist developers in performance-tuning and analyzing Visual Basic and Access applications. Limited test drive version. Analyzes any call to the Access Jet engine.

    JETINSP   220 K $495   *Blue Lagoon Software*

Jet Vs. Visual Basic — Sample contact database projects; one version uses the Jet Engine and the Data Control; the other version is Visual Basic only. Full source code.

    NOJET   125 K   Free   *Weber, Phil*

MDB Guru 4.2 — Generates VB code for creating an MDB file by reading the MDB structure from an existing MDB file. Understands tables, query defs, attached tables, etc. Generates forms from database attributes. Unregistered version only *prints* code. Source available.

    MDBGURU   118 K $30+SW   *Jones, Peter D.*

MQUERY — Significant improvements to the VISDATA and DATAMGR sample programs which are supplied with VB 3.0 Pro. Full source code.

    MQUERY   39 K   Free   *Smythe, Robert E.*

Nodes Database Grid — Database of Compuserve node codes. Record add, delete, and edit features. Source code included.

    NODEFI   34 K   Free   *Macedob, Antonio*

OLE To ODBC2 Using VB3 Objects — Example programs demonstrating techniques for reading and writing OLE2 objects to ODBC database fields using VB3 Professional database objects. Full source code.

    OLEDEM   39 K   Free   *Kosten, Michael*

Oracle VB Performance Tips — Document containing tips on improving performance, stored procedures, bound control issues, and attached tables when accessing Oracle from VB3 or VB4.

    CIDTIPS   6 K   Free   *Computer Interface Design Inc.*

Paradox Engine Demo — Two routines for working with database records created with the Paradox Database Engine. The Paradox PXENGWIN.DLL is required. Source code and a demo application are included.

    PDOXDE   14 K   *Jaster, John*

PowerTABLE 2.0 Data Manager — Replaces the VB Data manager. Create dBase and Access databases, compact and repair Access or dBase databases, create new tables, compact a single dBase table, delete multiple selected tables, etc.

    PWRTBL   285 K $55   *Bytes & Letters*

Programmatic Database Creation — Source code for creating a database definition report for an Access database.

    DBCSRC   5 K   Free   *Dirigible Software*

Query Def Utility 1.2 — Easy addition, edit, view and deletion of compiled Query Defs within Access MDB files. Open database and select MDB file. If any Query Defs have been compiled into the MDB, you'll see a list of them. DoubleClick on the Query Def to see SQL statement.

    QUERYD   43 K $10SW   *Winworks Software Corp.*

RI-VB Database Toolkit — VB/Access application development utility. Lets you execute single or multiple SQL statements on an Access database; add, modify, run, export and import query defs listings; and generate SQL from an existing database.

    RIDT10   682 K $34   *MIS Resources International*

Random File Access — Enhancement to the RECEDIT example included with VB. Lightning fast data access. Source code, working copy and data for a Random Access Address database. Demonstrates ideal database structure for small (2000-3000) record data files.

    RANDOMFA   191 *K*   Free   *Wood, Raymond*

Record Locking 1.0 — DLL provides record locking to your VB database applications. Record locking is in addition to VB's own locking scheme, and thus is invisible to inner workings of the Jet engine or ODBC drivers.

    RLDEMO   13 *K* $20   *Mey & Westphal*

Record Numbers Demo — Shows how to create a record number of total record numbers in VB using an Access database, i.e. [Record 5 of 1213]. Demo shows First, Last, Next, and Previous buttons to move through the record numbers. VB source code.

    RECORD   3 *K*   Free

SCRTEST Demo Of Browser/Scroll — Source code example of keeping the listbox and scrollbar in sync using recursion.

    SCRTES   33 *K*   Free   *Whittaker, Ross*

SQL 2 Variable — Utility used to format a long SQL statement so it can be assigned to a Visual Basic variable in small chunks.

    SQL2VA   14 *K*   Free   *Ferguson, Jim*

SQLSmts: SQL Statements — Source code demonstrates how to use the CreateDynaset method and a Dynaset object variable with a variable that the user selects from a Listbox. The result will bring up the entire record.

    SQLSMTS   4 *K*   Free

Sample — An interface to Btrieve for Windows which allows various file operations to performed from a pick list. Source code is included but the Btrieve.dll is required.

    WINBTR   31 *K*

Source Code Tool Box DEMO — DEMO of VB/Access Engine database utilities. VB source is included with purchase. Demo includes Code Librarian, SQL Tester, Database Printer, Data Control Form Designer, Database Compacter, Database Deleter, Database Viewers.

    DBTBUT   160 *K* $25+   *Bear Hug, The*

Table Doc — Reads an existing Access, dBase II, dBase IV, or Paradox database and creates a text file of its Database Object Properties and Field Properties.

TABLED 8 K Free *Nelson, John R.*

TimeTrak — A time tracking database application written in Visual Basic, using the Paradox Engine (Borland Int'l) Windows .dll. All code is included.

TIMETRAK 40 K Free *Jaster, John*

Trap Access Error — Source code module traps the Reserved Error 20 found in the Access 2.0 Compatibility Layer. A message box is displayed with the appropriate error message which can be handled by your program.

ACCESERR 5 K Free *Okapi (Pat Hayes)*

True Grid Demo — DEMO version of TrueGrid. Adds fully-editable database browser table. Based on Agility/VB. Supports all databases VB recognizes.

TGDEMO 149 K $69 *Apex Software Corporation*

VB And Jet 2.0 Demo — Simple project shows some of the new SQL features which are available from VB when using the new JET 2.0 engine. Examples of Union, sub-selects, top 'n' queries, data def. queries, etc. Source included. Requires Jet 2.0 engine and VB Compatibility Layer.

AC2VB3 6 K Free *FMS, Inc.*

VB Data Companion 2.1 — Utility contains many of the routine functions needed to build, specify, and maintain an Access database. Includes the data dictionary tools needed to build a database from scratch which are not included with VB3. Also includes SQL building tools.

DC 506 K $50 *MM Technology*

VB3 Initial Blank Record — Simple application shows how to create an application where the form is initialized with all fields blank vs. displaying the first record of the set.

BLANK 16 K Free

VBBtrv — Example code for using btrieve in Visual Basic applications.

VBBTRV 4 K Free

VBDB — No longer sold. A database engine which supports the dBase file format and operates as a DDE server. Several programs, forms, and routines are included to allow easy access to database functions for your programs.

VBDB 70 K $50CR *Marquis Computing, Inc.*

Vbrowser — Demonstrates a relatively simple way to construct a browser for Access 1.1 database tables.

    VBRWSR   *29 K*   Free   *ETN Corporation*

VideoMaster For Windows — Complete Shareware videotape catalog program written in Visual Basic using most features available in Visual Basic, including Access database engine.

    VIDEOMST   *993 K* $10 SW   *BMH Software*

VxBase Assistant — Utility designed to insert vxBase commands and functions into your Visual Basic code window while you are developing applications. DEMO version limited to 15 records. Professional version with more functionality available for $35.

    VXASSI   *23 K* $15   *Purcell, Tim*

VxC — C interface for vxBASE.

    VXC   *40 K* $100SW   *VXBase Systems*

Warning Ticket System — Application which tracks traffic warning tickets. Handles three related files, uses tabs, related files, has ability to sort or jump to any field. Full source code. Data (LDB/MDB files) are expected in the VB directory.

    VBWARN   *92 K*   Free   *Brown, Matthew*

Xtal Report Field Scaler 3.1 — Handy utilities for modifying reports designed with Crystal Reports. Includes DLL that allows you to get and set user defined labels, change face name and size; get report titles and comments; VB demo source code included.

    XTAL4   *73 K* $26   *Johnston, Robert J.*

Zip Code Database — Database of zip codes by city / state. Includes sample source code in Access Basic, similar to Visual Basic, for automatically filling city /state from Zip Code.

    ZIPCOD   *321 K* $18 SW   *HELP Software*

17
DESKTOP

Background Clear — Clears the Windows Desktop for running Visual Basic.

    BACKGND   8 *K*   Free   *Camarillo Technology*

Choyce — A program selection utility which allows you to associate several programs with one extension. When a file with multiple associations is double clicked in the file manager, the Choyce window pops up, allowing you to choose the preferred application.

    CHOYCE   15 *K* $10SW   *Amans, Robert L.*

Creating Toolbars In VB — Simple method requires no addons or toolkits to add Toolbars to a VB application. Full source code and documentation.

    TOOLBARS   17 *K*   Free   *Murphy, Stephen*

Cursor Position — Simple application shows the position coordinates of the cursor.

    CPOS   3 *K*   Free   *Joyce, Ben*

Drag And Drop Example — File Manager style drag-and-drop. Full source code included.

    FMDD   9 *K*   Free   *Brown, Jon*

Ed VB Editor Interface 1.0 — A simple Windows interface for non-Windows editors which provides a file open window to choose the text file you want to edit. The program then opens your editor with the chosen file. Source code is included.

    WEDI   8 *K*   Free   *Neal, Randy*

Floating Toolbox Demo — No longer supported. A simple source code demo of how to do a floating toolbox. Hides and shows the toolbox by menu control.

    VBTBOX   3 *K*   Free   *Dexter, Matthew*

Handle Windows Program Groups — How to handle Windows Program Manager groups. The first example shows how to install programs to the Program Manager. The second example counts all Program Manager groups. Full source code.

    PMXMPL   12 *K*   Free   *Germelmann, Christian*

Let's All Get Sick — A simple utility which rotates the desktop colors in Windows. The colors chosen are the weirdest color combinations possible. Possibly good for a laugh after a long day of programming. VB source code available on request from author.

LAGS 4 *K* Free *Smythe, William*

Odometer - System Resource Mon — Full source code for a program to monitor VB system resources and disk space. Includes interesting button array.

ODOSRC 36 *K* Free

Resource Bar — Time, date, memory, and percent of free resources on an icon like strip movable with mouse and arrow keys. Selectively chimes of hour and half hour. Source code included.

RESOCD 94 *K* $2+ *Denihan, Timothy J.*

System Color Finder — A program that finds your system colors and displays them. Full source code.

SYSCOL 6 *K* Free *Conger, Scott*

Tool Menu — Tool Menu modifies a host application, such as Visual basic, by appending a menu entitled "Tools". The Tool menu can be customized to spawn various applications. This has the effect of having a "desktop" of applications on your menu.

TM 59 *K* Free *Besset, Mark*

Tool Palette Launcher DEMO — Lets users launch other applications using a toolbox palette from within a VB app. If the selected application is already running, it will move to the top of the desktop. Source code with registration.

PRODEM 51 *K* $12 *Lee, Joseph*

Toolbar Demonstration — Full source code, (UNdocumented) for a toolbar including "Tooltip" captions for each button on the toolbar.

TSAF03 11 *K* Free

Toolbar Source 1.1a — Pure Visual Basic source code for a Toolbar. Includes QuickHelp. Full Visual Basic source code.

TBSRC 31 *K* Free *Fehr, Andreas*

Toolbox With Mini Title Bar — Program demonstrates a toolbox with a mini title bar. Source code (included) uses a main MDI form and a toolbox. It hides itself when its application loses focus and shows itself when its app regains focus.

TBOX100 36 *K* Free *Barham, Tim*

VB Icon Browser 2.2 — A simple viewer for icons which displays a group of 36 at a time. Many printing options. Source code available on request with registration.

  ICONB220   *42 K* $20 SW   *Valley Programming*

VB Task Switcher — This Visual Basic version of TaskManager comes with source code and a DLL that creates and returns an array of window handles to active applications on your desktop.

  VBSW11   *8 K* Free   *Morris & Steinwart*

Wallpaper Changer — Full source code to a replacement Wallpaper changer. Searches any directory and displays a thumbnail sketch of the graphic you are considering for use as wallpaper.

  WALPAP   *27 K* Free   *Rivers, Jerry*

18
DEVICE CONTROL

CD Volume Control — Source code needed to control audio volume from a CD player.
> VOLUME   4 *K*   Free   *Snyder, James Wj*

CD Volume Control 32-Bit — Source code needed to control audio volume from a CD player.
> VOLUME32   4 *K*   Free   *Snyder, James Wj*

Gameport DLL — DLL written in assembly language to provide all functions needed to use the PC's gameport in VB Windows programs. Reads all four trigger buttons, reads position of all four joysticks.
> GAMEPORT   20 *K* $40   *Innovation West*

PCIO DLL — DLL written in assembly language to provide all functions needed to use the PC's I/O ports from your programs. It provides functions to read and write 8-bit and 16-bit data. Sample source code and demo included.
> WINPCIO   17 *K* $25   *Innovation West*

Receipt (Windows For Pen Comp) — Sample Pen Computing application from Microsoft lets user complete an order form for Microsoft products, does a credit check and processes payment. Requires Pen Windows. Full VB source code.
> RECEIPT   120 *K*   Free   *Microsoft Product Support*

X10WIN — An interface for controlling the X10 CP/290 light/appliance controller, allowing you to monitor device activity as well as setting and maintaining a menu of commands. Partial source code included. Version 4.0 is available from the author.
> X10W11   51 *K*   *Tenholder, Edward J.*

19

DISK UTILITY

Drive Utilities DLL — DLL collection of disk and file utilities. Provides disk size, cluster size, sector size, and bytes used and free, file size, date, time, and attributes, allows date, time, attributes to be changed. Can "ZAPP" a file by writing over it with a pattern.

DRVUTL   26 K $20 SW   *TANSTAAFL Software*

EZDisk DLL Demo — DEMO version of a DLL for disk information. Returns strings to VB for disk type, disk size bytes, free space bytes, bytes per sector, and sectors per cluster. Full source code available with registration.

EZDISK   9 K   *CMC Systems*

File Search Utility — VB source code for a File Search Utility. Illustrates the concept of event-driven Finite State Automaton, a technique for handling long, involved calculations or manipulations in event-driven systems like Windows.

STATEMCH   10 K   Free   *Malik Information Services*

Find File — Searches a hard drive for files matching a filespec and/or containing certain text. Full source code.

FINDFL   12 K   Free   *Radford, Andrew*

Get And Put Disk Volume Labels — DLL to get, delete, and put disk volume labels. Also gets total disk space, available disk space, file date, file time, file size, and includes conversion routine to get plain English dates from the variable returned by the DLL.

VOLDLL   10 K   Free   *Guimond, Stephen C.*

Media ID — Source code for two routines to Get/Set the Media ID information on any disk - Serial Number, Volume Label, File System Type. Requires TIME2WIN.DLL.

MEDIAID   5 K   Free   *Renard, Michael*

QSetup — A solution to the slowness of the Visual Basic Setup program. QSETUP handles the version checking differently than the original VB Setup programs. Registered version includes a program to build a version info control file automatically.

QSETUP	20 *K*	$10	*Stillwater Systems*

Qsearch.Dll — String finding, file find and copy file functions. Source code included.

QSERCH	9 *K*	Free	*Simms, Jeff*

Retrieve Disk Volume Serial # — Sample source code shows how to retrieve the disk volume serial number for MS-DOS versions 4.0 and higher. Requires MicroHelp Muscle.

VOLSER	4 *K*	Free	*Mohler, David S.*

Tree — Example source code of using the outline control for displaying directory size, including subdirectories, summing

TREE	20 *K*	Free	*Aaerdeus, Inc.*

VBIO Disk And File VBX — Custom control allows you to set the volume-label, get total and free disk space, get and set file attributes, etc.

VBIO	37 *K*	Free	*Broeze, Arjen*

WinBack 3.0 — A basic backup program for Windows. Can create an "emergency system disk" automatically.

WB3	46 *K*	$15 SW	*Jurcik, Hal*

20
EDUCATIONAL

MathFlash — Electronic version of traditional flash cards. Addition, subtraction, multiplication and division are supported. Teacher can set the upper limit of the random numbers from 10 to 100. Full source code.

    MATHFL   25 *K* $15CR   *Kaufman, Brad*

Programmers Tool Kit — Series of Windows Help files covering an overview of programming topics and tools available. Includes mainframe, client/server, networking, Windows95, Visual Basic, Access, etc. Registered version includes over 35 in-depth topics.

    TOOLKIT   830 *K* $28   *Influential Technologies, Inc.*

Ruthie — Three programs designed to teach small children how to use a mouse. The child does not have to read to use them. Source code is included.

    RUTHIE   143 *K* $5CR   *Murdoch, John*

Tips Of The Day — Plug in form and code module that reproduces the Tip of the Day screen used by commercial software. Pure source code, no VBXs required. Includes TipEdit editor to create and edit tips. Source code key provided with registration.

    TIPDAY   55 *K* $24   *Anno Domini, Inc.*

VB Test Certification DEMO 4.0 — Tool for preparing for a VB programming certification test. Evaluates your programming skills. Evaluates potential employees. Can be used as an examination for VB students. A multiple choice exam of 200 questions.

    VBTEST40   195 *K* $80+   *Naroditsky, Vadim*

21
ENVELOPES

Envelogo 1.1 — No longer sold or supported. Print envelopes on HP laser printers, using template files (created with other programs) for speed and ease of use. Data can be copied from the Clipboard.

      HPENVLGO   41 *K*   *Pedersen, John*

Envelope Printer 2.0 — Prints an envelope on a Laserjet or compatible printer without requiring a change to printer setup in Windows. Source code included.

      ENVPRT   26 *K*   Free   *Federal Hill Software*

PrintEnvelope — Designed to print any size envelopes on dot-matrix or laser printers. Can print a company logo, and gives access to all printer fonts/sizes/attributes.

      ENVEL301   220 *K* $29SW   *Maurer Associates*

22

FILE COMPRESSION

ADDZIP Compression Libraries — Powerful PKZIP-compatible compression APIs for Windows. Includes VB3 source code for a drag-and-drop ZIP file manager.

    ADDZIP   211 *K* $50+   *Darlington, Stephen*

ArchiveLib 2.1 — Contains 4 classes and 100 functions for file compression and archiving. DOS and Windows platforms are supported. Complete source code is included. Windows 32bit support is integrated. Debug libraries are included, with ObjectGuard Debug tool.

    ALTD201A   2625 *K* $279   *Greenleaf Software, Inc.*

ICE-LHA Compression Library — DLL provides powerful functions to create and manipulate LHA 2.1x archives from within Windows applications.

    ICELHAB4   94 *K* $30   *Darlington, Stephen*

LZPACKIT.DLL — DLL provides LZ compress and uncompress functions.

    PACKIT   7 *K*   Free   *Taylor, Ian*

Stom.Dll — DLL with functions to compress and decompress a single file from Windows. Can be used with VB or C. Sample VB source code and demo EXE included.

    STOMP   19 *K* $25SW   *Dragon Software*

VBLZH Compression DLL — DLL for file management. Includes LZH file compression and decompression, 2 diskspace functions, and 13 file functions. Sample VB source code included. DLL source available for $99.

    VBLZH   96 *K* $30   *Macware*

Xceed Zip Compression Trial 2 — Library for creating and manipulating ZIP format compressed files. 35 functions including multiple disk spanning. Free trial version.

    XCEEDZIP   433 *K* $205   *Xceed Software*

Zip Master — A Zip file compression/decompression utility. Provides a consistent user interface for using zip/unzip, which must be in the DOS path.

Z_MAST   6 K   Free   *Saucedo, Rosary*

Zip Server 2.2 — Program allows you to create, view and extract PKZIP archives, including multivolume files. Can be called by any Windows application via DDE to perform zipping and unzipping invisibly. Sample Visual Basic source code included demos DDE link.

ZIPSERV   1054 K $40 SW   *Redei Enterprises Inc.*

23
FILE MANAGEMENT

Browse Folder OLE Control — OCX displays a dialog box that enables the user to select a folder.

    BF_OCX   23 *K*   Free   *Asik, Adil*

Compress Bucket 1.0 — A simple utility for use with COMPRESS.EXE. In File Manager, highlight the file(s) you wish to compress, and drag them to the Compress Bucket icon. The compressed files will be placed in a common directory. Full source code included.

    CBUKET   21 *K*   Free

Date And Time Stamp — Source code illustrates how to get a file's date and time stamp without shelling to DOS.

    DATTIM   3 *K*   Free

Directory To DBF File — Visual Basic source code to read directories and write to a dBase (DBF) file. For use with DBF compatible databases including ACCESS and FOXPRO.

    DIR2DB   63 *K*   Free   *Fabian, Imre*

DiskTrack — Disk cataloging program. Creates a database of your files on floppy. Lists the files within archives (ZIP, ZOO, ASRCF, etc.), if desired. Variety of report formats.

    DSKTRK23   149 *K* $25 SW   *Peninsula Software*

Drag And Drop — Small application demonstrating how to implement support for Windows 3.1 file manager drag and drop facility in a Visual Basic program. Includes source code.

    DD1A   4 *K*   *Bonner, Paul*

FCC File Access Library — File access library performs the functions of a disk cache and disk compression. Seven functions: Open, Close, Seek, Read, Write, Tell (retrieve position of internal file pointer), Length (find length of file).

  FCC110   41 *K* $95 SW   *Four Lakes Computing*

FileFind Subroutine — Source code for a fast file finder.

  FINDFILE   6 *K* Free   *Windley, Jay*

ISFILE Function — Source code example returns TRUE if a file exists, FALSE if file does not exist.

  ISFILE   4 *K* Free   *Carr, J. Frank*

Long File Names — Allows use of long filenames with a VB3 or 16-bit VB program when used on a Windows system supports long file names, using the native common dialog box.

  LONG16   42 *K* $50   *Internet Software Engineering*

Longfile — Using the enclosed source code modules will allow 16-bit Visual Basic applications to use long file names in user display while retaining short filenames for internal use.

  LONGFILE   16 *K* Free *Internet Software Engineering*

MC-Disk 3.40 — DLL collection of over 103 file management routines for VB 4.0 (32 bit) developer using Windows 95/NT.

  MCDSK340   341 *K* $10SW   *Renard, Michael*

MCDSK_32 — Dll collection of 100+ routines for file management.

  MCDSK_32   231 *K* $10   *Renard, Michael*

PKUNZIP Test Program — Source code for a small program to control the PKUNZIP control line from VB4. It allows you to extract files of type, and allows choosing source and destination paths.

  PKUNEXAP   9 *K* Free   *Beach, Chris*

Reading And Writing INI Files — Discussion and sample source code to read and write INI files.

  VB3EX   8 *K* Free *Marquette Computer Consultants*

Rich Levin's Toolkit Objects — 32-bit DLL (requires 32-bit VB4). Simulates DOS's DIR command. Give it a filespec, and it returns an array that contains a list of every matching file. Demonstration source code included.

  DIR3210   26 *K* Free   *LCI*

Search Subdirectories VB4 — VB4 subroutine searches for all files matching a given pattern, beginning at a specific directory or drive path.

    SUBDIRVB   *4 K*   Free   *Bercik, Bill*

VB-Drop (Dust Bin) — Utility allows you to delete files by dropping them on a trash can icon. Full source code included.

    VBDROP   *19 K*   Free   *Computer Technologies, Inc.*

Verinfo — Finds all available information about a file and lets you delete the file. Screen formatted for 1028x768. Source code available on request.

    VINFO   *102 K*   Free   *Clarkson, Charles K.*

24
FINANCE

Financial Func's From Excel 4 — These functions let you access financial functions from the Excel 4.0 FIN.DLL. Source code provided for Visual Basic and Access Basic.

      XLFINFUN   70 *K*   Free   *Scofield, M.L. "Sco"*

Loan DB Manager 4.0 — An amortization tracking application that creates a database of information on your mortgage and permits a number of reports and other options.

      LDBM40   37 *K* $25 SW   *Soft Solutions*

Moneybox Custom Control 1.79 — Custom control to get, filter and format currency or numeric data. Features an interface similar to a textbox, except that characters are entered in right-to-left fashion automatically.

      MONEYB   35 *K* $20SW *Richards Software & Consulting*

Solomon IV For Windows DEMO — Slideshow DEMO of Visual Basic Rapid Development Toolkit (VB RDT) for Solomon IV. Offers access to Solomon's 100 custom controls, Development Dictionary files, and Dictionary Manager.

      S4MMCD   897 *K*   *Solomon Software*

Writing DIF Files From VB — An example of writing DIF files from Visual Basic. Full source code.

      DIFEXM   2 *K*   Free

EZBanner 1.1 — VB source code routines that can be applied to any control with a text property to make text stream across the screen like a marquee banner. Controls speed, color, size, and other attributes. Source code with registration.

> EZBANN   35 *K* $10SW   *Robichaux, Roy J.*

Font Central 0.9 — A full featured font manager which allows displaying and printing of each screen or printer font in a wide variety of styles and sizes. Source code is available at additional cost.

> FNTCNT   29 *K* $15SW *American Computer Consultants*

Font Viewer For Windows — Font Viewer written using the Professional Toolbox. No source code.

> FVIEW3   103 *K* $15 SW   *Smart Typesetting*

FontShow 1.3 — Utility to print samples and character charts of any Windows fonts. Visual Basic source code is provided.

> FONTSH13   107 *K* $10 SW   *Alcott, Glenn*

FontShow For Windows 5.0, 1of2 — A font viewing and cataloging program primarily for use with third party font programs such as ATM and Facelift, and compatible with TrueType. Permits collection and printing of typeface catalogs of all registered fonts.

> FNTS5A1   225 *K* $15SW   *Kaye, Harvey J.*

FontShow For Windows 5.0, 2of2 — A font viewing and cataloging program primarily for use with third party font programs such as ATM and Facelift, and compatible with TrueType. Permits collection and printing of typeface catalogs of all registered fonts.

> FNTS5A2   196 *K* $15SW   *Kaye, Harvey J.*

FontViewer — Displays a sample of each installed font. It will show the effects of bold, italic, underline, and strikethru attributes. Source code included.

    FNTVIEW   15 *K*   Free   *Freeland, Frederick F. Jr.*

Fonter 6.0 For Windows — View any character in every font set you have installed. Fonter allows you to see it in different styles and sizes and even lets you print a "font book" which will yield a complete catalog of your font capabilities.

    FONTER60   55 *K* $15SW   *Campbell, George*

Lookie Here Fonts — A font comparison and sample printer. Prints a list and samples of all fonts. Source code included.

    LOOKHERE   9 *K* $5 SW   *Jackson, Jacob A.*

Other Fonts In Menu — A routine for using any installed font in menus. Contains routines to create a bitmap image of text in a given font, allocating memory for the bitmap, and freeing that memory. Full source code.

    BMPMNU   14 *K*   Free   *PTAHSoft*

PpFont — DLL returns number of available font families, arrays of info about font families, number of available fonts in a font family, retrieves arrays of info about fonts in a family. Demo source code included.

    PPFONT   23 *K* $10 SW   *Poellinger, Paul F.*

Printers' Apprentice 5.8 — A replacement for the Control Panel Font window providing WYSIWYG viewing of every character in your font sets. Printers' Apprentice interfaces with both the Windows' and Adobe Type Manager control panels.

    PA58   631 *K* $20 SW   *Lose Your Mind Software*

TrueType Font Specifications — TrueType font specifications in Windows Help file format. A complete tutorial on how TrueType is constructed and its various properties, and how Windows rasterizes a font for display or printing. (Where did this excellent file come from?!)

    TTFSPEC   577 *K*   Free

XLabel 2.2 — Extended label control. Enhancements: rotates TrueType fonts to any specified angle; provides shadowed text for 3D effects; allows horizontal and vertical alignment of text.

    XLABEL   35 *K* $15 SW   *Hanson, Mark*

3D Effects — DLL - Draw a standard form with standard controls, make a simple call, and instant 3D effects. Sample source code included.

    JR3DCT   16 *K*   Free   *Reynaert, John*

3D Frames Panels And Controls — Source code demonstrates 3D panels, frames, and controls.

    3DGD   4 *K*   Free   *DeBacker, Greg*

3D Look Using CTL3D.DLL — Demonstration of giving forms a 3D look using CTL3D.DLL, and making form stay on top of all other forms. based on code in the March 1995 Visual Basic Programmer's Journal. Full source code.

    X3D   13 *K*   Free   *Randriambololona, Roland H.*

3D Menu Demo — Small source code demonstration of 3D menu effects.

    3DMENU   2 *K*   Free   *Jwpc, Inc.*

3D Message Boxes — Custom control to allow a Visual Basic 3 application to display 3D Message Boxes and Dialog windows simply by placing the control on a loaded form. Sample source code included.

    VB3D101   23 *K*   Free   *Esanbock, Douglas*

3D Panel Demo — Example of what you can do with the VB Professional Edition to edit some Standard Edition controls and make them 3D. Source code included.

    3DDEMOJW   4 *K*   Free   *Jwpc, Inc.*

3D Routines — Simple routines (source code) that enable you to paint several kinds of frames around controls and forms, adding a 3D effect to an application.

    3D   2 *K*   Free   *Benito, Daniel*

3D Routines With Splitter Bars — 3D routines, with support for splitter bars. Example source code included. Enables you to paint several kinds of frames around or inside controls and forms, adding a 3D effect without the need for VBXs or DLLs.

    3D2SPL   8 *K*   Free   *Benito, Daniel*

3D Tabs — 3D Tabs. Supports multiple instances, up/down orientation, and more. All in VB source code, included and fully modifiable.

    3DTABS   33 *K*   Free

3D Tabs And Texts — DEMO of source code module to give 3D effects, including scrolling and tabs. Sample source code calling the commercial module is included.

    DEMORAPA   21 *K* $40   *Rapallo, Angel*

3d Frames And Borders — Tutorial on making frames and borders with a 3D effect in pure VB code. Source code to this tutorial program is available from the author.

    3DFAB   6 *K*   Free   *Wedergren, Kevin*

About Box Demo — Demo About Box shows system features. Windows version, DOS version, processor type, system resources. Full source code.

    ABOUTSG   11 *K*   Free   *Gotz, Steven*

AboutWin — Source code demonstrates a splash screen, using API functions and techniques for exploding windows, extract of icons and user information.

    ABOUTW   15 *K*   Free   *Stefano, David*

Access To VB Form Converter — Access 7.0 add-in that quickly converts Access Forms, Controls, and Code to Visual Basic 3 or 4 forms. Evaluation version is limited to converting three forms only.

    CONFORM   240 *K* $20   *Chambers, Lennox*

Another About Box Demo — Source code demonstrates how to make an About Box and start/restore programs if they are already running. Uses API calls and reads INI files.

    DEMO2   21 *K*   *Gotz, Steven*

App-Link Form Communication1.1 — Easily transmit and receive blocks of data up to 64Kbytes between VB forms. Easily create VB applications that talk to each other locally or over LAN. Demo version message length limited to 10 bytes.

    APPLIN   245 *K* $100   *Synergy Software Technologies*

Asgard Interface — VB source for Toolbox (3 styles), tabs, zoom, balloon help, status bar (buttons, pictures and gauge), 3D forms Guide (Wizard/Cue Cards).

    AIF   45 *K* $30 SW   *Asgard Software*

Autosize — Sample code shows how to make VB forms device independent for different screen resolutions.

    ASIZE   8 *K*   Free   *Scherer, Bob*

Balloon Form — Small source code demonstrates "balloon help" or tooltips.

    BALFRM   4 *K*   Free

Balloon Help — Small source code demonstrates "Balloon Help" or "ToolTips" in pure VB source code.

    BHELP   2 *K*   Free

Balloon Help Demo — Sample application which demonstrates balloon help. Uses no third party VBXs or DLLs. Allows balloon help to be displayed outside the form boundaries with no flicker. Source code upon registration.

    BALLOON   5 *K* $10   *PCs With Ease*

BatchEditor 1.2 — Program to edit and run batch files. Full source code.

    BATCH   12 *K*   Free   *Liebowitz, Jay*

Boxes — Another MessageBox/InputBox creator.

    UNREGBX   11 *K* $10   *Webster, Eli*

Bridgit 2.2 — Will read your form files and generate the code to resize your controls as the form changes sizes. Will recognize certain controls (e.g. catalog.vbx) that do not resize as well as controls that have limitations (e.g. drivelist boxes).

    BRIDG22   257 *K* $15SW   *Fishinghawk, James*

Bridgit 2.3 — Will read your form files and generate the code to resize your controls as the form changes sizes. Will recognize certain controls (e.g. catalog.vbx) that do not resize as well as controls that have limitations (e.g. drivelist boxes).

    BRIDG23   272 *K* $15SW   *Fishinghawk, James*

Build-A-Box MsgBox Generator — A MsgBox code generator. Has "Drag'n'Build" mode where icons can be dragged to the MsgBox, text is entered where it will appear in the generated code, buttons are previewed in rough placement.

    BUILDBOX   34 *K* $10   *Chameleon Group*

Burglar & Animate — Demonstrates popping forms up at random, and simple animation. Source code included.

    BURGLR   11 *K*   Free   *Campbell, George*

CTL3D Demo — Source code demonstrates how to create 3D dialog boxes in VB.

    DEMO3D   13 *K*   *Rodriguez, M. John*

CTL3D Demo (Rodriguez) — Shows how to create 3D dialogs using CTL3D.DLL. Shows a method for subclassing controls for 3D effects. Also has a routine which checks for CTL3D.DLL version 2.63 or later, and if not present, uses a native Visual Basic routine for lesser 3D effects.

    3DDEMOMR   18 *K*   Free   *Rodriguez, M. John*

CTL3D.DLL Example — Example of using CTL3D.DLL to create 3D Message Boxes and Common Dialogs. Full source code included.

    CR8IVE3D   20 *K*   Free   *Cre8tive Concepts*

Calling CTL3DV2.DLL — Demo source code shows how to display a message box, input box and common dialog using CTL3DV2.DLL.

    DMOC3D   12 *K*   Free   *Bridge, Inc.*

Colors.TXT — File of constants that can be used to set ForeColor, BackColor, or BorderColor properties to match the Windows system colors chosen by the user. Access and Visual Basic constants included.

    COLORSTX   2 *K*   Free

Control Toolkit 1.0 — 16-bit VB4 add-in that assists in managing controls in forms by providing a toolbar with buttons for aligning controls, spacing controls, and visually changing their tab order.

    CTLTK16   50 *K* $15   *Gower, Mathew W.*

Create Form — Utility to create forms from MDB or DBF files. Controls, buttons, and 3D effect can be added to the form from the utility.

    UTILFORM   57 *K*   Free   *Anderle, Michael T.*

CtFRMFX Form Effects — Custom controls lets you customize the background of a regular or MDI form. Bitmaps and Icons can be placed on the form. The background can be painted with a gradient color. A line of text can be placed anywhere on the screen.

    CTFMFX   21 *K* $99   *Gamesman Inc.*

Data Form Genie — Wizard type program that creates Visual Basic data forms.

    DFGENI10   234 *K* $17   *Krouse, Donald*

Desktop Changer — Applet to change Wallpaper. Source code included.

    CHANGE   5 *K*   Free

Dialog Box Wizard — Another Message Box / Input Box designer. Choose icon, buttons, message, and caption bar, and copy to the Clipboard.

    DMSGBOX   7 *K*

Dialog Source Code — Simple VB source code opens a Common Dialog box like that which comes with COMMDLG.DLL and various VBXs. Gives you freedom to place it anywhere on screen and add colors, bitmaps, and other controls. Does not need DLL or VBX files.

DIALOGJB   9 K   Free   *Bair, James*

Display Info Message On Form — Source and example shows how a status bar can be placed on a Visual Basic form to automatically identify the object the cursor is placed over. Also demonstrates how objects can be automatically repositioned as a form is resized.

DISPMS   31 K   Free   *Cath, Jeremy E.*

Drag And Drop From Outline Con — Source code demonstrates how to drag an item from an Outline control and drop it into a List box.

OUTLNDRG   3 K   Free

Drag/Drop Items Within Outline — Source code demonstrates how to drag and drop items within an outline box. Items are loaded from a file, and the new order is stored.

OUTLDRP   13 K   Free   *Van Der Sar, D.*

EZFace MDI Template — DEMO version of an MDI template. Provides a starting point for VB MDI projects. Uses many techniques including Toolbar, Tooltips, Help file access, Caps and NumLock status monitoring, etc. Full source code available with registration.

EZFACE   15 K $11   *CMC Systems*

EditDemo — Demo program and source show how to get the current cursor position and line number from an edit control.

LINENO   2 K   Free   *Campbell, George*

Elasticman — Small source code to turn any Form, in any scale mode, into an Elastic container. The controls and font sizes will expand or shrink when a form is resized. Also includes resizable tabs.

ELASTI   20 K   Free   *Stewart, Robert W.*

Enterkey DEMO — DEMO of a routine showing how to move through the fields of a form using the enter key OR the tab key. Instructions and source are available by registering with the author.

ENTERKEY   6 K $5   *Mattingley, Byron*

Exploding Windows Example — Source code demonstration of exploding windows using the Windows API.

    EXPLODIT   80 *K*   Free

Fade To Black — Sample project shows how to make the background of a form fade to black.

    FADE   3 *K*   Free   *Stine, Brian D.*

Fadeform 1.0 — Source code example creates a blue (or other color) gradient background on a Visual Basic form. Does not need VBXs. Changes depending on video available: EGA, VGA, SVGA, or 24-bit.

    FADEFORM   3 *K*   Free   *Jwpc, Inc.*

FocusPrb: Keeping Control — Source code to demonstrate how to design your own message box for validation checking - keeping control of the last control used after "MsgBox" is invoked in a LostFocus event.

    FOCUSPRB   3 *K*   Free

Folders — Folders module provides a Rolodex like tab folder system. By simply creating an array of Frames, you have a completely automated folder tab dialog box. All in pure VB source code.

    FOLDER   10 *K*   Free   *Parr, James*

Form On Top — Small source code project demonstrates a way to keep one form, out of a group of forms, on top while minimizing flashing, and without changing the focus.

    ONTOPFRM   2 *K*   Free

Form Refresh Workaround — Text describes a simple workaround for the strange repainting problems in VB. Using the "forms" collection, each form is "Refresh"ed. This solves the problem without DoEvents and its problems.

    REFRSH   4 *K*   Free   *Trahan, Jeff*

Form Wizard — Using a database and form template, the Form Wizard will generate a VB form containing the fields you select. All source code is included.

    FRMWIZ   288 *K*   Free   *Bacon, Royce D.*

Form Wizard 1.0 — Creates a simple Visual Basic data entry form based on a single table of an Access database using the Visual Basic data control. Additional features can be defined before the form is built.

    FRMWZ1   286 *K*   Free   *J&J Software*

FormSizer/VB — Custom control that automatically resizes controls on a VB form when the form's size changes. Can optionally resize at design time and resize the fonts on a form. Also works inside container controls.

    FRMSIZER   81 *K* $40   *DataObjects Inc.*

Forms Dispatcher — Source code "dispatcher" to invoke local procedures of a form from other modules/forms.

    DISPAT   5 *K*   Free   *Mangold, Oliver*

Gradient Background Demo — Source code demonstrates gradient backgrounds in forms and pictureboxes.

    GRADIENT   12 *K*   Free   *Flying Cows Productions*

Gradient Fill — Source code performs a gradient fill on the background of a form using any starting and ending color. It does this by creating a 1 pixel bitmap, saving it as a 256-color bitmap, then loads it into the form to give all the available shades.

    BACKGR   27 *K*   Free   *McCarthy, Michael*

Info Dialog Form — Dialog box form shows the following information: Windows version, Windows mode (standard, enhanced, debug), free memory, free system resources.

    INFO   4 *K*   Free

Kings Scrollable ContainerDEMO — 32 bit OLE control module to implement scrollable forms. Using this OCX you can place groups of controls larger than your form. The user can use the scrollbars to scroll beyond the visible area of the container. DEMO version only.

    SCLCON10   864 *K* $60   *Shanghai KingS Computer Co.*

LostFocus Field Validation — Not supported. Small project shows how to use the LostFocus event to handle field level validation. Allows the user to select a Cancel button using mouse, Esc key or hotkey.

    LOSTFO   3 *K*   Free   *Price, N.*

MDI Child Form From Dialog Box — Text and source file describes "How to Instantiate a MDI Child Form from a Modal Dialog Box, with control returning to dialog box when MDI Child Form is closed."

    MODAL   3 *K*   Free   *Rutledge, Thomas*

MDI Demo — Demonstrates an MDI (Multiple Document Interface) application that uses multiple instances of forms, data controls, and custom controls. Full source code included.

    MDIDEM   176 *K*   Free   *Radford, Andrew*

MDI Standard Application Shell — Source code - a skeleton MDI application. Features Compact/Repair of database; Helptips on toolbar items; support for help files; error trapping; "Nag" screen support for shareware authors; etc.

MDISHE 34 K Free *Blessing, John*

MSGBOX Code Generator — Code generator for Message Boxes. Full source code included. Can place generated code directly into your VB code window, or copy to the Clipboard.

MGBX95 48 K Free *Bunton, Vernon*

MSGBOX Replacement - Non-Modal — Allows you to implement MSGBOX non-modally so that timer events will fire and processing will continue. Form and BAS module, no VBX required.

DIALOG 5 K Free *Kornbluth, Aaron*

Make GRID.VBX Editable — Sample code demonstrates how to make GRID.VBX grids editable.

EDITGR 22 K Free

Manipulate Form Style Bits — Sample source code shows how to manipulate Windows style bits to add captions and sizable borders to every VB control.

MOVE2 15 K Free *Germelmann, Christian*

Message Box Boss — Assists in creating Message Boxes. Tests the Message Box visually, generates VB code which is placed on the Clipboard. Source code available with registration.

MBBOSS 370 K $10 *Burke, Eric*

Message Box Consultant — Another Message Box maker.

MBOXCONS 7 K Free *Gaughan, John*

Message Box Creator — WYSIWYG interface for creating standard Windows message boxes. Allows users to create a 3D box by using the included CTL3DV2.DLL. Clipboard functions allow an on-site test to be copied directly into VB with predefined SELECT CASE.

VBMB15 46 K Free *Wallette, Nick*

Message Box Designer 1.9 — A handy utility for designing message boxes. Allows you to build a Message Box, test it, modify it and test it again until it is correct. The code is then generated and can be pasted into a function or sub. Code can previewed before pasting.

MSGBX 99 K $15 *Burnham, Gordon*

Message Box Helper — A Message Box source code creator. Show the created VB source code and allows it to be copied to the Clipboard.

    MSGBOXJH   6 *K*   Free   *Hernandez, J. M.*

MessageBox Magic 1.0a — Utility to create all kinds of message boxes in Visual Basic. Takes the confusing, hard to remember options and handles them for you. MsgBox Magic generates the code for you. Requires VBRUN300.DLL.

    MSGBXM   41 *K* $6   *Extreme Software*

Module For 3D Effects. — Source code (BAS) file that calls some functions from CTL3D.DLL to create 3D effects on MsgBox, InputBox, and Common Dialogs.

    CTL3DBAS   1 *K*   Free

Move Form Without Title Bar — Source code from Visual Basic Programmer's Journal shows how to let the user move a form without a title bar.

    CALC1   7 *K*   Free   *Fawcette Technical Publication*

MsgBox Easy 1.2 (32-Bit) — This program is designed to help you quickly generate code for different message boxes and allows to save this code as template for future use. Quick comment/uncomment of code blocks.

    MSG12_32   195 *K*   Free

Multigrid — Source code workaround to a limitation of the grid control. Gives the ability to select non-adjacent rows from a grid.

    MULTIG   3 *K*   Free   *Desai, Anand*

Nomove Example Unmovable Form — Example source code for an unmovable form which contains a control box and title bar. Control box is simulated using an image control, the title bar is simulated using a label.

    NOMOVE   4 *K*   Free *Marquette Computer Consultants*

On Top - Keeps One Form On Top — Small source code project demonstrates a way of keeping one form out of a group of form on top while minimizing flashing and without changing the focus.

    ONTOP   2 *K*   Free   *Sigler, John*

OnTop32 — DLL easily creates stay-on-top windows in seconds. DEMO version.

    ONTOP32   151 *K*   *TAGS*

PARAMS — VB source code shows a method for passing parameters between VB forms when loading and loading forms. Also shows a method for setting application wide variables, not using Global variables.

    PARAMS   12 *K*   Free   *Carr, J. Frank*

PICTAB Picture Box Tabs — Tab control that is not a custom control. Two picture boxes, a data control, a list box, and sample code. Sample address book with tabs down the right side. Includes sample MDB.

> PICTAB 20 *K* Free *Crouse, Aaron P.*

PerfectTAB 1.0 — Perfect tabbed dialog boxes. Definable with BMPs and has normal and enhanced 3D effects. Included are four predefined styles, a demo, source code, and documentation.

> PERTAB 27 *K* Free *Bytes & Letters*

Picture Boxes As Controls — Source code contains 30 picture boxes with bitmaps used as control buttons.

> VP3DBOX 21 *K* $5 *Pozharov, Vitaliy*

PopUp Menu Reentrancy Problem — Demo project shows a reentrancy pitfall when popup menus are organized on an invisible menu container form. Demonstrates that a popup menu does not appear on a modal form when the form is opened by the entry of a popup menu. Full source code.

> POPUPRE 11 *K* Free

Position Forms Easily — Source code module, added to your project, positions your VB form on load event. Aligned perfectly regardless of the user's screen dimensions.

> POSITION 3 *K* Free *Briggs, Ryan*

Printed Label Class — Simple class module that will print text on a form as if it were a label.

> LBLPRNT 1 *K* Free

Quickform Form Generator 2.0 — Visual Basic program automates the creation of forms and controls. Reads an Access database and generates full functional forms from the tables you select. Automatic table and name generation; generates DataControl; generates code for all TextBoxes.

> QKFORM 121 *K* $20 *Mass, Martin*

Refresh Demo — Demonstrates the differences between VB's implicit refresh of text box controls during its idle loop and the explicit use of the refresh method. Source code.

> REFRES 6 *K* Free *Hartquist, Peter*

Restricting Mouse Movement — Example of restricting mouse movement to inside a defined region of a form. Full source code.

> INABOX 2 *K* Free *Leckkett, Blaine*

Sample MDI With Child Windows — Sample Multiple Document Interface demonstration, with common dialogs, child windows, fixed toolbar, and floating toolbar. Full source code.

    VBMDIXPL   27 *K*   Free   *Schmitt, Hans-Jochen*

Screen Size Template — Simple utility simulates different screen resolutions: 640x480, 800x600, 1024x768, and 1280x1024. Shows the form height and screen width values in TWIPS. Useful in the first design phase when positioning controls.

    GETSCR   9 *K*   Free   *MJ-Datatechnic GbR*

Screen Tester Utility 2.0 — Utility designed to assist the VB developer in designing forms at different screen resolutions. It places a floating form on the screen the size of a VGA, Super VGA, or 1024x768 screen. This can be useful in designing forms without changing video drivers

    SCRTST   19 *K*   Free   *Carr, J. Frank*

Scroll Demo — Example of using a Picture control and two scrollbars to provide the effect of a scrollable window.

    SCROLL   14 *K*   Free

Scroll Text — Example of scrolling text in a text box. Full source code.

    SCROLLTE   2 *K*   Free

Self Expanding Grid — Source code example of a self expanding grid. Data is entered into a text box above the grid and grid's cell dimensions change to suit the text.

    GRIDEG   3 *K*   Free

Setparent Demonstrations — Sample source code shows some techniques for moving one control from form to form. No docs.

    SETPAR   3 *K*   Free   *JSS Inc, Steve Shiavo*

Shareware Registration Source — Source code for a sample Registration dialog box, intended for shareware authors.

    REGSAM   11 *K*   Free   *Benignitas*

Spin Control Plug In Code — Spin control plug-in source code module. Eliminates the need for SPIN.VBX. 1K code is much smaller than the 22K Spin control. 100% pure modifiable VB code. (Source with registration.)

    SPIN   17 *K* $10   *Anno Domini, Inc.*

Splash Libraries — DLL allows developers to easily provide a splash, or startup, screen that is displayed while the program starts and initializes. This shows users that the program is indeed loading and initializing properly, a problem with large VB programs.

    SPLSH101   120 *K* $20 SW   *HSC Software Developers*

Splash Screen Demo — Three methods of creating splash screens in Visual Basic. (1) Modal splash form closes before continuing initialization; (2) continues initialization while splash is displayed; (3) use external program to display screen. Full source code.

    SPLASH   5 *K*   Free   *SoftCircuits Programming*

Splash Screen Demo - Dompier — Demo and source code for creating splash screens in VB4.

    SPLASHJD   45 *K*   Free   *Dompier, Jim*

Stay On Top Example — Simple "stay on top" or "floating" example uses one API call. Source code included. Useful for floating tool bars or custom message boxes.

    VBFLOATT   2 *K*   Free   *Temple, Tom*

Stay On Top Module — Source code module to make a form stay on top.

    ONTOPRB   3 *K*   Free   *Briggs, Ryan*

Stenklyft Form Wizard 1.0 — Automatically generates Visual Basic forms from Access database. Choose database, tables, and fields, and the Wizard generates a Visual Basic Database Input Form.

    STENKWIZ   1273 *K*   Free   *Stenklyft, Jason Lee*

Sticky Form — A source code example of how to make a "sticky" form. It acts like the Win95 taskbar - when dragged, it sticks to the nearest side of the screen.

    STICKY   3 *K*   Free

Subform Simulation Sample — Example of using an array of data control to simulate the subform capability of Access in VB3. (Compatible only with VB3 or above.) Source code. See VBZ01.ZIP.

    SUBFRM   2 *K*   Free   *User Friendly, Inc.*

Syscolor Module — Source code module gives programmer control over various Windows system components, such as Menubars and Scrollbars.

    SYSCOLOR   8 *K*   Free   *Bamber, Gordon*

TT Editor Rev. A — MDI version of Windows Notepad; a framework MDI application. Full Visual Basic source code. By changing a few constants, the framework of an MDI application is here without a lot of tedious work.

TTEDIT 46 *K* *Thorp, Ron*

Tab Demo — Custom control mimics the style of tabs found in Quattro Pro. Demo version handles maximum of 12 fonts and caption property is inactive. Allows setting fonts, color, angle of tabs, distance between tabs, etc.

TABSDM 16 *K* $10 SW *Gamesman Inc.*

TabFrame 1.4 Demo — TabFrame custom control allows tabbed dialogs to be included in a VB application easily. Supports multi-line, or stacked, tabs, as well as left/right tabs.

TABFRA 65 *K* $40 SW *GC Consulting Services Ltd.*

TabFrame 1.4.1 Upgrade — Latest version of TabFrame VBX. Requires the Tabframe.lic file supplied to registered users of TabFrame.

TFV141 45 *K* *GC Consulting Services Ltd.*

Tabbed Dialog Box Control — Custom control includes "invisible frame" control to group other controls for use with the tabbed control; NumberOfTabs; ActiveTab; Captions; TabHeight; TabPosition; Rows.

TABBED 22 *K* $35 *Ashton Information Services*

Tabbed Dialog Box Example — Source code and example of simple routine which simulates tabbed dialog boxes. Uses only VB 3.0 routines.

TABDIA 7 *K* Free *Eke, Richard*

Tabbed Dialog Demo — Example pure source code to create simple tabbed dialog boxes without any DLLs or VBXs.

VBTABDLG 11 *K* Free *Tanner, Ahto*

Tabbed Dialogs — Tabbed dialog source code. Produces file folder-like tabs. Full Visual Basic source code.

TDSRC 7 *K* Free *Fehr, Andreas*

Tabs2 — Demonstration of tabbed dialogs. Full source code included.

TABS2 9 *K* Free *Crawford, Ross*

Tip Of The Day With Editor — VB source code for a Tip of the Day implementation. Uses variable length files to save space. Provides a Tip Editor.

DEMOTOD 27 *K* $5 *Graham, Glenn*

Tips Of The Day Editor — Full source code for a Tip Of the Day dialog and an editor to easily add, delete, and search tips.

TIPOFDAY	21 K	Free	*InData*

Total 3D For VB — Source code demonstrations. 3D options for Visual Basic and other windows. How to make Windows search for CTL3Dxx.DLL. How to customize the Windows About box. How to cut the system menu of VB forms.

VB3D2	13 K	Free	*Germelmann, Christian*

TreeList 1.0 — Adds Tree functionality to listboxes. Full Visual Basic source code.

TLSRC	7 K	Free	*Fehr, Andreas*

VB Diner — Demonstration of drag and drop and MDI techniques from the August 1995 issue of VB Tech Journal. A graphical "diner" lets you choose menu food items, drop to the order pad, and automatically list and total your check. Executable and full source included.

VBDINER	715 K	Free	*Hoag, Steve*

VB Message Box Builder 1.0 — Simple utility to generate VB MsgBox code. Supports all possible message box styles. When finished, copy to the Clipboard for pasting into your project. Source code available, contact author.

VBMSGB	14 K	Free	*Hot Chilli Software*

VBMax Message Box Wizard 32bit — VB4 add-in simplifies the process of coding message boxes. Several configuration options and shortcuts. Full source code.

MSGWIZ	115 K	$5	*Stanley, Mike*

VBXtasy Volume 1 DEMO — Gives a photo-realistic feel to your VB application. Seven sets of designer controls. Including: brushed aluminum with black plastic; mahogany and brass; 90s psychedelic "rave"; textured corporate presentation. Royalty free.

SPINOZA	420 K	$149	*Spinoza Ltd.*

VGASize Form Template — Small application allows you to check the size and placement of VB forms against four common screen resolutions. Use its main form as a template to ensure your forms will fit in the screen resolution you choose.

VGASIZ	5 K	Free	*Dover, Bob*

VPFade Form With Gradient — Source code example shows a form with changing gradient colors as the background.

VPFADE	3 K	Free	*Pozharov, Vitaliy*

Window Treatments 1.0 Demo — Demonstration of "Window Treatments". Zoom windows open, 3D window frames, automatic 3D controls, window marquees, windows/forms which remember their previous location the next time they are opened. All in VB source code. Registration gets unlock code.

    WINTRT   28 *K* $17   *Lee, Joseph*

Wing3D - #D Made Simple — Code generator generates code to draw lines on your forms to give a 3D effect. Source code included.

    WING3D   15 *K* $3   *Silverwing Systems*

Wintab — Scalable 3D Tab Form, using no API functions. Uses a Paint event to draw, scale, and position tabs. All in standard VB code.

    WINTAB   10 *K*   Free   *Stewart, Robert W.*

27

GAMES

23 Pickup V2.1 — No longer supported. Player is matched against the computer in a match of wits. Player and computer take turns picking 1, 2, or 3 sticks from the pile. The player to take the last stick loses. Source code included.

    23PICK   12 *K* $5 SW   *Persky, Jonathan D.*

ABC Slots — Slot machine game. Source code included.

    ABCSLOTS   7 *K*   Free   *BMB Production*

Accordian Solitaire — Accordian Solitaire source code.

    ACCRD1   25 *K*   Free

Affirmations — A positive thinking program which pops up inspirational messages during a Windows session. Includes options to set the pop-up time period.

    AFFIRM   34 *K* $25CR   *Troy, Hailaeos*

Alex's Rocket Programmer — Educational programming tool. Allows kids to point and click to build simple geometric shapes or enter simple commands directly. Source code included.

    ALEXRK   32 *K*   Free

Bitmap Maze Demo — 3D maze type game written in Visual Basic. Not the typical wire frame maze but full color bitmaps. EXE only, source code provided with registration. Demonstrates BitBlt calls and matrix manipulation.

    KCBITMAP   219 *K* $25   *Krystal Cat Software*

CardPack 1.0 — Custom control for a stack of cards, useful for building games.

    CRDPCK10   116 *K* $25   *Zanna, A.*

Colorgam — Simple game to spell the names of colors. Source code included.

    CLRGAM   11 *K*   Free   *Sandell, David*

Crispy Solitaire — Another Solitaire variation, with source code. Requires VBCARDS.DLL - see CARDS10.

    CRISPY   19 *K*   Free   *Pando, Chris*

CyberSpace Cruiser — Demo of 3D graphics programming using the GEO.DLL library. CyberSpace game includes full source code and is free. GEO.DLL when used for programming has $50 registration.

    GEODEM   51 *K*   Free/$50   *Ivory Tower Software*

Engine Estimator — You are presented with an auto engine. Pressing "Start", the engine has a problem. The object of the game is to choose and replace the correct part to make the engine run. Illustrates simple animation - once you get the engine is running.

    ENGINE   25 *K*   Free   *O"Massey, Michael*

Executive Decision Maker — Tiny program, including source code for VB1, makes a random "decision" when you think of a question and press the answer button. (For use with VB 2+, copy the "GBL" file to a new module.)

    EXECSC   8 *K*   Free   *Mezaros, Mike*

Extended Reversi — Source code for the game of Reversi.

    XREVERSI   30 *K*   Free   *Rutt, Rick*

Grids 4 Kids — Four colorful games based on a simple grid pattern. Supports either EGA or VGA. Combines Tic-Tac-Toe, a Simon-like game, match the boxes, and a code-breaker with simple math challenges. Source code available - $60.00.

    G4K110   78 *K* $15 SW+   *Pritchett, Glenn*

Jeopardy Scorekeeper — No longer supported. Scoring program allows you to play along with the contestants on the Jeopardy! television show. Source code included.

    JEOPKE   12 *K* $5 SW   *Persky, Jonathan D.*

Knight's Tour Chess Problem — Source code and examples of solving the classic Knight's Tour chess problem. Contains examples of calls to the Windows CommonDialogBox API to Open/Save routines.

    KNIGHT   21 *K*   Free

Life — Simple implementation of the "Game of Life". Source code included.

    LIFE   4 *K*   Free   *Ivory Tower Software*

Memory Match 2.0 — Memory Match game. Source code included.

    MMATCH   78 *K*   Free   *Marino, Lou*

MyMemory Game — Memory/concentration-like game. Source code includes samples of drawing buttons, reading and writing INI files, determining screen resolution, and using floodfill to color screen areas. No longer supported by author.

    MYMEM1   *35 K*   Free   *Rogers, Dirk*

Nisus Missile Master 2.70 — Missile Command type game for Windows (inspired by original Atari game) written in Visual Basic. No source code here, but a fair demonstration of the speed and graphics capabilities of Visual Basic.

    MM270   *686 K* $17   *Nisus Development & Technology*

Number Crunch — No longer supported. Uncover 20 random numbers and try to put them in order at the top of the screen before time runs out. Source code included.

    NOCRUN   *13 K* $5 SW   *Persky, Jonathan D.*

Numbers Game — Game to help children understand the basics of addition, subtraction, multiplication, and division. Source code included.

    NUMGAME   *14 K*   Free   *Huss, Dennis L.*

Roll'em — A simple craps game with a graphic display of two dice. Source code and several alternative icons are included.

    ROLLEM   *19 K* $1CR   *Lewellen, Kirk*

Simon1 — Visual Basic game of sound and color memorization. Source code is included.

    SIMON1   *18 K*   Free   *Elkins, Jeff*

Switch — No longer supported. Game of logic. Switch shows nine boxes, blue in the left four boxes and red in the right four. The object is to reverse the order of the colored boxes. Source code included.

    SWITCH   *14 K* $5 SW   *Persky, Jonathan D.*

Tablenette — Card game for two players. Source code included.

    TAB100   *34 K*   Free   *Sycomp Limited*

TrafficLight — An icon in the form of a changing traffic light, to demonstrate how icons can display information dynamically.

    TRAFLITE   *3 K*   *Brody, Evan*

TriviaTron Trivia Game — Trivia question and answer game written in Visual Basic. "Movies and Actors" module included with the program. Visual Basic source code and additional modules available with registration.

    TTRON   *60 K* $14SW   *Nannini, Stephen F.*

VB Jigsaw — This program turns any bitmap (*.bmp) into a jigsaw puzzle which can then be solved by dragging pieces into place with the mouse. It's highly configurable with hints, various puzzle shapes, and automatic solving. Source code is included.

    JIGSAW   104 *K*

VBFlip — Pattern matching game in Visual Basic. Source code is included.

    VBFLIP   28 *K*   Free

WIN5x5 Solitaire — A solitaire game. Fill in a 5 X 5 grid by drawing cards from the deck.

    WNSOL5X5   30 *K* $15 SW   *Hilgart, John*

What's My Number — No longer supported. Guess random number set by the computer. Source code included.

    WHATSM   12 *K* $5 SW   *Persky, Jonathan D.*

WinShark Poker — Poker game for Windows. Illustrates use of CARDS.DLL (see CARD10 file).

    WINSHARK   81 *K*   Free   *Tyminski, James D.*

Wire Frame Maze Demo — 3D maze type game written in Visual Basic. The typical wire frame maze. EXE only, source code provided with registration. Demonstrates BitBlt calls and matrix manipulation.

    KCATWIRE   7 *K* $25   *Krystal Cat Software*

28
GENERAL

Cursor Position Example — Source code shows how to position the cursor using API declarations.
MOVECUR	2 *K*	Free	*Wisecarver, Mike*

Disk Space DLL Demo — DLL with the single function to return the disk space free. Sample source code for Visual Basic 2.0 included.
DISKFREE	6 *K*	Free	*Castravet, John*

Icon Extract — Icon extractor. EXE and source code included.
ICONEXT	8 *K*	Free	*Hill, Tim*

Load Time Problem Solution — Discussion of the apparent long load time required for some Visual Basic applications, which may lead the impatient user to double-click and try to load a second copy of an application, and one simple solution.
LOADTI	2 *K*	Free

Math Expression Evaluator — Basic module and sample program for a basic five function algebraic expression evaluator. Code is entirely Basic. Reusable for any project that needs to evaluate expressions with +, -, *, /,
BASEXP	8 *K*	Free	*Big Dog Software*

MsgBox Class — Class module provides a wrapper around the API MessageBox function. Includes code generator. Source code included.
MSGBXCLS	9 *K*	Free	*Irwin, Gregg*

Rdonly.Dll — Subclass standard VB edit control to intercept messages, eliminating any indication of a normal textbox. C source included.
RDONLY	5 *K*	Free	*Simms, Jeff*

Security Example — Security example - randomly selects a code which must be entered by the user. Source included.
VBSECEX	5 *K*	Free	*Miller, Bill*

Status Bar Demo 3.1 — Source code demonstrates how to create a Status bar using just a picture box and label control. No VBXs required. Solely VB code with only one Windows API call.

    SBARDEMO   39 *K*   Free   *Rodriguez, M. John*

Trig — Derived math and trigonometric functions.

    TRIG   3 *K*   Free   *Gorman, Robert*

VB Compress Pro 3.11 Demo — DEMO version does everything except print reports and optimize projects with more than eight files. Generates EXEs with no overhead from comments, white space, or descriptive names; with no unreferenced global constants, variables, types, or declarations

    VBCDEM   239 *K* $60   *WhippleWare*

VBZ Electronic Journal — VBZ Electronic journal for Visual Basic programmers. Windows Help file format (HLP). Unique custom controls, DLLs, tool-oriented VB coding techniques and utilities, with full source code. 1-yr. subscription published bimonthly.

    VBZ01   120 *K* $73   *User Friendly, Inc.*

32x32 Icon to 20x20 BMP Convt. — Converts 32x32 icons to 20x20 bitmaps. Includes source code. Useful for VB4 imagelists.

      32TO20   *7 K*   PD   *Rataycza, Richard A.*

3D Effects Demo — Shows how to achieve three-dimensional control effects, and how these are different than the effects from the THREED.VBX control supplied with VB 3 Pro.

      3DSDMO   *32 K*   Free   *Stewart, David*

3D Look Source Code — Sample program and source code to give a #D look to your VB projects. Uses CTL3DV2.DLL or CTL3D.DLL if found - but not necessary.

      VB3DSS   *8 K*   Free   *Sorrentino, Silvio*

3D Map Graphics Example — VB source code demonstrates a method for manipulating graphics off screen while also having "buttons" on screen that are not restricted to four sides - the outlines of each of the United States.

      3DMAP   *97 K*   Free   *Rogers, Kerry*

3D Meter Plug-In 2.0 — PLug-in code module that produces a 3D meter capable of 3 separate 3D effects and various colors that eliminates the need for METER.VBX. Pure modifiable source code (unlocked with registration).

      3DMETR   *16 K* $10   *Anno Domini, Inc.*

APM-Metafile Support Library — Library to support APM-Metafiles in Visual Basic. Library supports viewing and printing of WMF vector graphics files, as well as "Aldus-Placeable-Metafiles", which also carry to WMF extension. Source code and discussion of the differences included.

      APMMET   *21 K*   Free   *Reisewitz, U.*

Aarons; Color Mixer — Small Windows program allows you to mix the Red, Green, and Blue values of a color independently, see the results in real time, and get the corresponding numeric values used by Windows to identify the color.

    COLORMIX   36 *K*   Free   *Emke, Aaron*

Animation Code — Carl Franklin's ANIMATE code and bitmaps from "Creating Smooth Animation with Visual Basic", BasicPro magazine, Oct/Nov 1992.

    ANIMAT   297 *K*   Free   *Franklin, Carl*

Animation GIF OCX — 32bit OLE control module to display GIF animation files in an OLE container. It supports the GIF89a standard, including transparency, looping, delay time, logical screen, etc. Supports Netscape GIF extensions. Demo and sample source included.

    ANIGIF   287 *K* $20   *Gan Hui Mei*

Audio Video Demo — Sample source code programs demonstrate playing WAV sound files and AVI video files from Visual Basic.

    AVIDEM   8 *K*   Free   *Turpin, Jerry*

BARCOD 1.5 - Custom Control — Makes bar code display easy. Pick the orientation, set the size, pick bar code style. Then set the text to be shown as barcodes. Source code available at extra cost.

    BARCOD   210 *K* $15   *Mabry Software*

Barcode Plus 4.5 DLL Demo — 16-bit DLL allows creating and importing bar code graphics as standard bitmaps via the Clipboard. Using a single function call you can create many standard types of bar codes. Complete error checking. Sample VB source code included.

    BCP450D   82 *K* $150   *GRAFtech Development Corp.*

Biobears Bioryhthm — Simple biorhythm calculation and display. Source code included.

    BIOBEA   12 *K*   Free

Bitmap Catalog — Basic graphic catalog program. Searches the current directory for BMP and RLE files, uses StretchBlt to place each file in a 50x50 window. Source code included.

    BITCAT   6 *K*   Free   *Bishop, Shawn*

Bitmap Patternbrush — Adds bitmaps and patterns to windows, dialog boxes, statusbars, toolbars, etc. Uses a small set of API routines available as one line of code.

    BRUSH   12 *K*   Free   *Bytes & Letters*

Bitmap To Icon — Source code converts 32x32 256 color bitmaps to 256 color icons.
　　BMP2ICON　　　　　　8 *K*　Free

Chart FX 32-Bit OCX — 32 bit Win95/VB 4.0 OCX for charting.
　　CFXOCX32　　　　　210 *K*　　　　　　　　*Software FX Inc.*

Chess - The Queen's Problem — Source code shows the solutions to the "Queen's Problem" in chess. Demonstrates graphics and event programming.
　　QUEEN　　　　　　6 *K*　Free

Choose SavePicture Color Depth — Simple way to save a bit,map to disk from a picture box and choose the color depth, independent of the video driver. Processes the image one line at a time, avoiding high memory needs. Full source code.
　　SAVBMP　　　　　14 *K*　Free　　　　　　　*Deutch, Jim*

Classic Timepieces HC — Three animated raytraced clocks which take advantage of 24 bit color graphics. They will display in 16 colors on standard VGA cards. While this is interesting in VGA, under lower video modes it shows pitfalls in programming graphics.
　　CTHC10　　　　　279 *K*　$20SW　　　　　　*Brown, Richard*

Color Calculator — Utility converts color values selected by the user to hexadecimal values for use in Visual Basic programming, C programming, or HTML page authoring. Help file included.
　　CCALC　　　　　27 *K*　$7　　　　　　*Kinasevych, Orest*

Convert BMP To ICON — Sample source code to convert a BMP to an Icon.
　　PIC2ICON　　　　　8 *K*　Free　　　　　*Murphy, Michael J.*

Custom Cursor Demo — Source code demonstrates loading an icon as a custom cursor which changes over chosen hotspots on form.
　　CURSORPF　　　　　7 *K*　Free　　　　　　*Fillion, Pierre*

Custom Cursors (Updated) — Code and icons from Mike Stanley's article on Creating Custom Cursors, from Visual Basic Programmer's Journal, Dec. 1993. Demonstrates creating custom mouse pointers without using a DLL. 1/22/95 update.
　　CUSCUR　　　　　16 *K*　Free　　　　　　*Stanley, Mike*

DimLib Window Dimmer — DLL allows dimming inactive windows. Provides three dimming functions. Up to 64 windows can be dimmed at one time. Sample VB source code included.
　　DIMLIB10　　　　　44 *K*　$10　　　　　*Noonan, Timothy D.*

Draw On Iconized Form — OBsolete. Demo code shows how to draw graphics on an iconized form. Uses the timer to change what appears on the icon.

    ICONDR   2 *K*   Free   *Young, Ted*

EYECAN — Library of 40 icon animations for Visual Basic versions 3, 4, and 5. To use this library you will need a shareware copy of either Object Thing or Object Workbench.

    ANIICON   90 *K*   *Eye Can Publishing*

EZ-Screensavers — DLL to create 32bit screen savers. Screensaver template and sample source code make creating screen savers easy. DEMO version requires "DEMO" wording on your screensaver.

    SSAVE32A   154 *K*   *TAGs*

Example Percentage Bar — Example percentage bar fills from 0 percent to 100 percent. Full commented source code included.

    PERCENT   3 *K*   Free   *Carmer, Joseph T.*

Extract Pictures From FRX File — VB source code demonstrates extracting pictures from FRX source code files.

    FRXFILES   3 *K*   Free   *Gradowski, Mark D.*

FXTools/VB 1.3 Demo — Demo program for FX/Tools. Custom controls add image, text and shape effects to VB apps. 50 main and transition wipes; 42 dissolve wipes; speed control; image resize and transparency; 3D fonts, bevels, and shadows, multitasking, etc.

    FXTOOL   380 *K* $129   *ImageFX*

FXTools/VB Pro 3.0 DEMO — Set of 9 custom controls that add 100 professional special effects to images, text, shapes and video. Displays text with drop/block shadows, outline, rotation, 3D styles and 3D borders. Displays 19 image formats. WAV/MIDI audio, AVI/QuickTime Video.

    FXPRO3   883 *K* $349   *ImageFX*

Fade To Black — Source code paints a blue-to-black gradient on the background of any form. Has the capability to do horizontal and diagonal gradients, and the code is optimized for the bit depth of the display adapter in use.

    FADE2   4 *K*   Free   *Reed, Michael A.*

FastGraph Custom Control 0.9 — Custom control gives the VB developer much of the power of the Windows Graphics Device Interface API while maintaining the simplicity of VB. Uses properties for graphic objects which are similar to other VB properties.

> FG   115 K   Free   *Pienaar, Marc*

Floating Toolbar Example — Demonstration source code of keeping a VB form on top of only the selected window, not all windows. Lets you create a floating toolbar that stays on top of its app's window without staying on top of all windows.

> FLOT1W   2 K   Free

Folders-II — Use folders in your Visual Basic programs without custom controls. Three tab styles, overlapped tabs, color tabs. Full source code.

> FLD216   41 K   Free   *Cordero, Antonio*

Generic Screen Saver — Small screen saver can be initialized manually. Full source code included.

> SAVER   4 K   Free   *McLaughlin, Thomas*

Graphic Viewer — A graphics viewer for BMP, ICO, WMF, and RLE files.

> GV   18 K   Free   *Nordan, Matthew M.*

Graphic Viewer 2.0 — Displays BMP and PCX files. 2-color, 16-color, 256-color files and 24-bit color files are supported. It demonstrates the Custom Control available from C/Systems.

> GRAF20   47 K $5SW   *Cramp, Stephen*

Graphics Devel./Slideshow 2.6 — Program to help you browse, search, find, create, view, enhance, convert, and print your picture files. You can crop, adjust, size, reorient, and change aspect ratio. It works with picture file types such as BMP, PCX, TIF, GIF, JPG, PIC, RAS, TGA, more.

> GDWSS26   766 K $25   *SkiSoft Shareware*

ITGraph Diagram/Flowchart VBX — Diagram graphics custom control. Graphs are arranged automatically (hierarchical, compact, flowchart or tree) or by application control.

> ITGRAPH   259 K $80SW   *Indra Technology, Inc.*

Icon 2 Bmp — Utility to convert ICO files to BMPs.

> ICON2BMP   16 K   Free   *Endorphin Software*

Icon Extract — Sample program in French shows how to extract icons from a DLL or ICO file. Full source code.

> EXTRAC   4 K   Free   *Tisoft S.A.*

Icon To Bitmap Converter 3.2 — Converts icons from files or libraries (EXE, DLL, ICL) into 256-color bitmaps. Drag and Drop files from any file manager. Comes with detailed Windows Help.

ICBM32   46 *K* $15SW   *Germelmann, Christian*

ImageKnife/VBX Demo — Full demo of ImageKnife/VBX from Media Architects.

IKDEMO2   410 *K*   *Media Architects, Inc.*

ImageLib 3.0 Professional — Trial version of ImageLib Professional 3.0 for VB4/16. Features read/write 4, 8, 24 bits resolution JPG, PNG, PCX, GIF, and BMP image handling. Dithering support.

ILIB_VB   248 *K* $89   *Skyline Tools*

KingS ANI OCX — 32bit OLE control module to play an ANI animation files within an OLE container.

KSANI10   924 *K* $40   *Shanghai KingS Computer Co.*

KingS Anination Tray OCX — 32bit OLE control module to display animated icons on the taskbar tray of Windows 95. You can play the ANI directly, control showing or hiding the icon on the tray and get the mouse event at the tray icon.

ANITRY10   728 *K* $40   *Shanghai KingS Computer Co.*

KingS Screen OCX — 32bit OLE control to directly draw on and capture a Windows screen. Supports standard Line and Circle keywords as used in Form or PictureBox.

KSSCR100   655 *K* $20   *Shanghai KingS Computer Co.*

LEADTOOLS Imagehandler Demo — Demo graphics viewer and compressor demonstrating the performance of tools available from LEAD Technologies. JPEG compression as well as LEAD's own compression format are available as custom controls for Visual Basic and other Windows languages.

LEADTOOL   1396 *K*   Free   *LEAD Technologies*

LED Code Module — Source code module that produces an LED meter capable of three separate colors that eliminates the need for any VBX. Pure modifiable source code. (Source code with registration.)

LEDAD   15 *K* $10   *Anno Domini, Inc.*

LED Control — LED ActiveX control imitates a Light Emitting Diode display. Developed for use with SuperLog for Windows (a frequency display) and MilleniumCount (as a billboard type display unit).

SDKLED   1454 *K* $10   *SDK Software*

Manipulate Windows Style Bits — VB4 source code. Put captions and/or sizable borders on all controls on a form, and make them float. Realize floating toolbars of any style. Pure source code included.

    MOVE4   7 *K*   Free   *Germelmann, Christian*

Many Things Screen Saver 3.0 — Screen saver program written entirely in Visual Basic. Cycles between several screen savers. Source code included. Includes a DLL for reading GIF87a graphics.

    MNYTH3   101 *K*   Free   *McLean, Bruce*

Mapping With Visual Basic — DEMO of a Visual Basic program that provides thematic graphic mapping of the United States. Full source code with registration.

    MAPS   58 *K* $19   *Educational & Business Systems*

Marquee — Creates a moving banner or logo in your program. Source code.

    MARQUE   2 *K*   Free   *Campbell, George*

Meter 95 — Plug-in code module that produces a 3D meter that reproduces the Windows 95 style meter, yet allows various colors for customization and eliminates the need for METER.VBX. Pure modifiable source code (unlocked with registration).

    METER95   19 *K* $10   *Anno Domini, Inc.*

Morphing Demo — Demonstration of morphing using the T4DIBLIB.

    MSMORPH   856 *K*   Free   *Johnson, Nathaniel*

Multimedia Demo — Full multimedia demo of how to use the MCI control for sound and full motion video with sound. Contains all source, runtimes, VBXs, and setup files. Requires drivers for WAV and AVI files. Requires sound card for sound, MS Video for Windows driver.

    VBMMDE   972 *K*   Free   *Trimble Technologies*

NED Image OCX 32-Bit 1.45 — 32-bit OCX custom control which displays and prints image files. Works with TIFF, BMP, DIB, GIF, JPEG, and Photo CD files. Includes demo source code.

    NIMGVB14   238 *K* $199   *Northeast Data Corp.*

OLE Object-To-Bitmap 1.3 — Demonstrates embedding a VB picture box bitmap into an OLE2 control as a PaintBrush object, editing the object in Paintbrush from within a VB application, and retrieving the edited bitmap from the OLE2 control and into the picture box. Req. VB 3 Pro.

    OLE2BM   15 *K*   Free   *McCreary, Jeremy*

Orbital Motion — Planetarium style program. Executable and (troublesome) incomplete source code.

    ORBIT   103 *K*   Free   *Brown, Nathan*

PCSSave Screen Saver — Screen Saver written in pure Visual Basic. Source code included.

    PCS   61 *K*   Free   *PCSWare (Paul Coombes)*

PS-Out 1.0 — Prints bitmap images from the Picture Box to the Windows Printer. Source code included.

    PSOUT   22 *K*   Free   *Stephen Cramp*

Patterns — Background patterns created using VB's custom color features. Source included.

    PATTER   22 *K*   Free   *Speranza, Paul*

Pic Clip Tool (For VB2Pro) — PicClip bitmap array. Provides 100 toolbar type buttons with graphics for use with the PicClip VBX control. Requires VB2Pro or above.

    PICBTNFF   36 *K*   Free   *Freel, Fred*

PicClip Viewer — PicClip viewer gives an easy way to view the individual graphic cells of a PicClip.

    PCV   84 *K*   Free

PicScroll -Scroll Picture DEMO — DEMO of scrollable, clipable, zoomable picturebox for Visual Basic. Can be used for image display, simple animation or as a container control for scrollable forms. Unique features for handling metafiles.

    PICK_P   88 *K* $50   *Bennet-Tec Information Serv.*

Polygon — Draws polygons with connected vertices in various sizes and colors. Source code included.

    POLYGO   6 *K*   Free   *Mack, Jim*

Poorman's Percent — Source code module to draw a percent bar.

    PERCENTG   4 *K*   Free   *Gernaey, Michael*

Print Previewer 2.0 DEMO — Functions which help you create your entire printed document. You can place lines, blocks of text, triangles, circles, boxes, bitmaps, etc. When complete, the document is saved to disk. Because it is saved as a file, it may be previewed or printed again.

    PRINTPRE   79 *K* $30   *Lee, Joseph*

ProEssentials 1.5 DEMO — DEMO of VBX and DLL for presentation charting. Custom controls provide a turnkey graphic presentation subsystem for Visual Basic. This demo shows many of the graphic types available with ProEssentials. Double-click on any graph to change settings.

PEDEMO   390 *K* $395   *Gigasoft, Inc.*

QCARDS.DLL 2.0 — DLL that simplifies the creation of card games in VB. Easy access to over 40 card game specific functions.

QCARD   83 *K*   Free   *Murphy, Stephen*

Quick View BMP/DIB/WMF — BMP/DIB/WMF viewer and printer. Full source code included. Demonstrates the API calls needed to print a 256-color file.

QUIKVIEW   74 *K*   Free   *Woodruff, Ben*

RGBColor Class — Vb4 class. Get or set R, G, B color values independently. Set/get Hex strings or RGB value strings. Set form systems colors. GetNearestSolidColor. Source code included.

RGBCOLOR   7 *K*   Free   *Irwin, Gregg*

Resistor Color Codes — Resistor color codes; find the value of resistors by selecting the color bands. Source code included.

RCODE   8 *K*   Free   *Sheppard, Brian*

Resource-Only DLL For Bitmaps — Text describes how to make a resource-only DLL to hold bitmaps. Explains how to retrieve them, get their color tables, and how to handle them.

RESNC   4 *K*   Free   *ImageSoft Inc.*

Rotate.Dll — DLL with functions to rotate and mirror bitmaps with picturebox controls using VB for Windows. Sample source code, DLL and EXE file provided.

ROTATE   12 *K* $25SW   *Dragon Software*

Screen Saver DEMO — Screen saver source code (source available with registration) shows how to capture the Windows desktop and float a bitmap above the captured desktop around your screen. Includes password protection, "About" form showing Windows resources, etc.

DTSAVCOD   17 *K* $20   *Hudson, James A.*

Screen Saver Demo — Working screen saver application (template) developed in Visual Basic 3.0. Source code available with registration.

SCRNSA   5 *K* $20 SW   *INside*

Screen Savers Examples — Example of creating screen savers in Visual Basic. Full source code included.

    SCRSVR   31 *K*   Free   *Hunt, Rick*

Shoot The Dice — Dice game with full source code makes use of graphics and simulates sprites.

    DICE2   10 *K*   Free   *Clark, Jim*

Simple Animation Button Code — Code example demonstrates how to use a 16 or 32 bit resource file to add animation to a Threed command button.

    ANIMTB   15 *K*   Free   *Cunday, Richard*

Simulated Tab Control — A tabbed folder control emulation using only the THREED.VBX control and very little VB code. Automatically resizes and aligns the tab indexes according to the primary panel width.

    SIMTAB   3 *K*   Free   *Himmer, Eric F.*

Slider Demo — Slider control in pure Visual Basic source code.

    SLIDER   9 *K*   Free

Softcraft Graphic CC DEMO — Attractive graphic and flexible graphic shapes for use in VB. Closed polygons, graduated color fills. 256-color palette. Composite shapes can resemble 3-D objects and natural shadows.

    SCGDEM   75 *K* $295   *Softcraft, Inc.*

Splines DLL — DLL contains functions to create spline curves. Curves can be defined in 2 or 3 dimensions. A VB source code interface to demonstrate the spline functions is included.

    SPLINE11   55 *K* $25   *Dean, Andrew S.*

Store/Display Pictures In MDB — Demo application shows how to store Bitmap (BMP) and icon (ICO) files and store them, in an Access database, and display the files in a Visual Basic application. Sample MDB database and Visual Basic source code included.

    STOREBMP   30 *K*   Free   *Luhring, Mark*

Stretch — How to stretch a bitmap, icon, wmf, using VB source code.

    STRECH   4 *K*   Free   *Crouse, Aaron P.*

T4 DIB Library — DLL transforms BMP, ICO, RLE, WMF, and image files into DIB format and stores them as "members" in a single fast-loading library. See file MSMORPH for a user-created demonstration. Shareware version only builds libraries of four or less members.

    T4DIBLIB   724 *K* $99   *Staley, Marc*

TabStrip Control Demo VB4 — Simple source code demo of the TabStrip control in 32-bit VB4.

TABSTRIP	3 K	Free	*Jones, Michael*

Tile — Source code for a routine to tile a picture (GIF) on a form.

TILE	3 K	Free	*Law, Justin*

Tool Tips 2.0 — Tool Tips code module that eliminates the need for any VBX or OCX or DLL. Full source code.

TOOLTIPF	5 K	Free	*Friend, Jonathan*

ToolTips 3.0 — Plug-in code module that produces Microsoft style ToolTips, including ForeColor, BackColor and font styles. Pure modifiable source code (unlocked with registration).

TOOLTIPS	72 K	$24	*Anno Domini, Inc.*

Using CARDS.DLL — Sample application shows how to access the CARDS.DLL that shipped originally in the Microsoft Entertainment Pack. VB source code included. CARDS.DLL is NOT included as it is a commercial Microsoft product.

VBCARDS	9 K	Free	*Perrott, Ric*

VB Progress Bar Code — Source code adds a status bar showing the status of tasks completed.

STATUSRK	2 K	Free	*Kraft, Rob and Jeff Trader*

VB4 Splitter Classes — Source code for VB4 class demonstrates a horizontal or vertical splitter bar.

SPLTRCLS	9 K	Free	*Jones, Michael*

VBMax 3D Effects DLL — VBMax3D.dll is an in-process OLE server that lets you add the 3D effects that Microsoft forgot to your VB 4 applications without the overhead of third-party controls.

VBMAX3D	145 K	*Stanley, Mike*

VBMax 3D Electronic Message — VBMaxEM.dll is an in-process OLE server for adding electronic message style controls to your VB 4.0 applications.

VBMAXEM	173 K	*Stanley, Mike*

VBMax 3D Liquid Crystal Displa — VBMaxLCD.dll is an in-process OLE server for adding LCD/LED style controls to your VB 4.0 applications. There are tons of uses: clocks, timers, meters, calculators, dialers, etc.

VBMAXLCD	122 K	$10	*Stanley, Mike*

VBproFX Animated Demo — DLL provides a comprehensive collection of special effect subroutines for the animated display of bitmaps, and the movement and 360 degree rotation of text. All demonstrated in this demo.

    VBPRO   108 *K* $129   *Advance Animation Systems*

VisEFEX — Comprehensive collection of special effects for the animated display of text and for making dialog boxes and controls 3-dimensional. Choose the effect, destination, font, color, and VisEFEX generates code for a one-call subroutine.

    VISEFE   21 *K* $49 SW   *Advance Automation Systems*

Visual Basic 4.0 Animated Demo — Microsoft's original self-running animated demo/advertisement for dealers of Visual Basic.

    VB4PRES   592 *K*   Free   *Microsoft*

Visual Basic 4.0 Dealer Demo — Microsoft's original self-running animated demo/advertisement for dealers of Visual Basic. Explains the differences between the Standard, Professional, and Enterprise editions.

    VB4DEMO1   558 *K*   Free   *Microsoft*

WMF To BMP Converter — Utility program to convert WMF graphics to BMP format. Full source code included.

    WMFBMP   25 *K*   Free   *Campbell, George*

WMF Viewer / Printer — Source code for a simple WMF viewer/printer. Has zoom-in and zoom-out, and a custom cursor. Based on "Print Preview" in the Knowledgebase.

    VIEWER   11 *K*   Free   *Farber, Ryan*

Waldo Animation — Loads and unloads a brief animation of Waldo of the "Where's Waldo" books. Source code included.

    WALDO   19 *K*   Free   *Melanson, Leo M.*

Waving Demo Of A Bitmap — Source code demonstration of how to "wave" a bitmap in a sine wave style.

    WAVE   3 *K*   Free   *Rossow, Frank*

WinFlic FLI/FLC Player — Custom controls to play FLI and FLC animations in Visual Basic.

    WINFLIC   128 *K* $25   *Plieger, R.S.*

WinStep Toolbars Rollup Demo — Demo program shows you how to add CorelDraw style rollup windows, with mini captions, toolbars, and special scrollbars, to your program without a VBX.

    ROLLUP   60 *K* $14   *Winkelbach, Dirk*

Windows95 Style Tab Controls — Tab controls modeled after Windows95. Three different forms with 2, 3, and 4 tab bitmap control. Sample source and bitmaps included.

    WIN95TAB   22 *K*   Free   *Dompier, Jim*

Wmfpix — A group of 13 Windows metafile format pictures for use on controls in Visual Basic programs.

    WMFPIX   28 *K*

30
HELP

$20 Help Authoring Tools 2.0 — A beginner's Help authoring tool for use with Microsoft Word 6.0. Users work in a Word document which has active jumps for easy composition of hypertext. Help Project Editor assigns topic titles, keywords, browse sequences, and help compiler settings.

    20HELP   116 *K* $20   *Synergystic Productions*

$5 Help Authoring Tools 2.0 — Help authoring tool for Word 6.0. Users work in a Word document that has active jumps for easy composition in Hypertext. Use buttons to assign topics, jumps, etc. A macro converts the DOC file to RTF for processing with the Help Compiler.

    5HELP   48 *K* $5   *Synergystic Productions*

Add Help — Modified from the IconWorks file which comes with Visual Basic. The include file and form contain only the required code to use the Windows API for Windows Help.

    AHELP   3 *K*   *Microsoft (Modified By Unknown*

AnetHelpTool 1.2 — Tool for creation of Help systems. Fully WYSIWYG and looks exactly like the Help file. Has its own internal word processor with multifont and multicolor text, which provides full WYSIWYG presentation.

    ANETHELP   1591 *K* $75   *Anet Inc.*

Balloon Help Text 3.8 — Adds balloon help feature to applications. Help text is displayed in a popup window. Source code available at optional cost.

    BLUN20   38 *K* $18 SW   *Weimar Software*

Balloon Popup Labels — Routine displays a delayed popup help label (TheLabel) centered under TheControl whenever the mouse passes over the control. Position controls whether the label appears on top or bottom of control.

    LABELS   4 *K*   *Bencivengo, Nicholas Jr.*

Bubble Help — Example on how to add a help caption to any object on any form. Pure Basic source code.

TAGIT 47 K Free *Neese, Al*

Bubble Help Window System — A DLL to provide a quick semi-help system in VB programs. Sample source code included.

VBUBBLE 6 K Free *Gamber, Mark*

CreateHelp V3.03a — Authoring tool for writing help files. Requires WinWord 2.x. Point and click macro building, outline building from a list file, summary reporting, auto page building, etc.

CH3S 407 K $40 *Barnes, Nic*

Creating Windows Help Files — Article on how to create Help files. Includes info on macros and integrating Help into your program. Sample Help file and all VB source files showing how to implement many features.

HELPIN 103 K Free *Kahn, Theodore*

EZHelp Simple Help System — A simple "Help" system created from standard ASCII files. Source code included.

EZHELP 8 K Free *Campbell, George*

FTS Wizard — Helps you add full text search to existing Windows Help 3.x files. This tool automates, but does not replace, the steps required to add full text search to your help files.

FTSSUP 923 K $10 *Allman, Gary*

Flyhelp Balloon Help DEMO — Demonstration of balloon help without the use of a custom control or API call. Source is included, but encrypted, awaiting payment of the registration fee.

FLYHLP 8 K $5 SW *Streu, Randy*

FoCoach For Help Training Card — Controls the Training Cards found in the Windows 95 Help format. Allows your VB application to "drive" through a Help file, or allows the Help file to "drive" your VB app. 30-day evaluation copy.

FO951EC 1391 K $69 *Fundamental Objects Inc.*

GetHelp — Allows to to call Windows Help and jump to a specified page. Multi-colored icons are provided to select a Help file quickly by color without reading the caption. Full source code and icons.

GETHEP 12 K Free *Freel, Fred*

GetHelp — Scans project files, builds a list of all controls that have a HelpContextID, and an include file generates a name for each help topic for the help file. Source code included.

    GETHEL   35 K   Free   *Lorenzini, Greg*

Glossary How To — Windows Help file shows how to add a glossary feature to your help files; design issues, use of secondary windows; mid-topic jumps and keywords, extraction of files from baggage, etc.

    GLYHOWTO   675 K   Free *CNS - Companhia Nacional De Se*

Helllp! Help Authoring Tool — Windows Help file authoring tool for Winword 2 and 6. Automatically builds table of contents with hypertext jumps to topics in place. You add more jumps and popups by point and shoot. Can resize windows, add sound, etc.

    HELLLP25   448 K $30+SW   *Guy, Edward*

Help Balloons Example — Uses Windows API to create help balloons for an object on a Visual Basic form. BALLOON.BAS file can be added to any project to create Help Balloons. Sample project included.

    BALLOONC   4 K   Free   *ChimpWare*

Help Builder 1.07 — Application to build Help files. Supports Topic, Links/popup windows to other topics, keywords, browse sequences, bitmaps, fonts, colors, context identifiers, locking top of page.

    HB   591 K $65   *Plowman, Graham*

Help Compiler 3.10.505 — Update to the Help Compiler. Uses extended memory, is faster, produces smaller files. Updated to handle new RTF information generated by Word 6.0, increases internal compiler limit to 64K.

    HC505   214 K   Free   *Microsoft*

Help Compiler Shell — No longer maintained. Shell to assist in compiling Windows Help files.

    HPJ   64 K   Free   *Brown, Tim*

Help File To WinWord — Converts a Windows Help File to a Word for Windows 2.0 format document, including formatting information.

    HELP2DOC   43 K   Free   *Beyer, Wolfgang*

Help Maker Plus — Creates Help file with multiple fonts, font sizes and colors: however you want to express yourself. You can even make your help file come to life with graphics and sound!

    HELPMAKE   1201 K $20   *Ippolito, Ian*

Help Project Editor 1.0a — Program designed to help manage help project (HPJ) files required by the Windows Help Compiler. Allows you to easily get to and understand all the functionality of HPJ files.

    HPJEDI   1096 *K* $50   *Fletcher, David*

Help S12923 — An "Application Note" file from Microsoft, to convert Microsoft Excel custom help files to a format compatible with Excel 3.0. This file includes the Microsoft Windows 3.0 Help Compiler program, normally sold ($50) as an add-on for VB. See QDHELP also.

    S12923   105 *K* Free   *Microsoft*

Help Writer's Assistant 2.0 — Visual and easy way to create Windows Help files. Import/decompile existing help files. Full WYSIWYG editor that displays graphics and text, along with topic tree providing an overview of the topic structure. Create links by drag and drop.

    HWA20   1675 *K* $65   *Olson, Stephan*

Help Writing Help — Book for writers and developers who design and develop Windows online help for third party applications. Contains helpful information on writing and designing Help screens. Meant to be used as an online reference. Supplied as a Windows Help file.

    HLPWRT   376 *K* $32   *TechnoTrends*

HelpBreeze 1.6 Demo — Slideshow and Windows Help demo of HelpBreeze. HelpBreeze turns Word for Windows into a complete integrated environment for developing Windows Help files. Now includes the Topic Wizard which automatically structures and formats help files.

    HLPBRZ   162 *K* $279   *Solutionsoft*

HelpNavp Plus 3.2 — Windows help remote control. Open and close help files, browse through them, print out the topics, and copy entire topics to the clipboard. Gives you complete control over the Help files on your system.

    HELPNAV   45 *K* $10 SW   *Arnote, Paul*

HelpScre — A form that can be used to add help screens to your programs. A combo box is used to quickly locate topics of interest. VB 1.0.

    HELPSCRE   8 *K* Free   *Crygier, Ed*

HelpScrn — Provides a method of adding help screens to your VB program. Requires VB 2.0.

    HELPSCRN   9 *K* Free   *Crygier, Ed*

Hypertext For VB — No support available. A simple way to add hypertext to your VB programs as an alternative to using the Windows Help system. Basically a text box hack that works. Source code included.

    HYPER   11 *K*   Free   *Martin, Wendell*

Menu Help Text Custom C. 3.0 — Provides users dynamic menu help using a status bar. Allows user to search all menu choices before confirming selection from the menu.

    CLAK20   32 *K* $18 SW   *Weimar Software*

Microsoft Multimedia Viewer — FTENGINE.DLL, FTUI.DLL, and MVAPI.DLL add full text search capabilities to the Windows Help system. Just copy into your WINDOWSSYSTEM directory. Useful (not required) for Microsoft Knowledgebase files in HLP format.

    SEARCHMS   52 *K*   Free   *Microsoft*

MiniHelp Plus 3.2 — Complete Help Authoring Aid. Writing Help files is as easy as typing the text in an ASCII text editor and clicking a couple buttons in the MiniHelp Plus ToolPad.

    MHP32SW   402 *K* $25 SW   *Arnote, Paul*

Multimedia Help Viewer — How to use MVAPI2.DLL, the Multimedia Viewer, for context sensitive help in Visual Basic applications. Source code included, no other DLLs needed.

    MVHELP   14 *K*   Free   *McGregor, Rob*

Personal Helper — Utility for creating help files. Allows you to import your project files into an Access database, creating a context id for the project and all the controls for each form in the project. Creates a Visual Basic subroutine to merge into the main form.

    PERSHE   44 *K* $15   *FAR, Inc.*

Popup Help VB Source — VB source code example that emulates the popup help system for toolbars used in Microsoft products. Source code only, no VBXs required.

    POPHEL   4 *K*   Free

Quick And Dirty Help 3.0 — Utility to allow writing help text, to be compiled with the Help Compiler, in straight ASCII. Plays WAV files, creates UP buttons, automatically creates glossary topics.

    QDHELP   153 *K* $49 SW   *Allen, Phil*

RIGHTMOUS Help Text CC 3.8 — Custom control allows developer to provide the user with dynamic popup help balloon for each control on each form. when the user clicks the right mouse button on a form control. Source code available at extra cost.

RTMOUS	36 K $19 SW	*Weimar Software*

RTFMagic Help File Generator — Allows the rapid conversion of Word for Windows documents into Help format. Using the Outline feature of Word, RTFMagic creates a matching table of contents, jumps, popups, browse sequences, and buttons.

RTFMAG	34 K $20 SW	*Bainbridge Knowledge Mngt Arts*

RoboHELP DEMO Animation — Animated demo of RoboHELP Help authoring tool which uses Microsoft Word for Windows 2.0 or 6.0 (not required for demo).

ROBOHEDE	769 K Free	*Blue Sky Software*

STMOUS Help Text CC 3.8 — Allows developer to provide dynamic status line help for each control on a form. When the user moves the mouse cursor over a form control, status line displays the help. Source code available at extra cost.

STMOUS	23 K $18 SW	*Weimar Software*

Simple Tip Help — Source code for a simple way to add Tip Help to your application. Uses a label control positioned near the control like a "Tip Balloon".

TIP2	3 K Free	*Hipp, Frank*

SmartDoc 1.2 — Prints Windows Help files and extracts plain text from Windows Help files. Can also drive the Windows Help engine to print a complete Windows Help file or a portion of it.

SMTDOC12	40 K $25 SW	*Oakley Data Services*

SmtHlp — Winword authoring tool to create help files especially for VB applications.

SMTHLP	67 K	*Bytes & Letters*

Text File To VB Help — Visual Basic source code for a utility which converts an ASCII text file into a VB Subroutine, which can be used as a "help" message. Creates VB source code which is fed into a Textbox control.

TXTCON	69 K Free	*Rivers, Jerry*

Using WinAPI Calls W/ WinHelp — Help file describes some Windows API calls which can be used to extend the functionality of the Windows Help system. Includes Changing Title Bar Text, Writing Values to WIN.INI, Reading values from WIN.INI, and more.

WINAPI3	531 K Free	*Arnote, Paul*

VB AHA!!! 1.25 — Inexpensive and easy to use utility for writing Windows Help files. With simple mouse clicks and Drag 'n' Drop ease you will be able to construct your help files quickly without using any word processor.

    VBAHA125   147 *K* $50   *Villalon, Craig*

VB HelpWriter 2.5g — Automates the helpfile creation process. Reads a VB program to create a helpfile framework; automatically links to the program's forms; easy creation of hypertext jumps and popups; automatic Glossary generation; reads and writes RTF files (pro version).

    VBHW25   1166 *K* $59+SW   *Teletech Systems*

VB HelpWriter Dictionary — Dictionary file needed to add spell checking to version 1.8.5 of VB HelpWriter. For Professional Edition only.

    VBHWDIC   192 *K*   *Teletech Systems*

VBAPI Help 2.1 Program — No longer supported. Small program accesses VBAPI.HLP file.

    VBAP21   10 *K*   Free   *Bostwick, Marshall*

VBHelper Integrated Help DEMO — Integrated help system for VB. Includes ZIPping of help files, internal ZIP/UNZIP, integrates into VB menus, 3D look and feel, fast execution.

    VBHELP   253 *K* $25   *Disk And Desk Software*

Visual Basic Naming Convention — Add-in that displays a Windows Help file containing naming conventions from the Microsoft Knowledgebase and other sources. RTF and HPJ source files included for modification. 16 and 32 bit versions included.

    VBNAME   253 *K*   Free   *Macdonald, Peter*

Visual Help 2.1i — Authoring tool for Microsoft Windows Help files. Use drag and drop to quickly create help files with bitmap and sound support, allowing complete multimedia documents. Outline view of help file, assign macros to labels and images. Programmer support.

    VH   434 *K* $49   *WinWare*

Visual Help Pro 3.1e — WYSIWYG help development and runtime testing environment. Drag and drop visual objects using the built-in editor to create help files fast. Support for bitmap, sound, and video files. Save compile time with a runtime test.

    VHPRO   924 *K* $49   *WinWare*

WSHELP Help Text CC — Four custom controls; Composite containing balloon help for each form control, balloon help when right mouse button is clicked on a control, status line help for each control.

    WSHELP   144 K $45 SW   *Weimar Software*

WhizNotes S2.14 — Super-notepad with topic management features to organize your text. Use for random notes, research, to organize tasks, to make hypertext reference notes. One mouse click away from turning your notes into a Windows Help file.

    WHIZNT   546 K $50 SW   *Advanced Support Group Inc.*

Win Help Builder — A user interface to the Help Project File (HPJ) for compiling the Topic file (RTF) to HLP format.

    WHB13   76 K $20   *McFall, Pete*

WinHelp Extension Library 3.2 — DLL displays 256-color and 24-bit bitmaps in the Windows Help system. Also inserts BMPs, WAVs, etc., files into Help files, which are automatically extracted when needed and can be deleted.

    EW256BMP   762 K $20   *Arnote, Paul*

Windows Help Magician Demo 3.0 — DEMO of: Integrated help development system that simplifies the creation of help files. Create jumps and pop-ups by simply marking words or phrases within the help text. Include bitmaps. Create and dynamically order single or multiple Browse sequences.

    HLPMAG   274 K $199   *Software Interphase*

Windows Quick Help — Viewer for Windows Help files. Allows printing topics from help files.

    WQH111   32 K $15 SW   *SMI Enterprises Corp*

Xantippe 2.06 — Hypertext/hypergraphics authoring environment. Automates development of Windows help files.

    XANT206   283 K $15 SW   *IRIS Media Systems*

31
ICON UTILITY

ICOBMP — Converts ICO files to BMP format, either one at a time or by whole directories.

    ICOBMP   8 *K*   Free   *Campbell, George*

Icon Box 1.1 — Utility to extract icons from EXE, DLL, or other files. Save as icon or bitmap. Limited shareware version.

    ICONBOX   334 *K* $25   *Simha, Andre E.*

Icon Chooser 1.3 — An icon database and manager which allows grouping of icons into one of 12 predefined categories. It uses simple "drag and drop" operation and automatically checks icon integrity.

    ICCH13   21 *K* $15SW   *Ledbetter, Keith*

Icon DLL — A DOS program (NOT a Windows or VB program) designed to build a DLL from a collection of icon files. As a DLL, the single file requires much less disk space than the individual ICO files. (Limit 500 Icons per DLL).

    ICONDLL2   10 *K*   Free   *Curran, James M.*

Icon Extractor — Extracts all icons from one or more source files (EXE, DLL, VBX, DRV) to individual icon files, giving each icon a unique name based on the name of the source file. Full source code.

    EXICON   11 *K*   Free   *Mulks, Charles*

Icon Extractor — VB source code for extracting icons from programs and libraries. Uses functions in USER.EXE, KRNL386.EXE and SHELL.DLL. Shows how to create a multilingual program and obtain strings from Windows modules. Uses the original Windows About Box.

    ICONEX   14 *K*   Free   *Germelmann, Christian*

Icon Extractor — Extracts icons from Windows EXE programs, and saves as standard ICO files. Companion to VBICON12. Source code available with registration.

    ICONX113   22 *K* $15 SW   *Valley Programming*

Icon Extractor — Utility to extract the icon from EXE or DLL files and save each as a BMP. Source code included.

    EXTRICO   13 K   Free   *Tricaud, Christophe*

Icon Grabber — Lets you view all icons stored in a Windows DLL, print the icon library, save a selected icon to an ICO file, or copy the selected icon to the clipboard, to be pasted directly into the Picture property of a VB control.

    ICONGRAB   106 K   Free   *AndyD*

Icon Selector — A quick viewer for ICO files. Visually displays 36 icons per screen, with simple facility to copy a selected icon to a target directory.

    ICONSE   5 K   Free   *McNamee, Tom*

Icon Viewer — Icon viewing utility which can save to the clipboard. Source code included.

    ICONVIEW   5 K   Free   *Evers, Dave*

IconJuice Win95 Icon Extrac1.5 — Icon extractor for Windows 95 files. VB3 source code available for $50.

    ICOJUICE   13 K   Free+   *Hansen, Mogens*

IconLook — A viewer for ICO files. Full source code is included in the documentation (WRI) file.

    ICONLOOK   7 K   Free   *Pitts, David*

Programmers Icon Pack Vol. 1 — Twenty-five icons geared for applications development. Royalty-free use. Help file included which advertises graphic services. Icons include Open, Save, New, Print, Trash, Find, etc.

    PROICO   15 K   Free   *Creativision Graphics*

Shrink Icon Capture Utility — Utility to capture a portion of the screen for use as an icon. Edit individual pixels in colors, rotate by 90/180/270 degrees, convert to monochrome. Undocumented but simple and well done.

    SHRINKIG   31 K   Free   *Geron, Israel*

Visual Basic Icons — 15 improved icons for VB. 16 and 32 bit versions. Also 3D versions.

    VB_ICONS   3 K   Free   *Main, Mark*

32

INPUT ROUTINES

Blind Data Input — A SUB to call when user input should NOT be displayed on the screen - as with passwords, etc.

    BLINDI   *3 K* $10   *Woodward, Kirk*

Change Name To Initials — Short function to change a full name to its initials. Full source code.

    INITIA   *2 K*   Free   *Covell, Stephen E.*

Edit Demo - Input Routines — A form demonstrating several methods of advanced input validation and output formatting. Source code included.

    EDITDEMO   *19 K*   Free   *Milligan, Keith*

Masked Input Using Text Box — An attempt to do masked input with a regular VB text box using only Basic code. It will handle simple masked input such as a phone number, date, decimal number, or dollar amount.

    TBMASK   *5 K*   Free   *Craig, Bob*

NewInputBox — Create your own Input Box with command buttons and system menu in Visual Basic. Full VB source code.

    VBIBOX   *17 K*   Free   *Germelmann, Christian*

33
INTERNATIONALIZATION

Multiple Language Resource DLL — Sample VB application showing how to use a resource DLL with program text (captions, etc.) that is loaded at runtime. This lets programs change languages on the fly.

    INTLAN   19 *K*   *Little, Thomas*

VB Language Manager Demo — Easy and efficient multi-language support for Visual Basic. You maintain a single copy of source code and VB Language Manager manages localizing any VB app, old or new. Even create multi-language executables that run in whatever language the user selects

    VBLM2   326 *K* $100+   *WhippleWare*

DataPage Maker — A Web DataPage creation utility. Transforms information from an Access database into text files called DataPages, formatted to function as homepages on the World Wide Web.

    DPM1   1782 *K*   *Fashenpour, Dave*

FTP Server — VB 3.0 source code for a simple FTP server implementing most of RFC959.

    FTP_SRV2   70 *K*   Free   *Lorenzo, Anastasi*

Millenium Countdown Control — Millenium Count ActiveX control, intended primarily for web pages, that uses a scrolling marquee to count down to the year 2000, and then the year 3000.

    MILCOUNT   1469 *K*   Free   *SDK Software*

VBrowser — Well documented source code for a simple Internet World Wide Web browser. HTML tags and graphics are not supported - VBrowse makes the connection and shows exactly what has been transmitted (the HTML "source"). Foundation for a VB browser or a debug aid.

    VBROWSER   58 *K* $20   *World Wide Development*

WebLib Beta Demo — VBX/DLL toolkit for integrating Netscape or Mosaic with other desktop applications. Sample VB code incl. WebLib has the ability to control and monitor the Web browser without using DDE. A customizable toolbar attaches to the browser. 30-day evaluation de

    WEBLIBEV   1293 *K*   *Potomac Software*

LANGUAGE EXTENSION

Bobber And Sinker — A simple application with source code which demonstrates how to float an application's window above all windows.

> VBFLOAT 7 *K* Free *Stewart, David*

Coerce — Routine to force Currency variable amounts to 0,1,2,3 or 4 digits of accuracy.

> COERCE 5 *K* Free *Aaron, Bud*

Compare! — Interactive magazine, in Windows Help format, compares various add-on tools for Visual Basic with features lists and screen shots.

> WCSCMP 234 *K* Free *Wonderful Computer Services*

Ctlwhwnd.Dll — This library adds the function ControlhWnd, which provides a simple method to get the hWnd (handles to Windows) to a control. See VBZ01.ZIP.

> VBHWND 2 *K* *User Friendly, Inc.*

CurrencyFix VB — Assembly language module and DLL to fix the number of decimal places in currency values.

> CFIXVB 5 *K* Free *Mack, Jim*

EnumFont — Not needed with Visual Basic 3.0 and later. A DLL, with the C source code, to permit a call to the Windows API function EnumFonts.

> ENUMFONT 19 *K* Free *WinWay Corporation*

Error Handler — Development tool that will add ErrorTrapping code into every SUB and Function in seconds. Also has Sub/Functions Print and View. Unregistered version has restrictions.

> EH 122 *K* $100 *Micro90*

Extended Arrays — Manages the creation, accessing, saving to and restoring from disk of arrays with up to 4 Gigs elements and >64K of text strings. No VB imposed limits. Arrays can be of any type except User-defined, which is available in the registered version.

AAARRY	90 K $30	*Willy, C. Scott*

Formula One DEMO — Microsoft Excel compatible spreadsheet and grid tool. Includes 126 of the most commonly used spreadsheet functions. Virtual mode supports editing and reporting of any size database. Royalty free runtime distribution.

F1DEMO	507 K $249	*Visual Components, Inc.*

FreeVBX — DLL with VB versions of PEEK, POKE, INP, OUT, VARPTR, VARSEG, VARSEGPTR, SADD, SEGG, SSEGGADD. A small part of MicroHelp's commercial Muscle library. Free unrestricted use. Sample source code included.

MHELP	5 K Free	*MicroHelp, Inc.*

Hotkey Gosub — How to do a GOSUB without using GOSUB and how to put hotkeys in an application. Source code.

HOTKEY2	5 K Free

Huge Array Support — DLL which contains functions for creation, maintenance, and deletion of arrays larger than 64K. Also gives the ability to create arrays with more than 32,767 elements per dimension, and to redimension arrays while preserving their contents.

HUGEARAY	17 K Free	*Microsoft*

Huge Grid 1.0 — Example routine used to demonstrate the proper coding necessary to use Huge Array in conjunction with the grid control. Source code is included.

HUGEGR	12 K Free	*Ford, Nelson*

Huge Variable And Fixed String — Visual Basic provides string arrays limited to 64k. VqStrings can use all available Windows memory. DLL and sample source code.

VQSTRG	34 K $30 SW	*Vi Qual Software*

LZH Compression DLL — A DLL for compression and decompression, copying, appending, and deleting files.

WLZHCXP2	16 K Free	*Gamber, Mark*

MoreAPI — Additional API functions made available to Visual Basic. Source is included.

MOREAPI	11 K Free

Number — Additional math routines for Visual Basic, IEEE floating point and Binary Coded Decimal.

    NUMBER   3 *K*   Free   *Marquis Computing, Inc.*

Number To Text — Source code to convert any decimal number up to one trillion to a text string.

    NUM2TXT   3 *K*   Free   *Martinez, Brad*

Passing Character String DLL — Example Turbo C++ DLL that illustrates how to pass a character string from the DLL to VB for processing.

    CDLLVB   12 *K*   Free   *Aylor, Bill*

Pointers.DLL 1.1 — DLL contains a function that returns the pointer of any variable.

    PNTR11   5 *K*   *Blaum, Greg*

Profile — Two routines which use the Windows API to manipulate the application profile entries contained in WIN.INI. They will allow your programs to save and restore their configuration options.

    PROFIL   2 *K*   Free

RandGrid 1.0 — Example code used to demonstrate the proper coding necessary to use a random access file in conjunction with the grid control. This is usually needed if you need to use an array larger than 64k. Source code is included.

    RANDGR   12 *K*   *Ford, Nelson*

Registration Creator — Simple registration system for programmers and shareware authors. Implemented by using API calls to a small DLL. The Code Generator keeps up with customer data and calculates serial numbers and valid registration codes.

    REGMAKER   1556 *K* $41   *Hutchings, Donathan*

Screen Saver — A DLL that allows you to create Windows screen savers in Visual basic. The DLL notifies your app when the user is not using the keyboard or mouse. Simple source code for a screen saver is included. See VBZ01.ZIP.

    SSAVER   5 *K*   Free   *User Friendly, Inc.*

SearcHistory 2.3 — Provides a feature missing from the VB environment - a history list of the most recent text search arguments. This shareware version is fixed at the last 10 items; registered version can be set from 1 to 50.

    SEARCHIS   157 *K* $18   *Chiselbrook, Craig*

SearcHistory 2.3 — Provides a feature missing from the VB environment - a history list of the most recent text search arguments. This shareware version is fixed at the last 10 items; registered version can be set from 1 to 50.

> VBSRCH 157 *K* $15 *Chiselbrook, Craig*

Searching For Windows — A DLL to supplement the AppActivate command. With it, you don't need to have an exact match when searching for a window caption. Source code is included.

> WFIND 4 *K*

Soundex — Soundex function for Visual Basic. A .dll (dynamic link library) written in Turbo Pascal for Windows. See VBZ01.ZIP.

> SNDEX 4 *K* Free *User Friendly, Inc.*

Status Bar — A status bar .dll that can be incorporated in your Visual Basic applications as though it were a regular VB tool. Sample source code included.

> STSBAR2 12 *K* $10 SW *Staffin, Ed*

String Encryption — VB source code function to encrypt and decrypt strings. Uses a complex pattern based on a supplied password so every string is encrypted differently.

> KTENCODE 14 *K* Free *Albrecht, Karl D.*

String To Bitmap — Not supported. DLL converts VB bitmaps into strings and vice versa. Also supports bitmap comparison, ANDing, etc. C source code included for the DLL; sample VB source code. Version 1.1 is available from the author.

> STR2BM 23 *K* Free *Monasterio, Jorge*

Tooltips Bar Sample — VB source code implements a "tooltips" bar using pure VB code, no APIs, or DLLs. Documentation contained in the source code under Sub Readme().

> TLTIPS 4 *K* Free *Crouse, Aaron P.*

User Defined Labels For Crysta — XTALUDL.EXE allows you to set user-defined label dimensions at runtime for label reports created with Crystal Reports. Mat be freely distributed with your own applications.

> XUDL 8 *K* Free *Johnston, Robert J.*

Using Borland C++ For VB Contr — Information on using Borland C++ with the Visual Basic Control Development Kit. For version 1.0, no longer supported by author.

> CDK 8 *K* Free *Langley, Brent K.*

VB 3.0 Setup Bug Fixes 1.00552 — Bug fixes and new features added to Visual Basic 3.0 SETUPKIT and SETUP files.

    SETUPK   89 *K*   Free   *Microsoft*

VB Add-Ons 1.02 — Files to provide support in Visual Basic applications for huge arrays, and additional access to disk/diskette information.

    VBA102   26 *K*   Free   *Stewart, Michael*

VB-Awk — Productivity tool intended to simulate the power and features of the AWK programming language in the Visual Basic environment. Creates native Windows apps using Visual Basic with many of the powerful features of AWK.

    VBAWK   32 *K* $25 SW *SYNERGY Software & Services*

VBPtr — Provides for pointer support in Visual Basic. See VBZ01.ZIP.

    VBPTR   5 *K*   Free   *User Friendly, Inc.*

VBTools Demo — Interactive demo of VBTools shows the full impact of how language extensions can enhance your Visual Basic program. Features shown will remove any doubts about the capabilities of Visual Basic. VBTools is incorporated into newer MicroHelp products,

    VBTOOLS   170 *K*   *MicroHelp, Inc.*

Windows LZSS Compression Lib — Compression library for Windows for file-to-file compression. Example source code included.

    LZSSLI   18 *K* $25SW   *Eschalon Development Inc.*

Writing Custom Controls W/MFC — Using MFC (Microsoft Foundation Classes [Visual C++]) to write Custom Controls (VBXs) for Visual Basic and Visual C++. Details differences between regular DLLs and VBXs.

    CDKMFC   16 *K*   Free

36
LISTBOX

Add Item — Demonstrates fixed length strings, string expressions, and the Listbox AddItem method.

    ADDITM   9 *K*   Free

BndRead - Data Control — Data Control with Bound ReadOnly Text Boxes. Source code demonstrates how to make certain bound text boxes ReadOnly or Read/Write by the press of a button. Uses data from the Access sample database BIBLIO.MDB, not included.

    BNDREAD   3 *K*   Free

Combo List Box Incremental Sea — Combo list box with incremental search. Source code included. From Inside Visual Basic magazine Jan 92.

    CLBOX1   2 *K*   Free

ControlFill Class Module — Control to fill a ListBox or ComboBox from a recordset of your choice.

    FILLER   6 *K*   Free   *Lee, Michaelx*

DameWare Checklist OCX — 32bit "Check" List-Box custom control for use with Visual Basic and Visual C++. Many customizable properties (fonts, colors, 3D, etc.).

    CHKLST13   44 *K*   *Dameware Development*

Dragging A Line In Listbox — Demonstration, with source code, of dragging a line in a Listbox which is displaying only part of the available list.

    LSTDR2   6 *K*   Free   *Mosher, Sue*

Link Demo — Demonstration of an advanced Linked List/Listbox and Speedfill. The demo shows a Text Box and List Box that work together in locating a selection in the Listbox. "Great for database browsing." Source code included.

    LTDEMO   8 *K*   Free   *Presley, Jack*

List Box With Bitmaps CC 2.0 — Convenient way to have pictures in list box with text, item data, and all other normal list box properties. Picture bitmap is placed at a user specified distance above the text. Source code available for $25.

BMPLST20   51 *K* $20 SW   *Mabry Software*

List Control Demo — Source code demonstrates how to set tabstops in a listbox using a borderless, disabled text box for the column headings. It also shows how to preselect a listbox item using Windows API functions.

LBDEMO   7 *K*   Free   *Kaenel, Brad*

LstGrid — Source code demonstrates how to drag data from a listbox to a certain cell in a grid. Select an entry with the mouse, holding the left button, drag to the target cell, release mouse.

LSTGRID   3 *K*   Free

Message Box Designer — Another Message Box Designer. Interactively designs the combination of several constants to describe the message box. Pastes the source code into your VB project. Full source code included.

MSGBOXMW   38 *K*   Free   *Warwick, M. J.*

Message Box Editor — Utility assists in creating Message Boxes. Cuts the designed Message Box, as Visual Basic source code, into the Clipboard for pasting into your Visual Basic project.

MSGBXED   84 *K* $15 SW   *Durocher, James*

MsgBox Designer Addin For VB4 — VB4 addin helps create message boxes, especially those requiring multiple lines of text. A test feature lets you view the format of the message box. Support for help file and context ID is included. Requires VB4 Professional or Enterprise edition.

MBADDIN   14 *K*   *Morelli Systems, Inc.*

Multi Column Listbox 32 Bit — Function automatically calculates and sets appropriate tabstops for a multi-column listbox, based on the actual data in the listbox. Full source code.

LISTTAB   8 *K*   Free   *Wallace, Robert*

Multi-Purpose Combobox Control — Custom control manages the way your data appears in a combobox. mComboBox is a property replacement of the standard combobox control which comes with VB 3.0. Many other features.

MCMBOX   28 *K* $10 SW   *McKean Consulting*

Multi-Select List Box — Excel 5.0 spreadsheet with VBA function to return an array of selected items in a multi-select listbox.

    MULTIS   6 *K*   Free   *Hamilton, Peter*

Multicolumn Listbox — Demonstration of a routine that dynamically calculates and sets tabstops in a listbox, by examining the actual widths of the text strings in each column. Full source code with extensive comments.

    LBTABS   7 *K*   Free   *PC HELP-LINE*

Multicolumn Listbox VBX 4.6 — Custom control for managing listboxes. Replaces the standard listbox control of VB 3.0. Handle bitmaps, true multiple column listboxes with bitmaps and check boxes, etc. Source code available.

    MLIST46   102 *K* $25+   *Klasman Quality Consulting*

Multisel — This control adds to the normal listbox control. This control allows multiple selections from the listbox. Items are referenced by a control array. VBX and source code.

    MULTSEL2   8 *K*   Free   *Gamber, Mark*

NoBeep — Source code demonstrates how to silence the BEEP sound when ENTER is pressed in a single-line text box.

    NOBEEP   1 *K*   Free   *Leckkett, Blaine*

Search A List Box — Example source demonstrates control over list boxes.

    SEARCH   6 *K*   Free

Search For Nearest Match — Commented source code demonstrates finding the nearest match among stored strings.

    SEARCHLI   7 *K*   Free

Seek Table Object From Listbox — Sample source code demonstrates how to use the SEEK method and a Table object variable with a variable that the user selects from a Listbox. The result of the search will bring up the entire record to be read or updated.

    SEEKLST   4 *K*   Free

SortedCollection Class (VB4) — Replaces the generic Collection object of VB4. The Add method automatically inserts the new item into its proper place based on a required key. Helps simplify synchronization between Items and Listbox controls.

    SORTCOLL   24 *K*   Free   *Velazquez, Chris*

Templar List Collection VBXs — Overcomes the limitations of the standard VB Listbox. Enhanced listbox and tree controls plus a line-oriented parser. Easy and efficient way of storing, managing, and displaying many different types of data.

LISTCOLL   371 *K* $149   *RA-Ware Technologies, Inc.*

TestLay — Demonstrates how to save a TrueGrid layout and restore it. A TrueGrid can be changed by the user at run time; this routine provides a method for the user to save his customized layout and restore it, or also revert to programmer default settings.

TSTLAY   20 *K*   Free   *Bridge, Inc.*

Text Justification Function — Function allows programmer to align text in a given amount of characters. Intended for use with the ListBox control. Pads or truncates the string passed.

PADDA   1 *K*   Free

TextBox Plus 1.0 — Source code demonstrates and implements Overstrike mode in the standard Visual Basic textbox control. Toggles between Insert and Overstrike mode by pressing the Insert key.

TBPLUS   6 *K*   Free   *Trimble, Daniel*

Textbox Styles — Source code and DLL hows how to use API calls to define textbox styles (uppercase, lowercase, password, limited number of characters).

TXTYLE   4 *K*   Free   *Irwin, Gregg*

Virtual List Box — Demonstrates creating a "Virtual List Box" from a Picture Box and a Vertical Scroll Bar in order to view text files larger than 64K. The file is first loaded into a huge array. Full source code.

BIGLST   4 *K*   Free   *Craig, Bob*

Virtual Text Browser 0.9 — Unsupported. Do not contact author. An attempt to get around the 64K limit of the VB text box control without third party DLLs. Slow in some operations. Full source code included.

VIRTXT   20 *K*   Free   *Risholm, Bob*

Visual Basic Message Potato — Simple program to make Message Boxes. You create a Message Box by choosing options and typing in text-you don't have to memorize constants or look up values. View your Message Box, see the code, and the Potato will enter the code into the code window.

MNUSPD   76 *K* $5   *Stewart, David*

37
MAIL

MSlot.Vbx — Custom control that makes it easy to use Windows for Workgroups Mailslots.

    MSLOT   15 *K*   *Thomas, Zane*

BLINC — Mailing list with labels, reports, and merge capabilities. Sort on multiple fields by user criteria.

    BLINC207   121 *K* $235   *Eastern Digital Resources*

38
MENU

Clicking With Right Mouse Butt — Short source code shows a method of clinking with the right mouse button in a listbox and changing the selection. Also pinpoints an error in the WIN30API.TXT file.

     HEREIT   3 *K*   Free

FXLaunch — This mini-menu allows easy access to the four different utilities which make up Metz Software's FX file program. Source code included.

     FXLAUN   6 *K*   Free   *Snider, Charles K.*

Flyout Menus — Example of how to implement flyout menus similar to CorelDRAW with Visual Basic. Detailed documentation and sample source code. Requires SpyWorks-VB custom control.

     FLYOUT   123 *K*   Free   *Koch, Peter*

Menu Embedding Demo — Demonstrates a technique for embedding one VB form inside another, with special reference to embedding so that one form's menu looks and works like a control for the embedding form.

     VBEMBDMN   8 *K*   Free   *Stewart, David*

Menu Enable/Disable — Subroutine to enable and disable the menubar. This routine uses the Windows API instead of VB itself, and is faster and has no screen flicker.

     MENUON   6 *K*   Free

Popup Context Menu VB4 — Sample VB4 32-bit code demonstrates a Win95 style popup context menu from a right mouse click.

     VBCNTX   4 *K*   Free   *MMC Software*

Popup Menu Problem Fix — A simple fix for the auto-misfire popup menu problem in Visual Basic. The ZIP file gives two source code projects, one showing the problem and one fixing it, and a README file documenting the problem.

     POPUPF   12 *K*   Free   *Liblick, Dathan*

VB Menu Potato 1.1 — Program makes it easy to reproduce Visual Basic form menus without having to recreate them manually in the Menu Design Window. Simply select a source form, select a target form, and copy the menu from one to the other.
    MSPD11   79 *K* $5 SW   *Stewart, David*

Visual Basic Toolbar 2.0a — Runs VB.EXE and is built into the VB Toolbar. Writes DAT file and registers MAK, BAS and FRM files. Adds instant icons for Notepad, API reference, SDK reference and a drag and drop area.
    VBBAR2   13 *K*   Free   *Germelmann, Christian*

39
MISC.

3DDemo 2.95 — Demonstration program with tooltips, Win95 spinners, 3D controls, and more in VB code.

    3DDEMO   11 *K*   SW   *Nickle, John*

Astem — VB 3.0 program that uses a FORTRAN DLL to obtain properties of water and steam based on 1967 IFC fomulation for ordinary water properties. Full VB 3.0 source code included.

    WATER   654 *K*   Free   *Throm, Edward D.*

CTL3D4VB — Demonstrates the use of CTL3DV2 with ordinary VB forms. Just pure CTL3DV2 calls.

    CTL3D4VB   17 *K*   Free   *Kennedy, Ian 'Ken'*

CodeLock 3.0 DEMO — DLL used to provide the security of a hardware lock without the hardware. Sample code included, and you can incorporate a sample DLL into your existing applications.

    CL3DEMO   174 *K* $599+   *Robust Software*

Color Scheme Form Adapter — Windows 95 allows the user to change the colour scheme on the fly. Many applications contain controls that do not automatically adjust to these colors (threed.vbx, for example). This BAS file fixes this.

    COLOUR   5 *K*   *Williams, Charles*

Crawford Common Routines — Several commonly used routines in VB source code. Sub ExitIfAlreadyRunning, Function FormFloat, ProfileString functions, SaveWindowPos, PlaySound.

    VB3UTILS   5 *K*   Free   *Crawford, Ross*

Custom Control Toolbox — Custom controls collection. Text input, data input, time input, spinner, tooltip, and threed. All in a non-VBX/OCX/DLL format, for compilation with your EXE.

    MSTOOLBX   46 *K* $30SW   *Nickle, John*

DBGrid Unbound Sample — Sample project using DBGrid unbound.
    DBGRID1   9 K   *Apex Software Corporation*

Dialog Box Generator — Wizard to create the code for all kinds of dialog boxes using only your mouse. Passes generated code automatically to your form or module. Requires VB 3.0 Professional Edition.
    CTDIAL   37 K   Free   *Tisoft S.A.*

Find/Sort Window — Database record selection window that helps find and sort records. Sets the SQL statement in your database control. All VB 3.0 code. Fully customizable.
    RECSQL   44 K $17   *Lee, Joseph*

LogBook 1.0 — Custom control for a scrolling message console with flexible file logging and time stamping. Clients write messages to the object, which time stamps and formats them. Messages are then shown in a configurable scrolling window, and logged to a file.
    LGBOOK10   50 K $25SW   *Zanna, A.*

Mouse Pointer Push and Pop — MouseSet and MouseRestore functions push the current mouse cursor shape onto the stack and restore it. Handy when applications fail to restore cursor shape (leave it as an hourglass, etc.)
    MOUSESET   9 K   Free   *Bridge, Inc.*

Patch Kit for Access Apps. — Prototype tool to update an MS-Access application that has already been delivered to users.
    DBPATCH   316 K   *Hanson, Michael E.*

Rotato — Pen Windows screen rotator.
    ROTATO   5 K   *Michael*

QueryMaster — SQL query development tool for VB4 programmers using Jet 3.0 Access databases. Includes templates for SELECT, INSERT, UPDATE, and DELETE and all variations. Comes with table/column name cut and paste tools. Commit/rollback for action queries.
    QMASTER   70 K   *Barrett, Jim*

Random Number Generator — Simple program to provide a user-chosen amount of random numbers. Source code included.
    RANDOM   7 K   Free   *Jarvis, Jeffrey L.*

Rosettes Screensaver — Screen saver. Backcolor is a randomly selected RGB color while the drawing color is a randomly selected QBcolor.
    ROSETTES   9 K   *Bennis, Robert G.*

Samples2 Source Code — Nine sample source code files for VB. Create directory if it does not exist. GetDir and FileFind. Extract Icon. Create Multiple instances of a form at runtime. How to parse a comma delimited text file. More.

> SAMPLES2   *25 K*   Free

Scheduling Control DEMO — Adds visual scheduling and tracking capabilities to your application. No DLL or VBX so there is no overhead. Schedule items can be added, deleted, resized, and moved with the mouse. Source code is unlocked with registration.

> VBSCHED   *61 K* $24   *Wolfebyte Ltd.*

Set1 — Unknown.

> SET1   *24 K*

Stilson — Collection of useful VB utilities. Sub SetReadOnly (tControl as Control), Sub GoShell (eShellString as String, iWinType as Integer), Function GetUser, String Function GoodDate (First%, Later%) and Sub FloatWindow (F as form, i as integer).

> STILSON   *3 K*   PD   *Tilson, Steven W.*

TLBox — Best way to create mini title bars without a custom control or extensive API calls.

> SMTLBOX   *10 K*   *Noble, Jason R.*

Taskbar Like Win'95 — Taskbar which lies near the bottom of screen. When the mouse pointer touches it, it displays a window with buttons for each running application, like Windows'95. Programs activate if you click their button. 3D menu. Demo - source with registration.

> TASKBR   *36 K* $12   *Lee, Joseph*

Time 2 Win - 16 bit for VB4 — VB 4.0 DLL with 685 functions for 2D/3D geometry, array, binary, bitmap, compression, CRC32, date/time, encrypt/decrypt, file, file I/O from C, huge memory array, huge string, IEEEnum, interest rate, language control, matrix, network, object, etc.

> T2W16910   *458 K* $43SW   *Renard, Michael*

VB Code Help File 1.1 — Windows Help File contains over 50 different code snippets. Includes routines to send MAPI messages, center your form, draw shadows on any control, connect to a network drive, and many more.

> VBCODE   *33 K*   Free   *Williams, Jeff*

VB Source Code Only ToolTips — ToolTips made only with standard VB resource and with few API calls. No VBXs or OCXs. Uses only one timer control for all windows with tooltips.

MYTTIPS   11 *K*   Free   *Giovine, Gabriele del*

VB Wizard 3.X System Files — System files for VBWizard. See file VBWIZ.ZIP.

VBWIZ2   143 *K*   *Pocket Change Software*

VBFree Tips — A collection of free tips and tricks for the Visual Basic programmer. How to create the tabbed notebook look with simple bitmaps (included). How to create Flyout Help Tips using standard VB controls. How to create a Help Tip Bar using standard controls.

FREETIPS   65 *K*   Free   *Owyen, Scott*

VBLaunch — Used to run and compile Visual Basic projects.

VBLAUN80   385 *K* $149+   *VideoFax Ltd.*

Win Library 3.0 — General visual basic function library.

WINLIB31   807 *K*   *Joussellin, Henri*

Windows'95 Dialog Box Wizard — Dialog box wizard which can be used with Win 3.1 and Windows'95.

MSGBOX95   8 *K*   Free   *Allcock, Alun*

Abort Printer — Demo program illustrates a method of cancelling a print job started from VB. Source code.

    ABORTP   4 K   Free

Access Table Design Printing — Visual Basic source code (and EXE) to produce a hardcopy of Microsoft Access table structures including field descriptions. Requires MSACCESS.EXE. Tested only with Access 1.1.

    LAYOUT   11 K   Free

Barcode/VBX — Custom control used to create barcodes. 18 different barcodes are included: Code 3 of 9, Interleaved 2 of 5, UPCA, EAN, Codebar, POSTNET, etc. Allows rotation of barcode. Sample source code included.

    BARVBX   148 K $35SW   *Gottschalk, Jeff*

Clipprint — Utility prints whatever is on the Clipboard as long as it is standard picture (Metafile, BMP or DIB) or plain text. All source code included.

    CLIPPRNT   9 K   Free   *McIntosh, Rob*

Crystal Reports DLL Update — Updated PDSODBC.DLL for Crystal Reports in Visual Basic.

    PDODBC   27 K   Free   *Crystal Services*

Crystal Reports Sample Applica — Sample applications using Crystal Reports 3.0 Pro with VB 3.0. Sample application source code includes Print Engine calls such as formulas, selection formulas, SQL query, Print to Window, file, printer, exporting, group sorting, etc.

    CRWDEMO   152 K   Free   *Crystal Services*

DDRV Print Preview 2.1 — DLL allows the programmer to have a common print preview screen throughout his application. Registered version contains a dialog to change the default printer and a pass-through to go straight to the printer without previewing.

DDRVPREV   190 *K* $15   *Dickinson, Don*

Device Tester — Sample source code shows how to obtain list of currently available printers and select one by programming or interactively as the default printer.

DEVTES2   3 *K*   Free

DrawScript 0.8 — A set of routines to simplify text report generation and Print Preview type functionality. They allow you to format your report once, then play it back to screen or printer. Early (beta) version.

DRWSCR   6 *K*   Free   *McClure, Jim*

FPrint 1.53 — A print utility that will print multiple copies of any ascii text or prn file. Each installed parallel printer port is supported. Support Drag'n'Drop; just drag the file to the File Print icon.

FPRINT   10 *K*   Free   *Kapune, Albert*

FontView — Font previewer and sample font printing utility. Source code included.

VBFONT   10 *K*   Free   *Snider, Charles K.*

GENPRINT Generalized Printer — VB source which allow the user to use a printer other than the Windows default printer, abort a printout, and more.

VBGPRT   70 *K* $20 SW   *Unger, Guinn*

Grid Print 1.0 — Utility to help determine the X and Y coordinates of each field on pre-printed forms. All you do is place your pre-printed form in the printer and overprint the grid.

PRTGRID   5 *K*   Free   *Overstreet, Mark*

GsSetPageOrientation DLL — DLL for C or Visual Basic that provides two functions to control printer page orientation: GsSetPageOrientation and GsGetPageOrientation.

LSCAPE   4 *K* $50 SW   *Hopkins, Geoff*

HP Envelope Printer — The simple interface of this utility allows you to quickly enter an address then print an envelope on an HP Laserjet or compatible printer without changing the printer setup in Windows. Source code is included.

HPENV   21 *K*   *Federal Hill Software*

How To Add Print Preview — Source code demonstrates how to create printing routines that can print to the printer or to a picture box. the enables adding print preview capabilities to a Visual Basic application.

    PRTPREV   14 *K*   Free

Hypertext Printer 1.1 — A printing routine to be used with Crescent Software's Hypertext control (CSHT.VBX). Provides for print preview at five zoom levels. Executable program is called by your program. Full VB source code is available for $45.

    HTPRN   38 *K* $5   *Dass, Beena*

LPR Remote Printing — Custom control implements remote printing on a TCP/IP network using LPR/LPD. Sample source code included.

    LPR   19 *K* $12   *Bridges, Steve*

MegaPrint 1.0 — Complete printing control with pure VB code. No VBX or DLL. Print preview and change printing size on the fly. Images must be loaded before printing.

    MEGPRNT   35 *K*   *Teunis, William*

Orient — DLL provides means to find and change the Windows default printer orientation. Sample source code included.

    ORIENT   26 *K* $10 SW   *Poellinger, Paul F.*

Print Clipboard — Prints the clipboard when it contains valid data. Source code included.

    PRNTCB   9 *K*   Free   *Barnett, Clifford*

Print DLL Test Application — Demonstrates printing in VB. DLL contains printing functions which are defined in the VBPRINT.TXT file. The print control application, TESTAPP (full source code), demonstrates the printing functions.

    VBPRINTN   80 *K*   Free   *Nolte, Barry*

Print Grid — Source code and demo prints a spreadsheet-like grid.

    PRTGRIDN   10 *K*   Free   *New Leaf Software*

Print Multiline Textbox — Full source code demonstrates printing to the printer object a multiline textbox using VB commands and one API call. The FRM file contains detailed comments.

    EMFMT   3 *K*   Free

Print Preview 1.2 — OLE server that lets you add print preview capabilities to VB 16/ 32 bit applications.

    PRVIEW32   51 *K* $20+SW   *Waty, Thierry*

Print Preview DEMO — DEMO of a print preview function for Visual Basic. Previews landscape or portrait, text, wrap text, rotated text, shapes and lines; previewed in a zoomable print preview window. Example (nonworking) source code included.

    PRINTP   85 *K* $30   *Phase II Software*

PrintClip — Now you can print the contents of the Clipboard with one action. Simply double clicking on the PrintClip icon sends the Clipboard contents to the current printer. Source code is included.

    PRCLP2   4 *K*   *Krumsee, Art*

PrintFile Altern. To Spoolfile — The Windows SpoolFile API call has certain problems. Here is a workaround, PrintFile, in Visual Basic source code.

    PRINTF   3 *K*   Free   *Johnston, Scott*

PrintForm DEMO — DLL for printing and previewing structured documents. Well suited for typical database reports. Documents can contain bitmaps, icons, and strings. Fonts and word-wrapping are supported. Left, right, and center alignment is supported.

    PFOVBE   55 *K*   *KWG Software*

PrintWorks And VisualForm Eval — Printworks: Graphic/text tools. Format text left, right, centered, or fully justified. Print text on angles. Supports TrueType. Draw circles, ellipses, more. Supports color and BW printers. VisualForms: creates forms and positions data fields.

    VFWPW   380 *K* $149   *Bytech Business Systems, Inc.*

Printer Lines Per Page — Source code demonstrates calculating the default printer lines per page with the declared Fontname and Fontsize. Also allows the user to abort a print job, flushing the printer buffer.

    VBPDEM   12 *K*   Free   *Obeda, Ed*

Printer Pick / Printer Cancel — Source code demonstrates a collection of printer routines to obtain a list of the currently installed printers, change the default printer on the fly, and provide a status window and "Cancel" button for print jobs.

    PRTPIK   7 *K*   Free   *PC HELP-LINE*

Printer Scale Tool — Small printing utility shows how many lines can be printed on a page using a particular font and size, shows the x and y coordinates of a point on a page. By choosing font name and font size, this tool shows what can be printed.

    PRINTOBJ   9 *K*   Free   *Rezuke, Joe*

Printer SetUp — A DLL with source code for controlling and configuring system printers. Source code is included.

    PRSET   *8 K*   *Programmer's Warehouse*

Printer Setup (CK) — DLL to access the standard Printer Setup dialog box. Sample source code included.

    PSETUPCK   *4 K*   Free   *Kitsos, Costas*

Printer Status Demo 1.0 — VB 3.0 code and custom dll to check status of a printer under Win 3.1 or Win95.

    PRNTSTAT   *24 K* $15SW   *Bragg, Gregory*

Printing Forms — Source code shows how to print forms and controls with VB code only. You can choose the place and size of the printing.

    IMPDES   *22 K*   Free   *Tisoft S.A.*

Pulsar — A full featured printer management program which allows switching between Postscript and HP modes on HP and compatible printers. Virtually every possible printer feature can be assessed through its pull down menus or quick access buttons.

    PULSAR   *25 K* $15SW   *Tesserax Information Systems*

Queue Watch — This print queue allows you to manage network printer output from the server or any workstation with a simple graphical interface. Source code is included. The NetAPI.DLL is required.

    QWATCH   *25 K*   *Landgrave, Tim*

Togglprt — Simple program to toggle between to printers. Source code included.

    TGLPRT   *8 K*   Free   *Shiavo, Steve*

Two Form Print Sampler — Two form example prints a form minus the datacontrol. The control button is displayed, but the control is not printed.

    PRINTBW   *2 K*   Free   *Wojtczak, Brian*

VB Code Print — Utility to format and print Visual Basic source code. Additional features in registered version.

    VBPRINTT   *12 K* $10   *Thornton, Michael*

VBBook 1.2 — A Visual Basic utility that will print ASCII text documents to a Laserjet in booklet form. Source code included.

    VBBOOK12   *34 K*   Free   *Scott, Dennis*

VBrotary Rotary Card Printing — Source code for printing rotary cards (Rolodex style) to the printer object or a form. Example project files included.

  VBROTARY   19 *K* Free   *Antony, P. Scott*

VSView 1.07 — Preview multi-page docs with zooming and panning, print by line, paragraph, columns or tables. Many formatting options for easy printing in VB. Make controls float within your form or customize the form. Virtual scrollable areas on your screen.

  VSVIEW17   182 *K* $99   *VideoSoft*

Virtual VsView Printer Demo — A virtual-memory approach to workaround the 64K and 100 page printing limit of the VSVIEW control. Requires VB 3.0 Pro and VSVIEW.VBX.

  VIRTUA   16 *K* Free   *Hayes, Brain C.*

41
PRODUCTIVITY

Address Book — A small address book which was written without any non-native language calls or extended tools. This application demonstrates some non-standard methods for IO. Source code is included.

    KWI   20 *K*   *Knowledge Works, Inc.*

Contacts Manager — This phone/address manager sports a NEXT like interface which shows off the design capabilities of Visual Basic. With many free form and formatted fields, it can handle almost any entry. Source code available at extra cost.

    CM01   51 *K* $20SW   *Hardaker, Mike*

Schedule — A Visual Basic application for launching applications at user defined times. A more recent version, complete with source code, is available from the author.

    SCHEDULE   7 *K*   Free   *Kosten, Michael*

Time And Chaos — Time and appointment management system. Track appointments, make To-Do lists. Alarms and phone book are provided. Numerous configuration options.

    TCHAOS1B   231 *K* $25 SW   *ISbiSTER International*

Time Bandits — This multi-function utility adds a time and date display (even when iconized) and a single alarm feature to its primary function of a stopwatch. Source code is available on request.

    VBTIME   5 *K*   Free   *Snider, Charles K.*

Time It — This stopwatch with a two button interface, allows you to pause it so you may record cumulative times for an action. It displays hours, minutes, and seconds.

    TIMEIT   5 *K* $5SW   *Leithauser Research*

To Do List — A simple daily organizer with many handy features, including an alarm function.

    TODOV14   42 *K* $6 SW   *Schoeffel, Dave*

Tynee-Calc — A very small four function calculator with cut and paste ability. Source code is included.

    TYNCAL   11 *K*   *Wilson, Michael*

VB Clock — Not available from the author. A highly configurable desktop clock with a unique method for accessing the options window. Source code is included.

    VBCLK   20 *K*   Free   *Gagliano, Jim*

VBMail — Virtual Basic User to User mail application. Source code only.

    VBMAIL   16 *K*   Free

42
PROG. - SYS. UTIL.

GPF General Protection Maker — Utility program instantly causes a General Protection Fault, if chosen from the menu. Requires VBRUN100.DLL.

GPFMAK 3 *K* Free

Inifile — CopyFile, FileExists, GetWinDir, and GetWinSysDir functions intended to assist in dealing with INI files. Full source code.

INIFIL 2 *K* Free *Hegerty, Chad*

Keytest — A program that will return the hexadecimal code for any key pressed. Source code included.

KEYTEST 3 *K* PD *Mosher, Sue*

Some Information About Windows — Source code provides "some information about Windows" including date, time, whether in Enhanced mode, CPU type (up to 486), memory type, math coprocessor presence, free memory. Early VB code requires two tiny changes which VB 2+ will indicate.

WINFO 18 *K* Free *Phares, Wayne*

VBMem 3.2 — Utility that displays the Windows operating mode and the amount of free memory and resources available to Windows. The display updates in real time. Full source code included.

VBMEM 5 *K* Free *Snider, Charles K.*

Wintrace — Debugging utility to track resource usage, bad calls to APIs, memory overwrites, GPFs. Will display VB control properties and trace VB events. Full featured program.

WINTRA 349 *K* $20SW *Bridges, Steve*

PROGRAM CONTROL

3D4VB — A 3-D effect subroutine library. More than 20 different routines are included to draw 3-D frames, shadowed boxes, borders, print "labels" in picture boxes, and print "labels" associated with VB text and label controls. Source code included. See 3DDEM.

     3D4VB   13 *K* $10SW   *LAN Services*

3DDEM — Demo of 3D4VB.

     3DDEM   16 *K* $10SW   *LAN Services*

About — A technique to keep the control button inside the "About" box no matter how it is resized.

     ABOUT   4 *K*   Free   *Marino, Lou*

Add Run-Time Error Handling — Utility processes VB source code to add run-time error trapping routines to a project.

     DEBUGJL   33 *K*   Free   *Lorenzini, Jeff*

ClipSibling — A demonstration of providing overlapping controls by setting the Windows WS_CLIPSIBLINGS style bit.

     CLPSIB   12 *K*   Free   *Funk, Keith B.*

Custom Control Factory Demo — An interactive development tool for creating custom controls, including animated pushbuttons, multistate buttons, enhanced buttons, and option button controls which are added to the existing Toolbox. (Demo Only.)

     CCFACT   63 *K* $48   *Desaware*

Custom Controls — Not avail from MH. 3 custom controls and demonstration projects with online help file. MhGauge displays 2/4/16 color pictures and icons, MhState displays/modifies Caps, Num, Scroll and Ins keys. MhTag offers several enhancements to standard VB List Box.

     CUSCON   59 *K*   Free   *MicroHelp, Inc.*

DBA VB Error Handler — Error handler routine for Visual Basic, as published in Data Based Advisor magazine, January, 1994. Full source code and demo program. Traps user input errors.

    ERRORS   27 *K*   Free   *Murdoch, John*

Design-Mode Custom Controls — Four design-mode custom controls. Sample source code included. Includes two meters, 3D label, and spin control.

    VB4CTRLS   28 *K*   Free   *Jiang, Jeng Long*

DoDos — Utility to provide runtime arguments for DOS applications.

    DODOS   26 *K*   Free   *Dickson, David*

Grid 2 — This enhancement to the original Microsoft grid.vbx adds several features to allow better control of Visual Basic form grid properties. See VBZ01.ZIP.

    GRID2   21 *K*   *User Friendly, Inc.*

Grid Test — A utility to test the properties of controls on a VB form. Public domain from Microsoft. Source code included.

    GRID   22 *K*   Free   *Microsoft*

MDI Background Demo — Two sample applications demonstrate how to create interesting backgrounds on MDI forms. Demos resize "wallpaper" WMF and BMP files, tile bitmaps, create gradient fills and do other effects. One method uses pure VB3 code, the other a free custom control.

    MDIDMO   59 *K*   Free   *Petersen, Karl E.*

Message Blaster 2.2 — Custom control allows programmers to trap and modify virtually any Windows message. Includes samples on how to create a custom cursor using icons, how to create a captioned window, and how to display messages in a status bar while user navigates a menu.

    MSGBLA   99 *K*   Free   *Microsoft*

Meter — A routine to implement scrolling gauges in several orientations. Source code is included.

    METER1   3 *K*

Minifile - INI File Help — VB module for simplifying INI file operations. Includes ReadINI and SaveINI functions, and GetProfileString and PutProfileString.

    MINIFILE   2 *K*   Free

NoGhost — Tool which allows Visual basic to respond to Cascade and Tile messages properly. When the VB app is minimized, it does not interfere with the Cascading or Tiling of other apps. Configurable to allow or disallow sizing of the VB app's window. Source code.

    NOGHST   6 K   Free   *Blaum, Greg*

Power Buttons — A Visual Basic application manager that allows you to define 21 buttons for quick launch of your favorite applications. It also provides for a reminder system.

    POWER   34 K   Free   *Venema, John E.*

Program Manager Example — Small program manager example. Demonstrates launching applications from within a VB program. Source code included.

    SCOTTM   19 K   Free   *Conger, Scott*

Propview.VBX — A custom control (.VBX) which can display and permit printing of the properties of the current form.

    STDPRO   14 K   *Merriman, Loren*

Shell And Wait — Demonstrates copying a file by shelling to DOS. Full source code.

    EXWAIT   4 K   Free   *Caughran, Mike*

Slider — A custom slider control with C source and several sample .bmp files.

    VBSLID   15 K

Thermometer Demo — Source code demonstrates a wait box which displays a thermometer. This wait box acts modal - stopping all execution of the calling program - without declaring it as modal, by looping through all open forms and setting the DISABLE style for each.

    THRMDE   10 K   Free   *Integrated Data Systems, Inc.*

Toolbox — Utility provides a graphical program launcher with a smaller desktop than Program Manager. Applications can be launched by pressing buttons. Uses Windows API functions. Full source code.

    TOOLBX   19 K   Free   *Williamson, Gary*

VB-Switch — Utility which allows you to disable Windows task-switching by disabling ALT-TAB, CTRL-ESC, disabling "Switch To..." from all control menus, and disabling double-clicks on the desktop. Source code included, requires Desaware Spyworks-VB for modifications.

    VBSWIT   82 K   Free   *Computer Technologies, Inc.*

WinPS Flow-Control / Sort DLL — DLL contains the logic to control batch-like sequential programs. Supports up to nine sequential input streams and up to nine control break levels. A fast record sort (Like CA's SRAM) and several service functions are also included.

WINPS   29 K $35   *Muehlenweg, Ulli*

44

PROGRAM UTILITY

API Function Spy — This utility looks into actual running Windows code, allowing interception of function calls. When a function is called by any application, the function and its parameters are displayed in a listbox.

    APISPY11   29 *K*   Free   *Gamber, Mark*

API Servant — Fast database containing Windows API declarations. It allows quick substring searches and copying to the clipboard or directly to any VB code window.

    APISRV   55 *K* $15   *Hanson, Mark*

Add-In Magic 96 — VB4 add-in. Six utilities to speed program development. Contains MsgBox Magic, Dialog Magic, DataForm Magic, MDI Magic, Form Magic, AboutBox Magic.

    ADDINM96   320 *K* $25   *Extreme Software*

Add-In Potato — Visual Basic source code demonstrating the extension of the Visual Basic IDE by the addition of menus to the Visual Basic menu bar window.

    ADTOVB   95 *K*   Free   *Stewart, David*

Alignment For Windows — Developer's tool which creates a grid from your choices of background colors, foreground colors, and line styles, then replaces your wallpaper with that grid.

    ALIGN   17 *K* $15   *Graphical Bytes*

Analize Used DLL & VBX Files — Lists all .DLL and .VBX files that are used by a program. Doesn't search the .EXE file for filenames, but rather traces all the modules that are loaded and accessed when the program executes.

    VERSION   138 *K*   *Michael, Seelig*

Application Title Spy — Utility peeks into a Visual Basic generated EXE and retrieves its application title string using an undocumented exploration of how Visual Basic works. Full source code.

    GETTIT   23 *K*   Free   *Aziz, Atif*

AutoSaveIt — Automatically saves files to a network server. Intuitive point and click interface. 3-D controls. Checks for date stamp, archived flags, and saves subdirectories. No more typing long or nonexistent paths!

AUTOSV20	406 K	$15	*Gatti, Alessandro*

Autoexec For Windows — Augments the standard "Load" and "Run" of WIN.INI with an easily altered list of startup applications. Intended for persons who frequently modify their WIN.INI. Written in Visual Basic, although source is not included.

AUTOEX	22 K	$15SW	*Kostelecky, Will*

Autoload For Visual Basic — Utility that loads Visual Basic along with the last project automatically.

AUTOLO	82 K	$5	*Robar, R.*

Backmeup — Utility to back up your work to diskette. A click on the BKMEUP icon sends your current work to diskette.

BKMEUP	11 K		*Embrey, Leland E.*

Backup Utility — Backup utility uses PKZIP to backup your project files and store in another directory. Screen text is in German, English or stored in an INI file.

BACKUP	37 K	Free	*Fehr, Andreas*

Big Mak 1.0 — Utility launches VB with a project of your choosing and starts VB in the same directory as the MAK file. Four selectable interfaces make the most of your advanced video card.

BIGMAK	1076 K	$20	*Kilgore, Tim*

Brand An EXE File — Source code and documentation explains how to "brand" an EXE file in order to permanently install a user's name, company, and serial number.

BRAND	4 K	Free	*Teter, C. Mark, M.D.*

Buster — Development tools. Loads custom controls with one button; enhanced renaming of projects; 'blast' multiple statements and declares; automatic backup/ save at timed intervals.

BUSTE2	71 K	$40	*Biney, Dr. B*

ButtonBar Plus — Program Launcher that uses a toolbar concept. Can be configured for up to 66 programs. Has been replaced by buttonStar Deluxe.

BBAR18	108 K	$18	*DiBiasio, Mark*

CUSGEN 1.2 — A tool for Visual basic 2.0 programmers to package their application and generate a professional installation program that can be distributed with the application.

    CUSGEN12   298 *K* $10   *RMJ Software*

Calllist — Utility opens a VB project and creates a call list tree. You select any of the subroutines or functions, and find the subroutines that are called by that routine, and which subs call the sub you select. Full source code included.

    CALLLI   23 *K*   Free   *Denenberg, Steve*

Change Journal 2.2 — Tracks and maintains information related to software development, such as software change requests, error tracking, and design. Uses four lists: Users, Error Level, Status, Category to meaningfully group data. Limited shareware version.

    CJ22   1184 *K* $29/$69   *One Point Software*

Chief's Install Pro 2.0 — Setup/installation program for Windows. Can use Windows' COMPRESS.EXE, but not required. Can optionally create a Program Manager group and up to 45 PM icons. Includes UNINSTALL program to uninstall any program installed with Chief's Install.

    CHIEF200   554 *K* $60   *Olowofoyeku, Dr. Abimbola*

Clear VB Debug Window — Source code to clear a VB debug window. Automatically pauses VB to allow clearing of the Debug window; command line parameters allow placement of Clear button on Desktop. Modified from original code by Barry Seymour.

    DEBUG   7 *K*   Free   *Blaylock, Don*

Clip Watch — Utility traps all text activity sent to the Clipboard . Records up to 18 different clips and stores them for manipulation by the user in interactive mode.

    CLIP10   34 *K* $10   *Owens, Mike*

Clipboard Spy — Utility prints whatever it see going to the Clipboard. Can be toggled on/off.

    CLPSPY   44 *K*   Free

Cloning VB Projects — Tool to manage copying VB project source. Used to build new projects from reusable components in other projects.

    CLONER   35 *K*   Free   *Big Dog Software*

Co-Pilot 1.1 For Visual Basic — Utility inserts API declares etc. directly into VB code. REMs, unREMs, and indents VB code, multiple clipboard facility.

    COPILOT   15 *K*   Free   *ABC Software*

Code Arranger 1.03 — Reformats VB source code to be much more readable. Click on Project to arrange, click Files to choose the files to be include, click Process to begin.

      CARRAN   332 *K* $20 SW *Cactus Development Company Inc*

Code Assistant 1.0 — Tool for programmers using any programming language. Provides an open database engine that stores objects (ASCII text, executable programs). Can be used to build reusable code libraries and programs designed to assist in writing source code.

      CA100D2   822 *K*   *Bebber, Douglas A.*

Code Keeper 1.2 — Utility store segments of code with an easy browse and retrieval system. Features MDI, Import/Export, and much more.

      CODEKP12   869 *K* $10SW *Princeton Computer Consulting*

Code Librarian — Simple functional code database. Save your most used functions and they are available at any time. Use the Clipboard to copy the code.

      CODELI   32 *K*   SEE PROG   *Infobase*

Code Librarian 1.03 — Function/Procedure/Object and code fragment archiver. Allows you to place all your favorite code samples in one place, and have them at hand when needed. Uses the clipboard to transfer code back and forth, and the JET database to archive the code.

      CODLB103   461 *K* $10 SW   *McMullen, Leigh C.*

Code Librarian For VB 1.1 — Programming utility keeps code fragments in an organized database available from the Visual Basic button bar. Standard Windows cut, copy, and paste is used. Requires VB 3.0 and the JET 2.0 compatibility layer.

      CL11   315 *K* $15SW   *Okapi (Pat Hayes)*

Code Manager 3.0 — VB program that helps you maintain and manage reusable code routines. Sifts through existing projects to find reusable code.

      CM3_0   744 *K* $35SW   *Jeffrey S. Hargett Consulting*

Code Master Lite 1.01 — Extends the VB environment. Replaces the Project window and displays file, variables, and procedures in one window. Replaces the VB Toolbar with the Code Master Toolbar in the form of index tabs. MANY more features. Fully functional.

      CDMLITE   803 *K* $129   *Teletech Systems*

Code Print Pro DEMO — Professional quality printing tool. Format your code printouts for better readability. Use seamlessly with Visual Basic - intercepts Ctrl-P and gives expanded print dialog. This DEMO prints only the sample files supplied with VB Pro. Can unlock by phone.

    CPVDMO   535 *K* $99   *Pinnacle Publishing*

Code Stylist/VB — Source code formatting tool. Allows you to specify your personal or company standard formatting preferences, process and format all source code, and save the new clean code to a new directory. It spell checks and shows all changes side-by-side.

    VBSTYLE   679 *K* $79   *Cycloid Software*

Code Stylist/VB — Source code formatting tool. Allows you to specify your personal or company standard formatting preferences, process and format all source code, and save the new clean code to a new directory. It spell checks and shows all changes side-by-side.

    CSTYLE   758 *K* $79   *Cycloid Software*

Code To Word 6.0 — Macro template that inserts an existing Visual Basic form or code module into a blank MS Word 6.0 document. The module is then reformatted for better screen and printer output. Uses color and styles to highlight procedures, structures and comments.

    CODE2W   61 *K* $15SW   *Jacques, Robert R.*

Code-A-Line 1.1 — Outline editor and printer for source code. Represent structure by indenting lines; fold/unfold program elements to hide/reveal program details; edit and restructure with unlimited Undo; print file listings with line numbers; etc.

    CODE110   265 *K* $35 SW   *Optimax Corporation*

Code.Print For VB 2.25 (VB3/4) — Source code printouts with full font and margin control, headers, footers, annotation, line spacing, project title, page numbering and more. Sort routines and index. Supports VB4.

    CPVB25   330 *K* $32 SW   *Caladonia Systems, Inc.*

CodeDoctor 2.4 — Automatic tabbing of all controls on a form with 1 mouse click. Faster copying of Controls & Menus and all code behind them. One mouse click deletes all selected controls and their code. Clone Forms. External Editor.

    CD16   449 *K* $30SW   *Smith, Les*

CodeWiz 2 — Code librarian catalogs generic and reusable code. Also includes commenter/uncommenter utility, a .VBX database program and .MAKer, a windows spy utility similar to WinSpy. Fully with functional program with online help.

    CODEWIZ   773 *K* $15   *Rhind, Jeff*

Codegen 1.1 — Utility generates VB source for common dialogs and message boxes, prints source code, formats source code, prints database schemas, file version info, VB code template screen, code librarian, and more.

    CODEGEN   265 *K*   Free   *Perry, Stephen M.*

Commandline MAK Compiler — Allows drag and drop from the file manager of multiple MAK files. The RESET button clears your selections. Use this program to quickly recompile your Visual Basic projects.

    WSCMPILR   18 *K*   Free   *Whiplash Software*

Comment Add-In (32-Bit) — Add-in (32 bit only) enters comments easily in your code. Can directly pass code to your code module without using the Clipboard.

    COMMENT   13 *K*   Free   *Tricaud, Christophe*

Compress-It — Windows utility builds one or more batch files containing the COMPRESS or EXPAND statements as though you had individually typed them. For custom setups.

    COMP   454 *K*   Free   *Whiplash Software*

Control Changer — Changes type of existing controls. Will save as many of your perfectly set property values as possible. Requires VB 4.0 or later.

    APHCC   143 *K* $25SW   *Holupka, Andrew P.*

Copy/Move Project Files — Utility for copying all project files for one project into one place (directory).

    COPYUT   4 *K*   Free   *Lundberg, Thomas*

Copycode 6.1 — Edit a project in Visual Basic and have a second project at hand as a source for your code to copy. Automatically load all files from VB project files. Now VB4 compatible.

    COPYCD61   95 *K* $15SW   *Koot, Andre*

Copycode 7.0 16bit — 16 bit version of CopyCode (VB 3 version that can read VB 4.0 files). Edit a project in Visual Basic and have a second project at hand as a source for your code to copy. Automatically load all files from VB project files.

    CC70_16   101 *K* $15SW   *Koot, Andre*

Copycode 7.0 32-Bit — 32 bit VB 4.0 version of CopyCode. Edit a project in Visual Basic and have a second project at hand as a source for your code to copy. Automatically load all files from VB project files.

    CC70_32   121 *K* $15SW   *Koot, Andre*

Creating Program Group — Routine for creating a Program Group and adding two items to it from within an installation program.

    DDEPM   2 *K*   Free   *Decker, Mike*

DLL Extractor DEMO — This program demonstrates how you can extract sound and images from a DLL and use them in your programs. The demo uses 11 different sounds and 3 images, all included in a single DLL file. DEMO only. Source code for the technique avail. with registration.

    DLLTALK   99 *K* $10   *E & B Systems*

DLL Investigator — Discovers relationships among EXE files and DLLs. It will show the set of DLLs referenced by and EXE; and it will show the set of DLLs and EXEs that reference a DLL. Can search the drive for a referenced DLL that is not in the assumed disk directory.

    DLLMAN14   72 *K*   Free   *Press, Barry*

Decompiler Defeater — Utility to modify your code to defeat decompiling. Overwrites formnames and/or control names in the EXE file. Source code included, requires Crescent's QuickPak Pro or can be rewritten in pure VB.

    DECDEF   42 *K*   Free   *MCS Electronics*

Dialog Editor 1.0 (Win95) — VB4 add-in creates standard Windows Message Boxes, Input Boxes, and Dialog Boxes.

    DIALOG16   1734 *K*   *Osborne, Greg*

Document Visual Basic — Source code printing utility in toolbar form. Select any combination of projects to print; select margins and fonts to be used in the listing; print optional cover/title page; print table contents of procedures; orient DocVB toolbar horiz. or vert.; etc.

    DOCVB   108 *K* $10   *McPhail, G. E.*

E-code code recycler — Code recycling database. Easy to understand, allows the programmer to concentrate on programming while this utility makes it easy to keep track of programming code. Shareware version limited to 45 work sessions.

    CODE   3440 *K* $5+   *Enterprise Software*

EasyLock — Utility to "lock" and "unlock" unregistered version of a program. Locked programs show a customizable splash screen and allow the user to obtain registration information, and continue use if time or use limits have not been exceeded.

EZLOCK32	1734 K	$199	*CRA*

Exitman - Exit Windows — Windows utility gives the user the ability to exit Windows, restart Windows, or reboot the system at any time. VB source code provided with registration.

EXITMA	146 K	$10 SW	*McNeill Consulting Services*

File Stamper — File Stamper stamps the date and time on a file using. Drag files from File Manager onto the File Stamper icon. Intended use to stamp related VB files with consistent date and time; the time stamp can be used to indicate the version.

FSTAMP	48 K	Free	*Irwin, Gregg*

FilePak! DEMO — Lets you store groups of uncompressed Child Files in one Parent File using DDE. Can password protect each file and lets you describe each file. Full Visual Basic source code provided with registration.

FPSETUP	239 K	$44	*Inspired MultiMedia Inc.*

FileView 1.0 — Simple file viewer. Shows hex, octal, ASCII formats of any file. (Written in VB, includes an undocumented VBX; no source code.)

FILEVIEW	16 K	Free	*Praxis Software Developments*

FormTrak 1.2 — VB Debugging and Monitoring utility that reports the Windows Memory and Windows Resource usage of Visual Basic Forms at runtime and in the VB Design Environment. Statistics can be exported to a flat file for import to Excel, etc.

FORMTRAK	128 K	$20 SW	*Margraff, Tom*

GBLIB2 - Brands VB EXE Files — DEMO version of a utility to brand a Visual Basic 3.0 EXE file with registration details in such a way that it is difficult for an unscrupulous user to change it. Registered version is personalized to the registering user. Sample VB source included.

REGMAX	61 K	*Bamber, Gordon*

GetAPI 2.0 — Front-end to a relational database containing Visual Basic and Windows 3.1 API declarations grouped by functionality. Accesses relevant functions and constants automatically. Accessible from the VB menu.

GETAPI	327 K	$20	*Velazquez, Chris*

Global Error Handling — Global error handling routine will handle all errors in a module. It writes errors to a log file.

ERROR10	8 K	Free	*Graff, George W.*

Goliath 1.0 — Goliath converts VGA-format programs to higher resolutions. It reads the original forms and modules, and writes converted source code to a new directory.

GOLIAT	8 K	Free	*Koot, Andre*

GrabClip — Utility to instantly save bitmaps copied to the Clipboard to disk. Visual Basic source code available with registration.

GRBCLP	39 K	Free+	*Infocomm(UK) Ltd.*

HDC Function Library — Function Library and MicroApp Manager for the hDC Power Toolboxes. See file PWRTBOX.ZIP.

HDC320	299 K	$50	*HDC Computer Corporation*

HDC Power Toolbox — Adds predefined floating toolboxes to Windows programs, including Visual Basic. With the toolbox editor, you can customize a toolbox button to perform common operations in a single click. Requires file HDC320.

PWRTBOX	120 K	$50	*HDC Computer Corporation*

Handyman — Utility for working within VB. It saves keystrokes by automating many of the tasks that VB programmers must perform while writing code. Comment/uncomment several lines of code; swap sides of an "=" statement; Sub grabber from existing files; etc.

HANDYM	77 K	$20SW	*Whittlesley, Scott*

Harper Utilities — Project loader adds a System Tray Icon on your taskbar that allows you to quick load VB4 and the four most recent projects. Code Window resizer allows you to quick resize the active VB code window.

VB4UTILS	2300 K	$10+	*Harper, Thomas*

Hex Dump Utility — Utility program displays a numerical and ASCII character dump of a file. Full source code included. Also includes functions: ByteVal, WordVal, and DblWordVal.

FDUMP	336 K	Free	*Main, Mark*

IMPVB 2.0 Code Printing — French program allows you to print your code without saving files in the TXT format. Formats the Code and Comments to present all printing as clearly as possible.

IMPVBF	47 K	$15SW	*Tisoft S.A.*

INI Manager — Manage Windows INI files with this utility, which understands the internal structure of INI files and allows searches based on section headers. Maintains a list of INI files for easy opening.

INI   61 *K* $12SW   *Owens, Mike*

INI Navigator 3.1 — Manage any INI file or section in any drive/directory. View, edit, backup, restore, print files fast.

ININAV   107 *K*   Free   *Di Bacco, Daniel*

InstallWare 4.2 — Small and easy to program utility for installing Windows applications. Uses CTL3D.DLL for a 3-D look, and checks the target system for existing files with newer dates.

IWARE420   138 *K* $0/$35   *Dolan, Bob*

IntelliPrint DEMO — Stylize your VB code by setting font properties in 13 separate areas. Set margins, add header/footers, set up print queues, print selected text, set timed print, print Index/Table of Contents, more. DEMO version prints only included project.

IPRINT   526 *K* $50   *Alliance Software Specialists*

KopyKat — Utility to ease the function of applying the same code to multiple control/event combinations. Enables you to type code one time and have the code applied to a specific event for all selected controls in the project at one time.

KOPYKAT   50 *K* $23   *Wells, Terre*

Link Manager 2.0 — Set of Visual Basic modules which allow simple messages to be sent to other LinkManager applications across any network that supports NetDDE. Manages link connections internally via internal ques.

LM200   34 *K* $10SW   *Praxis Software Developments*

Lister Box — Sample VB application uses only VB code to display a custom list of any other type of control. For example: list of checkboxes, list of toolbar type tools, list of 3D picture boxes, etc. Source code available with registration.

LISTER   4 *K* $10   *Gallino, Jeff*

LocalDim — Utility w/source takes a VB module and locates the subs and functions. It identifies the locally-declared variables in the subs and functions, and finds the locally-declared variables that are NOT used, allowing deleting the variable declaration lines.

LOCALD   13 *K*   Free   *Denenberg, Steve*

Logfile 1.0 — Provides developers a straightforward method of recording and logging program internal data information as the program runs. Takes text lines passed to it and writes to a disk file. Source code available.

    LGFIL1   20 *K* $10   *Raffel, Matthew P.*

MC Security (VB 4.0 16-Bit) — Set of serialization routines for developers to append a serial number and 50 characters of text information to a file. Allows tracing the registered owner of any copy of a file. VB4 source code and demo program included.

    MCSEC16   272 *K* $10   *MC Security*

Macro Manager — Keyboard macro program for power typists. Allows users to assign a series of keystrokes to the letters A-Z and 0-9. Macros are played back by typing a user defined "trigger", then a letter or number. A 11-28-93 version is available from the author.

    MACROMAN   141 *K* $25   *Ruzicka, John*

Make Multiple Projects — Source code for a simple program to recompile all projects with a simgle mouse click. Conditional compilation assures that if nothing in the project has been updated, the program will not recompile.

    MAKEALL   9 *K*   Free   *Wicinski, Steve*

Make-MAK VB Compiler — Compiling utility works faster than VB itself. Makes smaller EXE files. Supports multi-project compiling. Accepts drag-and-drop from File Manager. Works with VB4.

    VBMAK4   51 *K* $25   *Germelmann, Christian*

Mantec Code Library 1.5 Demo — Code library program - collects VBXs and routines and declarations and transfer directly to Visual Basic. Demo version limited to ten "saves".

    MCC   246 *K* $10   *Mantec Development Group*

Mem Check — Simple program to keep an eye on the goings on in the Windows environment. Its various gauges are updated every two seconds. Displays DOS version, number of running tasks, disk space, free memory, GDI memory free, etc. Source code available with registra

    MEMK   20 *K* SEE DOC   *Hawkes, Peter R.*

MessGbox 2.0 — Utility flips through all boxes available with the MsgBox command to quickly view default buttons, return values, and get a visual preview of the result.

    MESSGB   90 *K* $7 SW   *Collado, Louis*

Message Box Wizard — Utility for creating Message Boxes. Simple to use - click on the type of message, enter title and message text, and the generated code is placed on the Clipboard.

MBOX   5 *K*   Free

Minimize Program Manager — Utility program minimizes Program Manager and starts Visual Basic or any program specified. Full source code only.

PM_MIN   2 *K*   Free

MsgBox Editor — This program determines what elements are desired in a MsgBox command by accepting point and click input from the programmer. The proper code is then generated and can be sent to the clipboard for pasting into a program. Source code is included.

MSGBOX   21 *K*   Free   *GeoDuck Systems*

MsgBox Editor 2.1 — Determines what elements are desired in a MsgBox command by accepting point and click input from the programmer. Code is generated and can be sent to the clipboard for pasting into a program. Now includes names of variables, etc. Source code included.

MSGBOX2   43 *K*   Free   *Pewitt, Woody*

Multiple App Project Launcher — A multiple application project launcher. Collects a number of applications and or documents together and launches them at the same time. (Written in VB, but no source code included.)

MIRB2   93 *K*   Free   *Truesdale, Greg*

Name Check 1.1 — Lets you define a prefix naming convention for variables, procedures, forms, controls, etc., then run it against your VB code to find violations. Results reported by module, can be viewed or printed.

VBNCK110   251 *K* $25   *Shaftel Software*

Object Library 1.2 — Code database which allows you to store and reuse objects implemented in native VB code. Provides a means of storing VB source code in a format which closely resembles the VB environment. Any type of code can be stored - routines, forms, modules, etc.

OBJLIB   254 *K*   *Exile Software*

Object Thing Demo — Reuse controls and code whenever possible. Select from a library of "objects" and drag and drop them directly into your programming window. Contains samples for Visual Basic and Access.

OBLIB   432 *K* $80   *Eye Can Publishing*

PR-Tracker 2.03 — Program helps manage software development projects by tracking software bugs with problem reports. Uses an Access database. Records problem reports in a network database that supports simultaneous access by multiple users.

    PRTRACK   915 *K* $60   *SOFTWISE*

Pack — Simple shell that allows files to be compressed using COMPRESS.EXE supplied with VB Pro.

    PACK   4 *K*   Free   *Summers, Judy*

Polisher DEMO — Working DEMO of a utility that takes the grunt work out of formatting, commenting, and spell checking your code. Can spell-check string literals and comments, resulting in more professional looking code. Working model with all functions except save.

    POLDEM   702 *K* $136   *Aardvark Software*

Power Toolz Code Manager — Visual Basic add-on allows cataloging and retrieval of code snippets for later insertion into any programming project. Appears as a button and icon on screen. Drag'n'drop interface allows you to takes snippets and drag them to VB, the clipboard, or trash

    PTCM10   201 *K* $50SW   *Haynes, Chris*

Pretty Print For VB 2.1 — Produces enhanced listings of your Visual Basic code that uses your choice of fonts, sizes, styles, color, which can be set for comments, identifiers, literals, and page headings. Optionally auto indents and corrects.

    VBPPDM   311 *K* $86   *Aardvark Software Inc.*

Print Clip CB — Simple utility to print the clipboard.

    PRINTCB   4 *K*   Free   *Barnett, Clifford*

Print Code As You Want 3.0c — Prints your VB source code with a professional look. User selectable fonts for form description, general, code comment, procedure names, header and footer. Margins control, editable headers, and much more.

    APRINT   215 *K* $35   *I.I.G. Development Ltd.*

Print Undocumented Win 3 Calls — Lists all undocumented entry points and external references in a Windows 3.x executable.

    UNDOCFCT   22 *K*   Free   *Murdoch, Duncan*

PrintVB — Formats and prints Visual Basic source code listings. User selectable font type/size, one or more individual procedures can be printed at user selection. Many more features.

    PRVB13   66 *K* $15   *Brant, Kyle*

Project Doc 2.2 — Helps VB programmers working on multiple projects have instant access to notes on each project. Open the required project and the program will load all related files and notes. By clicking on the Variables tab you can instantly see all variables.

PDV22U   147 *K* $20SW   *Software Factory UK Ltd.*

Project Manager 4 for VB 3 & 4 — Loads and unloads VB with project loaded. Tracks files used, including DLL, VBX & external modules. Records and totals time spent in each project. Writes error handling code for project. Unregistered version loads only two projects.

PM4100   433 *K* $40 SW   *A.F. Street Consulting*

Project Pal — VB MAK file compiler. This utility will compile and load your VB MAK files faster.

VBPP10   247 *K* $10   *Mech, Robert W.*

Project Print — Utility will scan Forms/Modules in your project for declarations/subs/functions that are new or have changed since the last print. You can print those changes at the push of a button or the entire project. Font sizes/styles can be set.

PJPRNT   129 *K* $20   *Grey Parrot Software*

Project Print 32-Bit — Utility will scan Forms/Modules in your project for declarations/subs/functions that are new or have changed since the last print. You can print those changes at the push of a button or the entire project. Font sizes/styles can be set. 32-bit version.

PJP32   198 *K* $20   *Grey Parrot Software*

Project Wizard — Add-in emulates the Repository of Borland Delphi for Visual Basic programmers. Includes two DLLs and sample source code.

SC4VB   446 *K*   Free   *Simon*

ProjectSnap 1.0 — Load, compile, execute projects in a snap. Select from a complete list of projects on your system. Saves time and needless directory navigation.

PSNP10   249 *K* $25   *Caladonia Systems, Inc.*

Properties On Top — Helps in the design process by giving the programmer the ability to keep the properties window on top always.

PROTOP   301 *K*   SEE DOC   *Sauve, Eric*

QB-VB Converter — Converts QuickBasic FILE I/O related statements to VB compatible code. Contains an INC file to be added to the project. Allows QB code to be more simply converted to VB/Windows.

QBVB11   62 *K*   *TransSend Technology*

Raven - Text Management 1.01 — Text management system lets you organize and manage multiple text files you frequently re-use. Perfect as a source code librarian, etc. Tabbed indexed sections let you manage hundreds of pieces of diverse text.
RAVEN   383 *K* $30   *Fineware Systems*

ReadForms — Quick and easy viewing and printing of VB code without all the unnecessary stuff VB prints. Select a directory where your VB code is, then view, edit, or print it from Word or Write. Full source code.
READFR   15 *K*   Free   *Ludwig, Bill*

Registration Editor — Utility to embed a registration number into your EXE file. The program maintains sequentially incremented sequence numbers. Allows maintaining separate database tables for different programs.
REGISTED   89 *K* $17   *Levy, Ronald S., M.D.*

Registration Information — Sample application to show how to add registration management to your application. Requires the TIME2WIN library. Source code included.
REGISTER   7 *K*   Free   *Renard, Michael*

Runfix - Minimizes Apps — Small utility which minimizes Program Manager when an application is run. Visual Basic source code included. Quite useful for running Visual Basic itself.
RUNFIX   4 *K*   Free   *Mezaros, Mike*

SCFILE 2.0 — Fast, easy way to view and print text files and Visual Basic arrays. Source code available with registration.
SCFILE   71 *K* $30 SW   *Garrison, Gary P.*

SETUP Enhancement By Barrett — An alternative to SETUP supplied with VB. This version copies all files to be installed to a temporary directory first, making it possible to install a VB program if another VB program is already running.
SETUPB   10 *K* $12   *Barrett, Simon*

SPY:FRX Graphics Recovery — Utility "spy"s inside FRX files. Shows the graphics from all ICO, BMP, and FRX files. When shown, a graphic can be copied to the Clipboard. Can be used to recover source bitmaps from within FRX files.
VBSPY   6 *K*   Free   *Koot, Andre*

Sam Spade Runtime Debugger — Utility to diagnose VB runtime errors. It writes to a log file if the application's command line contains "DEBUG" or "PAUSE". The dialog box displays system information and the current values of up to 10 variables. Adds about 18K to your application.

SPADE1   22 *K* $10 SW   *KnowledgeWorks*

Scoper B.10 — Analyzes VB3 project code and finds unused variables, constants, function/procedure declarations, and function/procedure code. Helps create the smallest, fastest possible EXE.

SCB10   509 *K* $19   *ISES, Inc.*

Scout Programming Utility — Display free system resources. List all loaded modules or tasks. List exported functions in module. Show modules implicitly linked to a DLL. Show modules loaded below 1MB. "Liposuction" shows extraneous debug info. Much more.

SCOUT   55 *K*   Free   *Bonincontri, Michael*

See VB 0.99 — Works in the background of Visual Basic 3.0 to automatically tile or cascade open form and/or design windows. You control when the windows are rearranged - manually or whenever a code window is opened or closed.

SEEVB   63 *K*   Free   *Collier/Rother, Jim*

Setup Factory 3.03 — Using a visual object-oriented approach, Setup Factory gives you the power and flexibility to create your installation program and disk sets without writing a line of code or filling in forms. Features data compression, gradient backgrounds, etc.

SUF303   1002 *K* $250   *Indigo Rose Corporation*

Setup Studio 2.4 — Allows you to create professional-quality installation programs for Windows 3.1. Contains the DLL with its C/C++ and Basic functions and a Wizard to manage files and create disk sets. English and French versions included.

SSETUP24   685 *K* $50 SW   *Chevron, Denis*

Shaded Blue Setup — VB source code replaces one of the functions in VB's SETUP1.MAK, to provide a shaded 3D look to your setup application like all standard setup programs. Source code provided.

SETUPTXT   2 *K*   Free   *Venugopalan, Vivek*

Shrink VB EXE Up To 50% — Investigation of the way VB stores color bitmaps. In some cases the final EXE size may be cut up to 50% by using the technique discovered and described in this text file.

SHRINK   2 *K*   Free   *Falconer, Jay J.*

Snippit 4.03 Code Database — Code database comes with a selection of code snips for immediate use. Creates picture buttons. Creates common dialog or message box code. Creates RGB color codes. Creates gradient box color codes. All code can paste to the current code or module window.

SNIP403	146 K	$20	*Slutter, Carl*

SourcePrinter 1.20 — Utility for printing Visual Basic source code. Features: prints headers, footers, margins, page numbers; procedure headings in bold, comments in italics; line continuation; prints all or user-selected procedures, files; etc. Prints Index.

SRCPRI12	221 K	$25 SW	*Ansuini, Doug*

SpaceTime — Program shows disk space remaining, and will copy date and time to the Clipboard. DLL and program. Source code included for the DLL, written in Quick C For Windows, and intended for use in Visual Basic. An example of using QCW to write DLLs for VB.

SPCTIM	8 K	Free	*Paul James Barrett*

Status — While programming, forces all instances of status bars to the bottom of the screen. Source available on registration.

STATUS	5 K	$10	*Staffin, Ed*

Strip — A conversion utility allowing you to filter a source file on several keys. Output is sent to a new file and the original source is not changed.

STRIP	9 K	*Quarles, Mark J.*

Subdoc 2.1 — Catalogs, displays, prints procedures, types, global variables, and constants with detailed catalog entries extracted from the original source. A 2.10 version exists. Works only with VBWIN 2 or later and needs VBWIN 3 runtime.

SDOC21	106 K	$35 SW	*Fox, Peter*

Task Killer — Program which displays all modules (DLLs, VBXs, EXEs) currently loaded in the system. Can terminate any module, determine the usage count of each module, save module lists to files, print module lists, display module version info, etc.

TASKKL20	146 K	$15SW	*Hyperion Microsystems*

Template MDI Demo — Application demonstrates floating help, floating toolbar, and multilingual capabilities. INI handling stores the last window position plus settings. Complete source code with registration.

VBTPL	22 K	$15 SW	*INside*

Testres — Simple utility tells the exact current screen resolution in pixels as well as number of colors.

    TESTRE   4 *K*   Free   *MJ-Datatechnic GbR*

The Code Artists — Code printing utility. Supports VB# and VB4 file structures. Word processor like page setup routines allow to select page orientation, header/footer, margins, custom fonts. Allows easy choice of functions or files to print. Limited shareware version.

    CODEART   542 *K* $79   *McGillicuddy, Rich*

The Nag — NAG will, at any user-specified interval up to 999 minutes, pop up and remind you to save your work.

    NAG   9 *K*   Free   *Forbes, Garry*

Thunderbolt For VB 1.12 — Wide assortment of control alignment tools. Freeze control and form positions. Bookmarks in form or control window. Tab order setting. One button commenting and uncommenting. Much more. Unregistered version handles up to three forms.

    TBOLT   708 *K* $33   *Software Savants*

Time And Date Stamp — Windows utility to change the time and date stamp of multiple files. (No source code, but written in Visual Basic.) Useful to keep track of release version dates and version numbers.

    JGSTDS   174 *K* $1+   *John Galt Software*

Tom's Happy Constants — From the code window, the programmer can highlight the constant name and press a hot key to have the corresponding Global Declaration loaded into the Clipboard.

    THC   48 *K*   Free   *Bassal, Thomas*

Toolbox On Top — Utility that places the Visual Basic Toolbox on top of all other forms. The status can be toggled on/off.

    TBONTOP   10 *K*   Free   *Carr, J. Frank*

Tools On Top 1.0 — No longer supported. Utility helps developers manage the Toolbox, Project Window, Properties Window, Color Palette, and Debug Window when in design or debug mode. Stops those windows from being hidden during design.

    TOT   120 *K* $10   *Bits & Bytes Solutions*

TrapIt! — Debugging tool (wizard) that helps shorten the development and maintenance cycle. Trap FRM, BAS, CLS, MAK, VBP or HTM (with embedded VB script) files. Trap SUBs, FUNCTIONs, PROPERTYs Let/Get/Set. Built-in editor for unrestricted complete error trap cust.

    TRAPIT   565 *K*   *Lapides Software Development*

Universal Code Indenter — The Universal Code Indenter is a software developer's tool that automatically indents Visual Basic code. It works for Visual Basic 4.0 (16- and 32-bit versions) and Excel Visual Basic for Applications.

    INDENTER   115 *K*   Free   *Hoeltge, Chris*

VB 3.0 Stack Patch — This program patches a copy of VB 3.0 to increase the available stack space for compiled applications from 20K to 40K. Full source code included.

    SPATCH   6 *K*   Free   *Monro, Chris*

VB 4-to-3 — Convert projects from Visual Basic 4.0 to 3.0.

    APHVB423   148 *K* $30SW   *Holupka, Andrew P.*

VB API Assistant 1.0 — Easy way to copy & past Windows API functions/subs, constants, & types into a program. Uses text files, like those provided with VB Pro. Includes small DLL to get pointers to VB data types & user defined types, extracts LOWORD/HIWORD from long, etc.

    APIAST   26 *K*   Free   *Fry, Brian W.*

VB Add File Utility 1.0.5 — Allows the programmer to multi-select a group of files (VBXs and DLLs) to add to VB projects. Includes the ability to read the file descriptions which may be embedded in VBXs and DLLS.

    AF105B   393 *K* $10SW   *Manoogian, Paul J*

VB Addins 1.5 — VB Design Environment utility. Features: 10 save Code Window bookmarks per project; Load Picture Dialog enhanced with picture preview; Find/ Replace Dialog enhanced with scrolling text; View Procedures dialog expanded; more.

    VB_ADDIN   243 *K* $20 SW   *Margraff, Tom*

VB Assistant — For Visual Basic 1 only. A small utility to save and run your VB application in one mouse click, or access help files with two mouse clicks. Source code included.

    VBASST   6 *K*   Free   *English, Donald R.*

VB Backup 2.2 — Utility for backing up VB projects. Backs up all parts of a VB project.

    VBACKUP   249 *K* $35   *Gentils, David M.*

VB Backup And Restore — Backup and restore VB projects. VB Backup will remember a unique backup path for each project. It will create a directory if it doesn't already exist. Multiple backup generations can be maintained automatically.

    VBBAKRES   38 *K* Free   *Kearney, Stephen*

VB Bookmark — Lets you place bookmarks in your Visual Basic code and easily jump around later. Any bookmarks inserted will be saved with the code, preserving them from session to session. Transparent to the VB compiler.

    BOOKMK   170 *K* $25   *Peopleware*

VB Clean — Loops through all forms and modules in a project, doing a save and a load for each file. Automates this task, which will reduce the size of the final Visual Basic compiled EXE files. Source code included.

    VBCLN   9 *K* Free   *Hite, David*

VB Code Analyst — Utility tokenizes an entire VB project. Prints many detailed reports on the contents of a project, illustrating the architecture of the project. Code Sculptor tool allows reorganizing code. Code Architect prints all caller relationships within the projec

    ANALYS   1243 *K*   *Bergmann, Ken*

VB Code Assistant — Contains databases for code snippets, project information and version changes. Includes bitmap viewer. Message Box and Input Box builder, and code generators for common code. Shareware version limited to seven records.

    VBCODEAS   1086 *K* $25   *RDB Knowledge Systems*

VB Code Browser 2.0 — VB 4.0 add-in enables the programmer to browse all VB files - frm, vbp, bas, and cls. Browse all functions and subs without opening another instance of VB. Allows modifying the code before reusing it.

    CB20   39 *K* Free   *Takriti, Nick*

VB Code Manager 1.7 — Utility makes it easy to copy or print code for the Subs and Functions of your project. You can load all the forms and modules (FRMs and BASs) in an entire project or load only an individual form or module. You can copy or print a single Sub or Function.

    CODEMGR   20 *K* $15SW   *Burnham, Gordon*

VB Code Recycler — Code library attaches to the Visual Basic environment. Create new code libraries or use existing; printed report of any code segment; can add info such as author, date, source, etc.; interface uses tabs and toolbars. Limited shareware version.

  CODERECY 856 *K* $25   *Bryte Ideas Software*

VB Code Wizard 1.1 — Coding aid includes database storage of all forms of VB source code and sub modules, including Constants, Functions, TYpe Declares, bitmaps, icons, etc. Allows for easy multiple storage and retrieval of all forms of ASCII code.

  VBCODWIZ 1075 *K* $40   *Taylor, Jonathan B.*

VB CodeSecure 4.0 — Utility protects VB3 and VB 4 programs from the Visual Basic Decompiler. Your application's source code remains safe by using data-protecting algorithms including form overlays, and object and control de-referencing.

  VBCS 177 *K* $25   *Clay, Jason*

VB Comment Potato 1.0 — Small but helpful debugging aid. It temporarily neutralizes sections of code on the fly, to help narrow down problems with a program, by commenting out lines in bulk. Also allows indenting and un-indenting blocks of code.

  CMSPUD 137 *K* $6SW   *Stewart, David*

VB Compile — Utility to allow choosing a MAK file from a file dialog, and Visual Basic is invoked to compile and create the EXE file.

  VBCOMP 14 *K* Free   *Buchholz, Elliot C.*

VB Convert — Interactive utility to convert VB/DOS code to VB/Windows. Several keywords in VB/DOS cannot be used in VB/Windows, and several other things must be changed. This utility automates the conversion.

  VBCONVER 122 *K* $25   *CC Advies*

VB Documentor 2.1 — Replaces Visual Basic's code documentation functions. This program can organize, index, consolidate, outline, format, block diagram, and print VB code. Gives an organized view of VB forms and modules down to the control, menu, and procedure level.

  VBDOC 240 *K* $50SW   *Lake St. Clair Publishing*

VB Escort For Windows 2.1 — Logs time spent on each Visual Basic programming project and creates billing reports to send to clients.

  VBESCT21 289 *K* $30   *Full Sail Software*

VB Global Help File — Direct translation of the Visual Basic 3.0 "constant.txt" file into a Windows Help file.

    VBGLOB   31 *K*   Free   *Thorp, Rick*

VB Launcher — Launches VB and loads the project file you wish to use immediately. Can minimize Windows, can load up to three utility programs along with VB. MDI code window can load code from other projects allowing cut-and-paste.

    VBLAUNDH   593 *K* $10   *Harris, Dave*

VB Librarian 2 — Utility stores VB file objects in an Access MDB database. Designed to allow source code, documents, etc., to be stored in a central location that can be accessed remotely. All objects stored are fully text searchable, uses Category and Reference types.

    LIB   1272 *K*   *Bergmann, Ken*

VB Make 1.11 — VB Make makes clean compiles easier. Add your projects to the list, select the ones you want to compile, and VB Make takes care of it.

    VBMAKE   15 *K*   Free   *Irwin, Gregg*

VB Menu Printer — Scans one or more VB forms, and prints out a formatted report showing the menus used.

    MENUPR   139 *K*   Free   *Transact Software*

VB Print 1.3 — Improves on the printout capability of VB. Selectable print sizes for Code, Headers, and comments; customizable code highlighting; right justified line wrapping; selectable project components; project and page header options; icon printing option, etc.

    VBPRINT   37 *K* $25 SW   *In Touch Software*

VB Printing Template For Word — Template file for printing VB source files from Microsoft Word 6 or 7. It will paginate and create a table of contents with page numbers.

    VB4PRINT   5 *K*   Free

VB Profiler 0.6 — Utility checks your application's speed and process flow. Easy handling and full power of accurate data. Test and improve the performance of your code.

    VBPROF   82 *K*   Free   *Fehr, Andreas*

VB Project Analyzer 0.3 Beta — Analysis tool for VB project files. Allows programmer to visually see how the project is constructed along with a variety of statistics. Time-limited INCOMPLETE BETA version, but usable. See files VBPRJ2, VBPRJ3, VBPRJ4 for support files.

    VBPRJ1   59 *K*   *Chapman, Mike*

VB Project Analyzer 0.3 Beta 2 — Support files for VBPRJ1, as supplied from author.

    VBPRJ2   218 *K*   *Chapman, Mike*

VB Project Analyzer 0.3 Beta 3 — Windows Help file - support file for VBPRJ1, as supplied from author.

    VBPRJ3   104 *K*   *Chapman, Mike*

VB Project Analyzer 0.3 Beta 4 — Support file for VBPRJ1, as supplied from author.

    VBPRJ4   26 *K*   *Chapman, Mike*

VB Project Backup — Quick and efficient way to backup your VB projects. Backs up all files in a project to a specified directory.

    VBBACKU   69 *K* $6   *U-Turn Productions*

VB Project List Spy — Demonstrates the use of Windows messages to analyze and retrieve the contents of the Visual Basic project window whether the window is visible or not.

    LSTSPY   13 *K* Free   *Stewart, David*

VB Project Protector — Allows you to make backup and archival copies of your VB project files in ZIP format, directly from the .MAK file on hard or floppy disks.

    ARCHIVE   124 *K* $30 SW *Professional Software Systems*

VB Project Spell Check — Utility to spell check VB user interface objects and text strings. Simple point-and-click interface.

    VBPSC   955 *K* $25   *Roland, Al*

VB RecentFiles — Simple program reads the name of the last used files from VB.INI, then loads VB with the last file accessed.

    VBREFI   4 *K* Free   *Joyce, Ben*

VB SNR - Global Change Automat — Helps make global changes to a VB Windows project based on search-and-replace techniques. Useful for changing hard coded drive/path or other variables. Extremely fast. Works on forms and modules stored in ASCII form. Complete logging shows changes.

    VBSR   110 *K*   *TARDIS DP Consultants*

VB SNR Search And Replace — Utility to help make global changes to files which make up a Visual Basic project. Can perform in search only mode, or search-and-replace. Helps change variable, control, or control options.

VBSNR 117 *K* $8 *Pride! Software Works*

VB Servants (Working DEMO) — Collection of "Servants" to provide assistance on over 140 statements, functions, and methods. Fill in the blanks and VB Servants puts the written code on the Clipboard.

SERVANTS 643 *K* $53 *Barnes, I. D.*

VB Setup Kit 1.00.02 — Replacement for the VB Setup kit. Includes all features of the VB Setup kit, plus background graphics, 3D message dialogs, About box that you can edit and change, etc.

JWPCSTP2 32 *K* Free *Jwpc, Inc.*

VB Sniplets — Organize frequently used code snippets in this fast, lightweight, 32 bit app. Full searchable for easy retrieval, VB Sniplets features a customizable toolbar. One mouse click places your selected code into your project.

VBSNIP 376 *K* $15 *Dompier, Jim*

VB Space — Scans VB projects and tells approximately how much Global Name and Symbol Table space is being used. It also gives a module level breakdown to see what is adding to each table.

VBSPAC 40 *K* Free *Irwin, Gregg*

VB Squeeze — Performs a Save Text/Load Text combination on each file in the current project, to eliminate bloat in VB source files.

VBSQZ 7 *K* Free *Irwin, Gregg*

VB Tracer/Profiler 3.0 — Program to add or remove tracer-profiler information in all files (BAS, FRM, INC) included in a VB MAK file. Traced/profiled information shows the path of your application run and the speed of each routine.

VBTRCPRF 132 *K* $43 *Renard, Michael*

VB Witch — Set of utilities for VB: Icon-based project launcher; tool to automate the parsing of Sub, Function, and other declarations; open binary source files which VB refuses to load because of name conflicts; desktop sweeper; etc.

VBWTCH 150 *K* $10 SW *Ling, Sui*

VB-Clip Space Saver — Adds quick buttons for find text, replace text, stop, break, single step, show and hide forms, tile or hide forms.

VBCLI 12 *K* Free *Stewart, Robert W.*

VB-Make ISNT — Utility for working with multiple projects. Creates multiple EXE files with one click. Searches across sub-directories, can be left to run without attention. Saves time keeping EXE objects up-to-date. VB3 version.

    VBMAKEIS   10 *K* $45   *ISNT Limited*

VB-Tools 1.0 Toolbar — Toolbar adds "On Top", close, MDI, Save, Open, Copy, Paste, Add icons. Source available at extra charge with registration.

    VBTOO   36 *K* $25 SW   *Disk And Desk Software*

VB/Error Handler-Tracer Profil — Combination of VB/Error Handler and VB/Tracer Profiler. Contains 16 and 32 bit versions for use with VB 3 and VB 4.

    MCVBEHTP   245 *K* $25   *Renard, Michael*

VB/Rig Standard 2.0 — Specialized code generator for VB developers. Creates graphical error-handling subsystem to trap run-time errors gracefully and allows program execution to continue. Your application instantly becomes bullet-proof. Pro edition can "rig" only part of app.

    VBRIG   302 *K* $29/$59   *PC HELP-LINE*

VB2Doc7 — Adds a Table of Contents, showing all Subs and Functions within your project and to what pages they may be referenced. Also creates an index on ALL the variables used within your project and what pages they are found on.

    VB2DOC7   98 *K*   *Juden, Eddie*

VBCode 1.01 — Add-in adds tools to VB4. Creates an "About" box; inserts 32-bit APIs into your code; recreates the structure of an Access database; arranges VB windows.

    VBCODE1U   651 *K* $20   *Bourderson, Benjamin*

VBE Enhancements — Adds two enhancements to the Visual Basic environment. 1) "Save Selected Text as File" in one step; 2) "Print Selected Text".

    VBE   11 *K* $15 SW   *Northington, Otha L.*

VBPLUS Toolbar — Toolbar which adds over 30 shortcut keys, a project ZIPper, quick Help access, full time resource and memory gauges, a multi-file dialog, and more.

    VBPLUS   194 *K* $25 SW   *Pennington, Bill*

VBPlus — Three components: Quick Click enables you to drag and drop text in the VB code window. InLaunch adds a customizable launch menu to the VB environment. Fast Access enables you to add, delete, or save files inside the Project Window.

    VBPLUSG   288 *K* $20SW   *Gottlieb, Daniel*

VBScript 1.1 — Scripting language that can be used to manipulate properties of VB controls at design time and perform batch operations on controls and forms.

VBSCRI11　　　　56 K　$20SW　　　　　　*Simmons, Jason*

VBTiler — Adds code window management to your VB design environment. Will cascade, horizontally tile, or vertically tile your VB form and module windows.

VBTILER　　　　354 K　$80　　　　　　　*Clark Software*

VBTrace 2.0e — Utility program gives the ability to obtain a listing of the procedures executed by a Visual Basic program in the order they are executed. There are times when the user clicks, tabs, or Alt-keys and you have no idea in what order. VBTrace shows you.

VBTRACE　　　　387 K　Free　　　　　　　*Stuart, Chuck*

VBTree Lite DEMO 1.01 — DEMO of structural cross reference and optimizing tool for VB source code. Graphical tree display shows the overall structure of an application and calls to related forms and modules. Redundancies in Dims and Constants are highlighted.

VBTREED　　　　892 K　$159　　　　　　　*DataSys Pty Ltd*

VBUSE - VB Usage Reader — Utility tells which version of VBRUN is required for a particular EXE file compiled by VB.

VBUSE　　　　　13 K　$5 SW　　　　　　　*Mabry Software*

VBView 1.1 — Utility lets programmers view and search VB source code without the overheads of switching projects or starting multiple copies of VB.

VBVIEW　　　　118 K　$10　　　　　　　*PD Consulting*

VBWerx 2.0 — Makes use of Visual Basic's command line switches. Select MAK file and then choose to RUN, MAKE, or just LOAD the file. Includes VBWERX 2 update along with original version.

VBWERX　　　　49 K　Free　　　　　　　*Joyce, Ben*

VBcheck 1.01 — Source code control for Visual Basic. Allows you to manage VB source code among a team of developers. Check-in, check-out system, keeps original copies as read-only.

VBCHEC　　　　53 K　$15 SW　　　　　　*Colton, J. E.*

VER Version Info / File Instal — Lets you use the functionality of VER.DLL through VB properties. It makes getting version info from a file (EXE, DLL, VBX, etc.) easy. Also gives you installation flexibility. Sample installation/setup utility included.

VER10　　　　　54 K　$20SW　　　　　　*Mabry Software*

VEXE 1.0b EXE File Embedding — Full function DEMO version. VEXE embeds supporting files (DLL, VBX, LIC, HLP, etc.) inside an application's EXE file. Allows improved version control, file security without additional programming chores. DEMO places a DEMO screen on compiled EXE files.

    VEXEDEMO   381 *K* $104   *Versatile Control Systems Inc.*

Valet 1.0 — Visual Basic 1 only. Utility which enable quick access to CONSTANT text files, help files, VBX, FRM, BAS files, custom controls. PLus logging feature tracks time spent working on a project; and support for drag-and-drop.

    VALET   66 *K* $15   *English, Donald R.*

Vb Add-On Witch (BETA) — Brings order to the chaos of VBXs, DLLs, and related HLP files. Provides quick access to these files with a simple directory tree. Creates VB project templates including the appropriate set of VBXs and DLLs etc.

    AOWITC   240 *K* SEE DOC   *Mey & Westphal*

Vb Shade Selection Assistant — Assists the developer in selecting shades of color, especially for apps designed for use on monochrome systems. Enables the user to select a color using the QBColor() function.

    QBCSA   3 *K*   Free

VbValet Print 1.4 — Word for Windows 6.0a template. Formats, prints, and cross references VB source code. Prepare Table of Contents, Index (of all or unreferenced Global Consts, Declares, and Type Statements), modify styles. Brings power of W4W6a to your document prep.

    VBVP14   74 *K* $30SW   *Haduch, Robert Wydler*

Vbtidy — Utility indents your VB3 code, reports code and adds or removes line numbers.

    VBTIDY   24 *K* $20   *RGS Software*

VerInfo Demo — Source code demonstrates how to use VER.DLL to extract the version information for any type of file using VER.DLL and Windows API calls.

    VERDLL   21 *K* Free   *De Palma, John R*

Version Browser 1.0 — Examine the various executable files on your disk, and see the hidden version information contained in many of them. Program and source code from the "Power Windows" column in the Dec. 1993 and Jan. 1994 issues of WINDOWS magazine.

    PWBROWSE   32 *K* Free   *WINDOWS Magazine*

Version Information 2.0 — Utility checks the version information for files on your disks. Check your VBXs and DLLs to be sure you have the latest versions.

    VER200   10 *K* $10 SW   *Jones, Graham*

Version Viewer 1.0 — Windows utility for examining version info in EXE, VBX, DLL, etc. files. Find out what those stray DLLs are. Also helps when installations won't work due to VBX conflicts. "Wizards" help find duplicate files, build system reports, etc.

    VERVIE   563 *K* $10SW   *Lose Your Mind Software*

Versions/VB 1.1c DEMO — Version control system. Streamlines the process of managing all project resources - source code, documentation, project plans - either on or off a network. Compatible with all programming environments.

    VVBDEM   753 *K* $99   *StarBase*

Vision Storyboard 3.006 DEMO — Tool for planning, documenting, and presenting Visual Basic applications. SpecMaker records and present information about forms and controls; SlideShow generates illustrations of forms and illustrates program flow; etc. DEMO has limited use functions.

    VSBEVAL3   2064 *K*   *Vision Software Tools*

Visual Basic Access Key Potato — Small utility helps you figure out what letters are used, and which are still available, for use as underlined access keys on Visual Basic controls with text.

    XKSPUD   5 *K*   Free   *Stewart, David*

Visual Basic Formatter 1.0 — Formats Visual Basic source code into easily read structured lines. Customizable printout of form and module source code. Automatically extracts form and module files from MAK files.

    VBFMT10   193 *K* $30   *Kohn, Joseph*

Visual Basic Listing DEMO — Utility to provide documentation of forms, controls, and code used in a project.

    VBLIST   67 *K* $5   *VanBrocklin Technical Services*

Visual Basic Office 1.2 — VB environment add-in which provides popup windows which give quick button bar access to program, help, document and VBX files. Handle list and spy mode. Scratchpad code collector for creating new procedures.

    VBO120   201 *K* $40 SW *Marquette Computer Consultants*

Visual Basic Quick Start — Auto-Launcher utility that resides as an icon in your Windows95 Taskbar. With one click you can start VB3, VB4/16 or VB4/32 or launch any of your last four projects. Simply copy to your Startup Group.

    VBQSTART   16 *K*   Free   *PCG Associates, LLC.*

Visual Basic Toolbar 2.0 — A Visual Basic Toolbar. Runs VB.EXE and is built into the VB Toolbar. Writes DAT file and registers MAK, BAS, and FRM files. Adds instant icons for Notepad, API reference, SDK reference, and trace.

    VBBARCG   13 *K*   Free   *Germelmann, Christian*

Vprint 2.2 — Prints Visual Basic source code in a more readable fashion. Options for different fonts for headers, code, subs/functions, comments, declarations. Optional line numbering. More.

    VPRINT22   167 *K* $15   *Pazur, Scott*

WINstall — Windows installation utility. Totally automated and supports installation from multiple floppies of any size or directly from hard drive or CD-ROM. At only 25K, the smallest program of its type for the flexibility it offers.

    WINS10A   35 *K* $43 SW   *Dovcom*

WinHelp 1.10 — Utility to help the VB programmer snoop around a windows' attributes. Based on a utility in "Visual Basic Guide to the Windows API" by Daniel Appleman.

    WINVIEW   35 *K*   Free   *Torralba, George R.*

WinPRT 1.0 — Version 2.0 is available. Allows you to easily print the contents of any window. Can print the entire window or the client area of the window.

    WINPRT10   168 *K* $10 SW   *Shaw, Kevin*

WinPtr Printer Control 1.04 — Capture - via icon menu and hotkey - screen, window, client or rectangle to printer, clipboard, or fax. Send clipboard to printer, file, or fax. Change printer defaults, route all output to files, etc.

    WINPTR   194 *K* $20 SW   *Poellinger, Paul F.*

Window Info — Utility reports the caption, window handle and class name of (1) the window under the cursor, (2) its parent window, and (3) its progenitor window (the parent of its parent's parent for as many generations back as its ancestry goes.) Full source code.

    WINFOPB   9 *K*   Free   *Bonner, Paul*

Wiper — Source code from the April 1994 issue of Visual Basic Programmer's Journal. Finds and closes all the various Visual Basic windows at design and run times.

    WIPER   7 *K*   Free   *Pleas, Keith R.*

XBAK Backup Utility — Simple utility to maintain backups of Visual Basic source code. Keeps three generations of backups, eliminating the oldest and renaming the last three.

    XBAK10   3 *K*   Free   *LCI*

45

PROGRAMMING

AAVBSORT.DLL — DLL provides routines to sort Visual Basic arrays. The routines are written in C++ and are much faster than equivalent routines in Visual Basic. SortAry sorts the elements directly; SortIdx sorts via an index.

    SFTGRD   31 *K* $35 SW   *Willy, C. Scott*

API Helper 3.0 — Beta version. Online reference to API calls including the Windows multimedia library MMSYSTEM.DLL. Requires VBRUN200.DLL. An enhanced 5.0 version for $10 will be available from the author. See file AHDAT.ZIP for updated data files.

    AH30   123 *K*   Free   *Bostwick, Marshall*

API Helper 3.0 New Data — New data files for API Helper, file AH30.ZIP.

    AHDAT   52 *K*   Free   *Bostwick, Marshall*

About Your Application — Source code provides framework for an About box with a 3-D look, containing various system information.

    ABOUT3D   5 *K*   Free

Adialer — Phone dialing program. Source code included, shows API calls needed for comm port and modem access from VB.

    ADIALR   20 *K*   Free   *Lamson, George*

Allocating Protected Memory — Document describes how to allocated protected memory in Visual Basic. Contains source code for a DLL (in C) and a method of using VB and Windows API calls alone to allocate/lock/unlock and free memory.

    VBLOCK   5 *K*   Free   *Langley, Brent K.*

Amaza Messagebox Creator — Fast and easy way to create MessageBoxes for VB. Type the title, choose the buttons, windowstyle, icon and defaults, enter your message, and the box is created.

    AMASA   43 *K*   Free   *Joyce, Ben*

ApiMan For Windows APIs 2.3 — Utility reads information from Windows API files, lists all available function names. Copies into the Clipboard. Tracks all used modules from a DLL, DRV, or EXE. View VersionStamps. Etc.

    WAPI23   102 *K* $20   *Germelmann, Christian*

App Shell — Applications shell. Includes mini text editor. Source included.

    APPSHL   30 *K* Free   *Presley, Jim*

Appointment Book — Appointment book application from BasicPro, April/May 1993 issue. Complete implementation of drag-and-drop techniques including cell-to-cell grid dropping and user-feedback issues.

    APPTBK   21 *K* Free   *Visual Basic Programmer's Jrnl*

Areacode — A program which displays the city and local time for any U.S. or Canadian area code entered. Source code included.

    AREACODE   8 *K* Free   *McGuiness, Charles*

Arrange Icons — Arranges icons at the bottom of the screen. Uses SendKeys and Taskman. Source code included.

    ARRANG   4 *K* Free   *Brown, Martin*

Asynchronous/Synchronous Shell — A subroutine for synchronous (wait until terminate) or asynchronous shelling from VB 3.0. Addresses the problem that "GetModuleUsage" under Win 3.1 does not perform under Windows NT.

    EVOKE   2 *K* Free   *Barber, Jim*

BAS Viewer 1.0 — Utility reads BAS files saved as text without starting Visual Basic.

    BASVIEW   43 *K* $3   *Slickware*

BEST0894 Program Listings — Contains listings from the 8/94 issue of B.E.S.T. Source code for ACLOCK animated clock icon (Visual Basic) and TEXTFX (C++) projects, and address for magazine subscription.

    BEST0894   15 *K* Free   *Digital PowerTOOLS*

BMP Kit — Toolkit to permit scaling, printing and displaying bitmaps from within your Visual Basic applications.

    BMPKIT   21 *K* Free   *Campbell, George*

Bars — Bar code and label printing utility. All source code included in this shareware program.

    BARS3   40 *K* $25   *Eclipse Software Programming*

BaseConverter — Converts numbers between bases.

    BASECVRT   10 *K* Free   *Huss, Dennis L.*

Basic Code Cache — Electronic magazine covers Basic. This issue features

| BCC101 | 58 *K* | $24/Year | *Basic Code Cache* |

BasicBasic For Windows — Basic interpreter/compiler for Windows. (Not related to Visual Basic.) An alternative to VB for smaller projects. Also includes compiler for DOS.

| BB15 | 436 *K* | $30 | *Davidsaver, Mark* |

Basically Visual Magazine #2 — Electronic magazine. This issue features: Visual basic for DOS review; Visual Basic for Windows columns; ObjectVision review; tips and tricks.

| BV2 | 147 *K* | $20/Year | *Basically Visual Magazine* |

Bitmap — Obsolete. Several forms demonstrating various methods of working with bitmaps. Many manipulations are included - loading, saving, drawing, refreshing, and clipboard operations. Source code included.

| BITMAP | 20 *K* | Free | *Young, Ted* |

Buddy System — Two VB4 add-ins. One copies controls with all associated code between modules and merges customizable code templates into existing modules. The other generates a form with controls based on properties and methods of a class module.

| BUDDY | 199 *K* | Free | *Krueger, Eric* |

Buttons — Application form to show how to simulate Windows command buttons with pictures. Source code and sample BMPs included.

| BUTTON | 9 *K* | Free |

CANZ Demo - Linked Lists/Trees — CANZ custom control provides Smalltalk-like collections - linked lists, stacks, queues, and balanced trees to Visual Basic. Supports the creation of collections containing and one of the fundamental VB data types. Fully functioning DEMO.

| CANZ | 145 *K* | $295 | *Cz Software Corporation* |

CFGTEXT — Routines to reconfigure a text box for maximum length and upper/lower case translation. Text format source code.

| CFGTEX | 2 *K* | Free | *McClure, Jim* |

CRC Algorithms — Collection of CRC algorithms in Basic. Includes CRC16 and CRC32.

| BASCRC | 10 *K* | Free |

Card10 — A dynamic link library for card game programming in Visual Basic. A library of routines allowing applications to share common bitmap resources. A more recent version (VBCARDS.ZIP) is now available in this collection.

CARD10   33 K   Free   *Sands, Richard R.*

ClassAccelerator — VB4 add-in that allows accelerated development of Class Modules. It will create a class template from variable names entered into Wizard-like Acceleration Frames.

CLASSXCL   761 K $25   *De Herrera, Felix*

ClockFrame — Has been renamed ClockFrame from Time Frame. Shows current date and time in the frame of the active Window. The display can be configured to show date and time in almost any way.

TIMEFR   6 K $7   *Braeuchi, Jakob*

Code Fragments — Utility stores code fragments in a personal database. Reference pieces of code by groups and item names. Use the clipboard to cut and paste code from this utility to VB.

CODEFRAG   20 K   *Knippennerg, Jim*

Colors — A calculator of color hex values for programmers. Using simple slide bars, it generates any color mix. Colors will also accept a hex value and display the corresponding color. Source code included.

COLORS   6 K   Free   *Evers, Dave*

Common Dialogs Made In VB — Demonstrates calling the Windows 3.1 Common Dialogs of File Open, File Save, Printer Setup, Font Selection, and Color Selection directly from VB. Full source code.

DIALOGS   8 K   Free   *Kitsos, Costas*

Creating Program Group Workaro — Workaround for the problem of attempting to create a Program Group using an existing Program Group filename, but a different group name. Normally Program Manager fails silently.

DDEFIX   8 K   Free   *Hardin, Todd*

Custom Properties — A way to associate values with a particular visual object and get them later using a text key. Simple to use and understand. Source code included.

CUSTPROP   4 K   Free   *Bliss, Steve*

D&DSERVE.DLL — DLL to support Win 3.1 Drag 'n' Drop capability. Sample VB source included. From the August 1992 Windows Tech Journal article.

DDSERVE   11 K   Free   *Zuck, Jonathan*

DB-XL Database To Excel — Source code demonstrates how to convert the data from any database which can be accessed by VB 3.0 and convert the data into an Excel 5.0 spreadsheet.

    DBXL   6 *K*   Free

DDD Professional Toolkit '95 — Plug-in code module that eliminates the need for THREED.VBX and does much more. Includes source code for a 3D Spin BUtton without using SPIN.VBX. Does the work of 100K of VBX controls in fully modifiable source code. (Source with registration.)

    DDD95   56 *K* $21   *Anno Domini, Inc.*

DLLManager — Load and unload DLL, VBX, XLL, FON, EXE, DRV files, and also setup modules to be preloaded when you enter Windows. Requires VBRUN100.DLL, CMDIALOG.DLL and TOOLHELP.DLL, CMDIALOG.VBX and THREED.VBX, available in Win 3.1 or in other files here.

    DLLMGR   12 *K*   Free   *Woodhouse, Mike*

DOS Shell Launcher — A simple exit to DOS shell. Source code included.

    DSL100   11 *K*   Free   *Meredith, Chazz*

Delayed Drag Demo — Source code puts in a delay that determines how long the mouse is moved over a particular item before dragging begins.

    DLAYDR   8 *K*   Free   *Simms, Jeff*

Directory Structure Scan — Not supported. Source code to scan directories for a filename.

    DSCAN   4 *K*   Free   *Rose, Joel*

DoDi's Developer Tools Demo — Demonstration versions of DoDi's VBPro Project Manager, VBMap Project Browser, VBDiff File Compare. Full source code is available with registration.

    VBTOOLSD   185 *K* $50+   *Rofail, Ash*

Drag Form — Source code demonstrates dragging a form with or without a title bar and also dragging a textbox.

    DRAGFO   4 *K*   Free   *Simms, Jeff*

Dropdown Box — Combo Dropdown Box. Source code included.

    DROPDO   5 *K*   Free

EZData Database Creator — Complete MDI Application skeleton with an easy-to-implement tabbed data editor to help speed project completion.

    EZDATA   138 *K*   145PST   *Leigh Business Enterprises Ltd*

Electrified Visual Basic #1 — Electronic magazine. This issue contains: reviews of VB 2.0, Muscle, VB Superbible book review.

    EVBMAG01   82 *K* $3.50   *Pro-Data / EVB Magazine*

Electrified Visual Basic #2 — Electronic magazine. This issue contains: Code Fragments column; Writing Help Files with Word for Windows; Robohelp review; Help Magician review; etc.

    EVBMAG02   321 *K* $3.50   *Pro-Data / EVB Magazine*

Electrified Visual Basic #3 — Electronic magazine in Windows Help format. This issue contains: Agility/VB review, company profiles, mini-reviews, etc.

    EVBMAG03   214 *K* $3.50   *Pro-Data / EVB Magazine*

Electrified Visual Basic #4 — Electronic magazine in Windows Help format. This issue contains: reviews of VBAssist 3.0, QuickPak Pro 3.0, VBTools3.1, and several shareware products.

    EVBMAG04   283 *K* $3.50   *Pro-Data / EVB Magazine*

Endprn — Source code which make Print manager the active application, or close Print manager.

    ENDPRN   3 *K*   Free

Enhance Spin Source Code — Spin buttons in pure VB source code. No VBX. Starts slow, then speeds up. Left mouse button spins by ones, right mouse button spins by tens. The button has a middle segment which can be dragged up or down like a scroll bar.

    ESPIN   9 *K*   Free   *Deutch, Jim*

Error Trap — Self-installing program adds code into Visual basic 4.0 projects to totally error trap the program.

    ERRTRAP   834 *K* $25   *Kappel, Jay*

Example DLL Programming — BC++ 3.1 and VB source demonstrating how to write a simple DLL and use it in VB.

    DLL4VB   4 *K*   Free   *John*

Expression Evaluator — Algebraic expression evaluator function. Expands on BASEXP. Full source code.

    CALC1A   3 *K*   Free   *Big Dog Software*

Favorite — Program adds parameters for your most frequently used programs and builds a list that you double-click to launch a program. Source code included.

    FAVORI   20 *K*   Free

FileOpen — Two routines to implement an advanced file opening method and to capture and format the information returned from opening the file. Source code included.

      FOPEN   9 *K*   Free

Filebox — VB source code for a File open dialog box that works just like the Open Project dialog box in the VB environment.

      FILBX2   9 *K*   Free   *Kiehl, Thomas*

Fileboy's Runway 1.2c — An applications launcher with source code.

      FBR12C   44 *K* $5.00   *Homegrown Software*

Find Program Manager Groups — Visual Basic source code for finding Program Manager Groups. Uses DDE and functions in USER.EXE for fast display of Program Manager groups in a listbox.

      PMLIST   7 *K*   Free   *Germelmann, Christian*

Find Screen Saver Password — Source code demonstrates finding the default Windows Screen Saver password from CONTROL.INI.

      SSPW   3 *K*   Free   *Hayward, John*

Find Window — Allows you to type a caption and/or classname into the textboxes on the form and see if a window exists. Provides a good way to test API FindWindow calls before committing them to code, or for debugging.

      FNDWND   4 *K*   Free   *Irwin, Gregg*

FindPrt — How to use the FindFirst method on partial strings. Demonstrates how to search for whole strings or partial strings in an Access database, with the results populating a Listbox. Full source code.

      FINDPRT   3 *K*   Free

FindVBID — A programmer's utility file written in Turbo Pascal for Windows. It permits the programmer to determine the IDs of Visual Basic Controls during the development process.

      IDVB   9 *K*   Free   *Kitsos, Costas*

Focus U-Turn Test Program — Demonstrates how to control focus transfers. Also shows how to divide form code between form and corresponding module. (Also shows ad for the author's book.) Source code included. See file FOC002 for extended version.

      FOC001   14 *K*   Free   *ETN Corporation*

Focus U-Turn Test Program #2 — Version 2 of Focus U-Turn. New features include using option buttons and text boxes on form. Source code included. See file FOC001.

    FOC002   12 *K*   Free   *ETN Corporation*

Font Rotate — Print text sideways, or anyways, from VB. Uses Windows API calls to rotate a font and print it sideways.

    FONTRO   4 *K*   Free

Form Scroll 200 — Not available from MicroHelp. A sample from the MicroHelp series of Visual Basic tools. This custom control adds horizontal and/or vertical scroll bars to forms. Full documentation in Windows Help format.

    MHFS200   22 *K*   Free   *MicroHelp, Inc.*

GENERIC Sample Files — GENERIC sample files and source code that should have been shipped with Visual Basic 3.0 Professional Edition but weren't.

    GENERC   15 *K*   Free   *Microsoft*

GRID.VBX Updated Ver 3.00.058 — An updated version of GRID.VBX that ships with VB 3.0. This version fixes an infrequent error which breaks backward compatibility with executables created with previous versions of Visual basic.

    GRIDVBX   26 *K*   Free   *Microsoft*

GeeWiz — Seven wizards that generates source code for Visual basic. MsgBox makes MsgBox code; InputBox makes InputBox code; four CommDlg wizards handle all arguments for Open/Save, Color, Font, and Print; Listbox table builds multi-column listings.

    GEEWIZ   30 *K* $69   *Resolutions Now*

Grid Routines — Examples of grid manipulation. Source code included.

    GRDRTN   9 *K*   Free   *Ford, Nelson*

HLPKEY.DLL — Sets task-specific F1 hook. Eliminates need for separate keypress events for F1 help. Demo and C source.

    HLPKEY   4 *K*   Free   *Simms, Jeff*

Huge Array DLL 9/11/92 — Modifications to Microsoft's Huge Array DLL.

    HUGE2   21 *K*   Free   *Microsoft (Mods By Scherer)*

Huge Array DLL 9/16/92 — Modifications to Microsoft's HUGEARY.DLL to support huge string arrays. The VB source builds a huge string array that is sent to the clipboard. VB and C source included.

    HUGSTR   35 *K*   Free   *Microsoft (Mods By Seale)*

Huge String Array Manager — Basic source code huge array manager. Create huge arrays of 16 MB on 386 or 1 MB on 286. Sample code for evaluation of this early "as-is" version.

    HUGE   *7 K*   Free   *Marquis Computing, Inc.*

I Declare API/Multimedia Decla — Accesses hundreds of the Windows API and Multimedia declarations quickly and easily, and copies them into your project in one pass.

    IDECLA2   *62 K* $20 SW   *Mullin, Dan*

INIUPD INI File Source Code — Simple VB source code that allows the user to update Windows INI file entries. You can add, change, or delete an INI entry. An example of good programming practices and the use of a few Windows API calls.

    INIUPD   *11 K*   Free   *Jniblack*

Icon Browser — Demonstrates ExtractIcon in SHELL.DLL and DrawIcon in USER.EXE. Source code included.

    ICBROW   *2 K*   Free   *Bonner, Paul*

Implement Object Oriented Prog — Text describes how some features of Object Oriented programming can be implemented in Visual Basic. Key features covered are Encapsulation, Polymorphism and Inheritance. Demo VB source code is included in the document.

    VBOO03   *8 K*   Free   *Harrich, Jack*

Inifile - INI File Wrapper 3.0 — Source code module contains "wrappers" for INI file access. Greatly simplifies the task of repeatedly reading and writing INI files. Parallel functions for WIN.INI and Private.INI files. Manipulates system.ini "device=" lines. Much more in 41 routines.

    KPINI   *12 K*   Free   *Petersen, Karl E.*

Junque - Open-Ended Activity — A method of displaying open-ended (unknown completion time) activity in VB. Emulates blinking lights on old computers. Includes EXE and source.

    JUNQUE   *5 K*   Free   *Merriman, Dave*

KillDLL — A way to dump a DLL from memory. Adapted from a Windows Tech Journal article. VB source included.

    KILLDLL   *4 K*   Free   *Brown, Carl*

Kwikpix 1.0 — Utility to find Subs/Functions in FRM or BAS files for cut/paste/editing; block indent/unindent comments; list Global Constants by type; list controls by type; remove unused variables; etc. Encrypted VB source included, unlocked for $35.

    KWSHARE   645 K $12   *Solomon, Maareyes*

Labtab — This program demonstrates how to use label controls to display tabular data. Under this method you are not restricted from using proportional fonts. Source code is included.

    LABTAB   6 K

Liberty Basic 1.1 — A shareware Basic interpreter for Windows inspired by GW-BASIC and QBASIC. (Not directly related to Visual Basic.) Useful for its ability to upgrade old GW-BASIC programs into Windows more easily than in VB.

    LB11W   768 K $35SW   *Shoptalk Systems*

Licence Pro For Visual Basic — Licence Pro is an advanced, powerful, yet intuitive, licence file protection package for VB authors. It insures protection against people who copy and give your program away for free.

    LICPRO4   444 K $30   *Tabb, Marchan*

Linked Text Box And Smartfill — Source code shows how to create a linked textbox/listbox and simulate Speedfill in a textbox linked to a listbox. The linked box performs a greater than/equal to match, highlighting the closest match.

    LTBDEM   9 K Free   *Presley, Jack*

Listdrag — A routine to demonstrate a method of dragging a text line from one location to another in a list. Source code is included.

    LISTDR   7 K

Lottery Numbers — Source code for a lottery game random number generator.

    LOTTER   9 K Free   *Riley, Ian*

MLISTBOX.VBX — Custom control which provides support for extended and multiple-selection listboxes.

    MLISTBOX   9 K Free   *Warning, Mike*

MRB Drop 'n' Comp — Drag 'n' drop front end for the Microsoft Multiple Resolution Bitmap Compiler. Select files with file manager and drop onto the MRB icon.

    MRBDNC10   40 K Free   *Barnes, Nic*

MSGDemo — A demonstration on ways to simplify message display while looping routines are active.

    MSGDEMO   4 K Free   *Campbell, George*

MWATCH.DLL — DLL to monitor the position of the mouse and provide dynamic feedback to the programmer in the form of a status bar. Can display a help message when a normal menu item is chosen. Now included and supported within VBZ.ZIP subscription service.

    MWATCH   4 *K* $73   *User Friendly, Inc.*

Marketing Demo — An example, with source code, of using a Visual Basic Windows program as an advertisement or marketing demo. Source code demonstrates using drag-and-drop, cut/copy/paste to the Clipboard.

    LANDAU   19 *K*   Free   *Landau & Associates*

MaskDemo — An example of creating a Mask from an image and Screen object using the API function BitBlt. Source code included.

    VBMASK   8 *K*   Free

Message Blaster — 32-bit OCX allows programming access and response to the various system messages generated by Windows applications. Trial version limited to 30 days use.

    MSGBLAST   1033 *K* $80   *WareWithAll, Inc.*

Message Box Generator 1.1 — Utility program generates code for the MsgBox() function. Select desired graphical and textual characteristics and then click "Clip" to write the code to the Clipboard. Includes code customization, 3D boxes and more.

    MBGEN1   48 *K* $10SW   *Taylor, Rick*

Message.VBX 1.75 — VBX and DLL allow you to intercept any window messages. With this added capability you can respond to right-mouse clicks and double-clicks, set minimum and maximum window resize dimensions, respond to custom menu items, etc. Sample source code included.

    MESSAG   220 *K* $10 SW   *Digital PowerTOOLS*

Method Maker For VB4 — Add-in provides a more complete set of procedure insertion options. Evaluation version lets you insert predesigned procedure templates complete with a general error control block.

    MMMAKER   57 *K* $15   *Malluf, Ibrahaim*

Migrating From 16 To 32 Bits — Microsoft Word document covering migrating to Visual Basic 4.0 and some considerations of migration efforts.

    16TO32AP   35 *K*   Free   *Microsoft*

Minimize Demo — Source code routine to minimize the current form or program.

    MIN   7 *K*   Free

Movtxt — A demonstration of how to use a picture control to give the impression of dragging a text control.

    MOVTXT   6 *K*   Free   *Funk, Keith B.*

MsgHook Control — MsgHook provides a way for VB programmers to intercept and respond to messages which VB does not provide events for. For example, MsgHook can intercept taskbar related messages, enabling you to write a program which displays on the taskbar.

    MSGHOOK   150 *K* $25+   *Mabry Software*

Multipik — Demonstration on how to create a multipick list box in Visual Basic.

    MULTIPIK   6 *K*   Free

Nabit 2.0 - The Snatcher — Spy on listboxes and comboboxes of other programs from your VB program. Reads every list or combo of other programs. Searches in foreign lists or combos - highlights items and scrolls the list.

    NABIT2   58 *K* $20   *Germelmann, Christian*

NetPrn — Source code and executable for linking a printer to a Local Area Network.

    NETPRN   10 *K*   Free   *Krumsee, Art*

New Composite Controls — Demonstrates how to create a new instance of a control, such as a frame, that has other controls associated with it, using the SetParent API call. Source code.

    CNTRLC   2 *K*   Free

OXDisplay 1.0b — Make 3D controls quickly using the PropertyMenus and ControlWiz to control all aspects of picture and text placement. Includes: OXLabel-label control allows rotated, multiline, 3Dtext; OXMeter-3D meter or graph control; OXClock-adds clock to any VB app.

    OXDSP   81 *K* $22 SW   *Opaque Software*

Order Form — A VB form of an "Order Form" to be included in shareware applications. Figures sales tax, totals the order, and prints a "professional-looking" order form. Source code included.

    ORDER   5 *K*   Free

Outline Control Sorting — Routine to sort an outline control with one level. Can be modified to sort more levels.

    OUTSRT   2 *K*   Free

PSetup — A dll with source code for accessing and integrating the standard Windows' printer setup utility in your Visual Basic programs.

    VBPSETUP   4 *K*

PTips — 32-bit OLE DLL allows adding Tool Tips to almost any control of a 32-bit VB program. Uses the Win32 API. Gives Tool Tip support to many older controls which lack Tool Tips.

    PTIPS   67 *K* $5   *PDC*

PX Create — A routine allowing the creation of Paradox tables (from the Borland Paradox Engine) in Visual Basic. Source code is included.

    PXCREA   7 *K*   *OutRider Systems*

Password — Simple source code to add a password system to your program. Documentation and sample password contained in the code.

    JSDNPASS   3 *K* $5   *JSD Software*

Password Program — Set of forms and procedures to add full password and task level functionality to your VB programs. No VBX needed. Pure source code. Features include: User ID, User Name, Password, Task Level, Setup Date, Expiration Date, etc.

    PASSWD1   36 *K*   Free   *Point Systems, Inc.*

Password Program 2.0 — Set of forms and procedures to add full password and task level functionality to your VB programs. No VBX needed. Pure source code. Features include: User ID, User Name, Password, Task Level, Setup Date, Expiration Date, etc.

    PASSWD2   41 *K*   Free   *Point Systems, Inc.*

Peacock - Color By Name Databa — VBX or DLL - A color by name system which allows you to create applications which can have their colors configured by symbolic name rather than by RGB values. Comes with a predefined database of hundreds of color names, and sample source code.

    PEACOC   59 *K* $23SW   *Maplerow Brothers Software*

Picture-Button Demo — Source code demonstrates a method of creating command buttons containing pictures.

    BDEMO   20 *K*   Free

PowerBasic DLL Compiler DEMO — Compiles Basic code to a DLL. Complete demo written in VB, source code incl., with benchmarks and technical comparisons. Allows VB programmers new data types: Byte, Word, Double Word, Quad Integer, Extended Precision, etc.

    PBDLLDMO   698 *K* $149   *PowerBASIC Inc.*

Printer Setup — A printer setup dynamic link library (DLL) that can be called from a visual basic application to set up the printer. A make file demonstrating how to list the library is included.

> PSETUP   9 *K*   Free   *Palmer, Joe*

Profile — Source code module for reading and writing INI files. See also INIFIL by same author.

> PROFILCH   3 *K*   Free   *Hegerty, Chad*

ProgGuide — Source code from the book "Visual Basic Programmer's Guide".

> PROGGD   18 *K*   Free

Program Picker — Program launcher with source code demonstrates stay-on-top technique, 3-D buttons, date and time display.

> F12SHE   13 *K* $5   *Force 12*

Programming Conventions (MS) — Microsoft technical note of Visual Basic programming and naming conventions. Goes beyond those in the Visual Basic Programmer's Guide.

> VBCONV   10 *K*   *Microsoft*

PropertyCreator 1.2 — PropertyCreator is a utility for VisualBasic 4.0. It creates property procedures and the associated member variables.

> PCREATOR   29 *K*   Free   *Baar, Michael*

RDB Library 1.4 — Common error handler and subroutines. Subroutines for string centering, right justifying, formatting long strings for printing, validating dates and more.

> RDBLIB   394 *K*   Free   *Bacon, Royce D.*

Report Generator For VB — Demonstration on how to include report generation capabilities in your Visual Basic applications.

> RPTGEN   34 *K*   Free   *Hobson, Graham*

Restore Add-In — VB4 add-in provides automatic reloading of the project which was active when VB4 was closed. Source code provided.

> RESTORE   9 *K*   Free   *MainSoft*

Revisited Generic Application — A simple generic application framework. The only special feature is it will randomly change the font as you click in the form.

> RGA   7 *K*   Free   *Perrin, Charles L.*

Save Me — A form with buttons to quickly save the current file or project. Source code included.

   SAVEME   5 K Free   *Irwin, Gregg*

Scroll — A routine, with source code, which demonstrates scrolling procedures on a form.

   VBSCRL   6 K

Sending Escape Sequences — Text discusses a technique for sending printer escape sequences to HP laser printers.

   HPESC   3 K Free   *O'Roarke, Peter*

Sendmessage API Listbox — Source code demonstrates some SendMessage API commands which should help overcome the limited set VB offers for simple list boxes.

   LB_FUN   5 K Free   *Hutmacher, Dave Th.*

Shell Sort Example — Source code demonstrating the Shell sort. Sorts an array of strings into ascending order.

   SSORT   2 K Free   *Wykes, Harry*

Simulate Custom Control In VB4 — Instructional demo simulating a custom control in VB4. Shows how to use a picturebox as a container, then customizes it for use with graphical option buttons that act like real option buttons.

   BTNDMO   11 K Free   *Marquardt, Doug*

Snatch — Utility to snatch function declarations from the WINAPI.TXT and other specific files for quick pasting into VB projects.

   VBSNAT   26 K Free   *Bergh, Arild*

Soft CodeBlocker 32 for VB4 — VB4 add-in simplifies repetitive procedures. Allows adding templates of up to eight tokens and paste them in a single-click operation. Demo shareware edition allows up to four standardized "codeblocks".

   WSCB3205   910 K $20   *Winchester Soft srl*

Sorts — Not supported. An in-memory sort routine, based on the Comb sort. Source code included.

   SORTS   5 K Free   *Dacon, Tom*

StrField — Inspired by the StrField$() function in Ami Pro. Extracts a field from a string containing fields delimited by a specific character.

   STRFLD   5 K Free   *Williams, Cris*

String Studio — Add-in brings the power of C-like String Tables to VB, and the ease of use of visual String, MsgBox, and InputBox editors, with no manual coding required. Visually edit every String, MsgBox, and InputBox in your project with one click.

    SSTUDIO   276 *K* $30   *NorthStar Solutions*

TPW2VB — A framework for using Turbo Pascal for Windows to write Custom Controls for Visual Basic. Supplements (not quite replaces) the Microsoft Control Development Kit (CDK).

    TPW2VB   14 *K* $20 SW   *Opaque Software*

Tag Environment Subsystem — Not supported. Routines to provide support for tagged string fields in a VB Form or Control tag property. Source code and demo.

    TAGENV   7 *K*   Free   *Dacon, Tom*

TestIni — Sample program shows simple routines for INI file management. Includes dynamic change of some system variables such as the Wallpaper, the BorderWidth, etc.

    INITES   12 *K*   Free   *Tisoft S.A.*

Text Editor — ASCII text editor written in VB. Full source code. Similar to Windows Notepad with additional features. Version 0.5 and not polished.

    TEXTED   25 *K*   Free   *Huskins, Douglas A.*

The Creator — Utility to automate program installation. Creates a SETUP.INI file to use with the SETUP.EXE program included. Registration gets full VB3 source code for this SETUP.EXE.

    CREATOR   74 *K* $17   *SNS Software*

Tip Of The Day — Displays tips about using program features. Similar to Microsoft's and other products. Shows tips at startup of a program. Shows "Next Tip" if selected or list of "More Tips". Full source code available for $35.

    TOD   44 *K* $20   *Marquis Computing, Inc.*

ToolHelp 32 Declarations VB4 — ToolHelp32 functions, constants, and types for Windows 95 and Visual Basic 4. Translated from TLHELP32.H from Microsoft's Win32 SDK.

    TH32   3 *K*   Free   *Lambrellis, Michael*

Trapper 2.1 — Code Generation tool reads your Visual Basic source files and generates standard error trapping code for each file.

    TRAP   30 *K* $10   *Presley, Jack*

Trapper Error Handler — Utility generates error handler subroutines, adding the required code to subroutines and functions found in forms and modules. Registered users get full source code.

    TRAPPER   349 *K*   Free   *Gandolf Development*

Txthook.DLL — Subclass VB textbox to add ES_NOHIDESEL functionality. Also adds caret choice and overstrike mode. VB samples and C source included.

    TXHOOK   6 *K*   Free   *Simms, Jeff*

Unload — A small utility that lets you remove any Windows program or DLL from memory.

    UNLOAD   7 *K*   Free   *Sax Software*

Update ODBC Oracle Driver — Update to the ODBC Oracle Driver for VB 3 and Access 1.1. Removes 2000 character limit. Updates SQORA.DLL and SQORASTP.DLL.

    ORA110   109 *K*   Free   *Microsoft*

VB Bar — Floating toolbar provides access to many of VB's most-used commands.

    VBBAR100   5 *K* $15 SW   *Rathwick, Zane / Addsoft*

VB CONSTANT.TXT Help File — This is the CONSTANT.TXT file that came with VB 2.0 Pro edited into a Windows Help File with hypertext links and keyword searching. Allows importing via the clipboard the sections that are needed.

    CONHLP   21 *K*   Free   *Buhrer, Richard*

VB Code Flush 1.1 — Performs the Save Text and Load Text commands for every form and module in your VB project. This procedure eliminates useless code left over by the VB 1.0 editor.

    VBFLUSH   6 *K* $4.00 SW   *Moccia, Lou A.*

VB Compress — Utility offers a Windows interface to compressing files using Microsoft's DOS-based COMPRESS.EXE program. It makes re-compressing groups of files fast and easy. Also supports drag and drop from the File Manager.

    COMPRIT   17 *K*   Free   *Buchholz, Elliot C.*

VB Icon Extraction — Use VB and Windows API SHELL.DLL to extract icons from Windows EXE and DLL files.

    ICOXTR   2 *K*   Free

VB Install — A modifiable installation program to install your completed programs into Windows. Source code included.

    VBINST   61 *K*   Free   *Kallonen, Jari*

VB Key Code Generator — Enables you to build into your shareware program a built in registration method for your registered users. Add or inhibit features based on a key code. This shareware version handles only four projects; registered version handles 99 projects.

    CGEN   22 *K* $30SW   *Reinstein, Robert*

VB Messenger - Owner-Draw LB — Sample program uses VB Messenger (file VBMSG) to show how to draw an owner-drawn listbox in Visual Basic. Owner-draw lets you display items in a list box with pictures.

    ODLIST   7 *K*   Free   *JOSWare, Inc.*

VB Tips 07/02/94 — A collection of tips for programmers of Visual Basic. Arranged by subject area. 7/2/94 update. See also VBTVWR for companion viewer source code.

    VBTIPS   134 *K*   Free   *Ford, Nelson*

VB Tips And Tricks '94 — Newsletter in Win Help format with help for VB Win, programming VB apps with MS Access, Win Help Files, advanced programming techniques and business solutions. Includes modules for use in your programs and sample programs with source code.

    VBTT21   286 *K*   Free   *NicheWare*

VB Tips And Tricks '95 — Newsletter, in Windows Help format, with help for VB Win, programming VB apps with MS Access, Win Help files, advanced programming techniques and business solutions. Includes modules for use in your programs and sample programs with source code.

    VBTT95   626 *K*   Free   *NicheWare*

VB Tips And Tricks 3/1996 — Newsletter, in Windows Help format, with help for VB Win, programming VB apps with MS Access, Win Help files, advanced programming techniques and business solutions. Includes modules for use in your programs and sample programs with source code.

    VBTT0396   667 *K*   Free   *NicheWare*

VB Tips And Tricks Saver — Multimedia screen saver with graphics, animations, sounds, and a VB trivia module to test your VB code and history knowledge.

    VBTTSSVR   1177 *K*   Free   *NicheWare*

VB Tips And Tricks Thru 10/96 — Newsletter in Win Help format with help for VB Win, programming VB apps with MS Access, Win Help Files, advanced programming techniques and business solutions. Includes modules for use in your programs and sample programs with source code.

    VBTTFULL   1720 *K*   Free   *NicheWare*

VB Tips Viewer — A file viewer for the VB Tips series. Source code included to compile in Visual Basic.

VBTVWR	11 *K* Free	*Ford, Nelson*

VB To Visual C++ Forms Convert — Assists programmers in turning prototypes forms written in Visual Basic and other Windows prototyping tool into Windows 3.x Resource Scripts. Demo. Captures any Windows form, together with its menus, controls, color, font and position.

STORC10	94 *K* Demo	*PractiSys*

VB Toolbox Pro 3.0 — Toolbox featuring printing of all code; F6 hotkey for quick code printing; list of all available VBX files used in project; launch programs from within VB; help files include declarations for most public domain DLLs. For VBWin 2.0 and 3.0 only.

VB3_TB	382 *K* $25 SW	*Jurcik, Hal*

VB appwizard — Utility generates complete VB4/16 or VB4/32 applicatiion templates including toolbar/tooltips, status bar, help file, and more. 30 day evaluation version.

VBWIZPM	397 *K* $22	*Macdonald, Peter*

VB*Alyzer — Utility scans a VB project's files and counts number of lines, variables, constants, etc. Includes a "McCabe Complexity" measure to find routines of high complexity. Full VB source code included.

VBALYZ	11 *K* Free	*Woodhouse, Mike*

VB-Tools Discomppiler And More — Set of tools for Visual Basic 2.0 and 3.0. Includes VBDis Discompiler for VB 2/3; VBMDis3 optimization tool; VBCtrl2 custom control analyzer; VBDiff comparison tool for VB modules; VBMap project browser; VBpro2 project manager and preprocessor.

VBDIS9E	317 *K*	*Diettrich, Dr. Hans-Peter*

VB/DLL Library Builder Demo — Custom control add-on allows a Visual Basic executable to simulate a Windows DLL while remaining an executable program. Allows Visual basic programs to be called from any other language that can call a Windows DLL. An alternative to DDE or OLE.

DLLDMO	199 *K* $249	*DataObjects Inc.*

VBA Disable Break On Errors — Excel 5.0 file uses Visual Basic for Applications to test for and disable the 'Break on All Errors' setting in the Tools-Options-Module General dialog box.

ONERR	5 *K* Free	*Hamilton, Peter*

VBArray — Source code demo of using the Windows API's fast I/O routines to load or save arrays without the use of for/next loops. Arrays are subject to the usual 64k limitation of Visual basic.

    ARRAY   6 *K*   Free   *Kitsos, Costas*

VBDOS — A DLL which can be integrated into your own programs to access and modify file attribute and disk information. Source code is included.

    VBDOS   8 *K*

VBINST Install Program 1.30 — Visual Basic source for installation program. Copies files, creates Program Group if needed, etc.

    VBINST13   25 *K*   Free   *Kallonen, Jari*

VBMEM V3.1 — Utility that displays Windows operating mode, presence of math coprocessor, system resources, and the amount of free memory. Updates in real time. Source code included.

    VBME31   4 *K*   Free   *Snider, Charles K.*

VBMenu — Program with source code for creation of Bit Map Menus in Visual Basic.

    VBMENU   16 *K*   Free

VBPaths — Utility to show the path specifications which are stored in VB make files.

    VBPATH   60 *K*   Free   *Brown, Tim*

VBQuirk — Not available from MicroHelp. A text file describing known quirks or bugs in Visual Basic.

    VBQUIRK   4 *K*   Free   *MicroHelp, Inc.*

VBSort — A QuickSort routine in Visual Basic. Source code included.

    VBSORT   4 *K*   Free   *Ford, Nelson*

VBToolbox — A small toolbox that remains on-screen while programming in VB. One click to "Save and Run", "Save/Load Text", "Call Help", "Call Text", "Call Paint" and "Call Icon Editor".

    VBTX1B   83 *K* $10 SW   *Jurcik, Hal*

VBUtils — Two (pre VB 1.0 only) utilities to copy or delete Visual Basic project files. They allow you to act on an entire project with one command and are very useful for cleaning up directories quickly.

    VBUTIL   44 *K*   Free   *White, George M.*

VBX Control Development Wizard — A class library for developing VBXs using Microsoft Visual C++ and the Microsoft Foundation Classes. No documentation in this shareware version; documentation available with registration.

MFCVBX   376 *K* $25 SW   *Bish Programming*

VBX Wizard For MS C++ — Creates a custom class for VBX controls in MSC++, allowing for more compact and efficient programming of VBX controls. Creates an include file that defines a custom class for every custom control in a VBX file.

VBXWIZRD   61 *K*   Free   *Sax Software*

VBX Wizard For Pascal — A program to simplify the development of VBX custom controls using Borland Turbo Pascal for Windows. Creates the framework of an application that creates VBX controls. Consists of four dialog boxes where controls, properties, and events are specified.

VBXWZ   153 *K* $55   *Zeitlin, Eli And Dani*

VBXRef Demo — Not available from MicroHelp. X-reference utility for VB applications. Lists all forms, controls, properties, variables and procedures. This crippled version is limited to a single form or module and 5 standard control per form.

VBXDEMO   199 *K*   Free   *MicroHelp, Inc.*

VB_APPS — Library of applications and add-on modules. Includes a log, multiple simultaneous timers, encryption front end, password protection, enhanced scroll bars, multiple file starter, font viewer. Registered users receive full source code.

VBAPP01   185 *K* $30 SW   *Resolutions Now*

Visual Basic Project Tools — Tools to view and copy project files.

VBPT16   19 *K*   Free   *Dombroski, Bob*

Visual Basic To C Resource — Reads a Visual Basic form file and creates a resource and header file which can be read into resource editors and included in a C/C++ project, Beta version.

VBTORC   18 *K*   Free   *SoftBit Enterprises*

Visual DLL DEMO Program — Animation DEMO of Visual DLL. Provides the capability of creating true Windows DLLs from Visual Basic. Automatically creates C header files and Basic Declare statements for access from third-party applications.

VDLLIF   1249 *K*   *Simply Solutions*

Wallpaper Changer — Automatically changes wallpaper at selected intervals. Source code included. Continuously displays time, free resources, free memory, and free disk space.

    WALLCH   24 *K*   Free   *Hitchings, Tim*

Wampus Tracker — Formatted scratch pad to be used with "Hunt the Wampus" game (not included here). Source code included.

    WTRACK   5 *K*   Free   *Fuller, H. L.*

WinAPI And API Crossref — This file contains both WINAPI.TXT and APIXREF.HLP files provided with the "Microsoft Windows Programmer's Reference Book and Online Resource". WINAPI.TXT contains most VB Declare statements to access the Windows API. See also APIREF.

    WINAPI   54 *K*   Free   *Microsoft*

WinBasic 1.2 — Shareware basic interpreter for Windows. Full documentation (English) included.

    WINBAS12   180 *K* $30   *Zimmer Informatik*

WinRC 2.00 — Standalone Resource Compiler for 16- or 32-bit modes. Accepts bitmap, icon, string, or wave resources.

    WINRC2C   1623 *K*   Free   *Deleau, Jean-Marie*

Wrapping Legacy Code In VB4 — Microsoft Word document. Code that has functioned for many years could be a candidate for reuse. Visual Basic provides many new ways of integrating legacy code into new applications.

    LEGACY1   80 *K*   *Microsoft*

Write VBX Control Using MFC2.0 — Sample C source framework for writing generic VBX controls using Microsoft Visual C++ and Microsoft Foundation Classes.

    MFCVBXMS   10 *K*   Free   *Microsoft*

XTASK.DLL Monitors Termination — Allows detecting a terminating EXE. Pass a window handle of the calling application along with the task handle of another running application, and a number of your choice. The function returns immediately. On termination, window receives WM_KEYDOWN.

    XTASK   4 *K*   Free   *Stam, Pieter*

46

PROGRAMMING DEMO

Automated Questionnaire — Designed to administer a questionnaire to a group of networked users. Written to look for information on four servers. Graphs the information collected. VB and Access source code included.

      IPROJ   45 *K*   Free   *Houtari, Scott*

ButtonTool Demo — Demo of this vendor's custom button toolkit, providing 3-D effects, raised buttons, icons and bitmaps, and other custom effects.

      BTDEMO   40 *K* $49.95   *OutRider Systems*

Toolbar Demonstration — Rough demonstration of building a Visual Basic program that is a "toolbar" to communicate with other Windows programs. Demonstrates building a minimizable window that stays on top of all other windows. Full source code.

      TOOLBA   7 *K*   Free   *Milbery, Jim*

VB3 For Dummies Example — Source code and executable file of the "Hello World" example from the book "Visual Basic 3 for Dummies" by Wallace Wang. Also description of the book and other books by the same author.

      VB3DUM   16 *K*   Free   *Wang, Wallace*

Visual Basic 2.0 Primer Editio — A working but limited demo version of Microsoft Visual Basic 2.0. Runs as an interpreter, does not create EXE files. Apparently from the United Kingdom. Freely distributable.

      VBPRIMER   1126 *K*   Free   *Microsoft*

47
REFERENCE

API Reference — Function names and corresponding DLLs of the Windows API. See VBZ01.ZIP.

    APIREF   4 *K*   Free   *User Friendly, Inc.*

APIX — Utility gives the programmer instant access to the Windows API Declares, Constants, and Types. Select from the appropriate lists and selections are copied to the Clipboard. Source code included.

    APIX   26 *K*   Free   *Simms, Jeff*

Borland Visual Controls Info — Full information of the Borland Visual Controls Pack. Comprehensive set of more that 25 custom controls. Database (access dBase and Paradox), Spreadsheet (500x500 grid), Word processor (WYSIWYG), Communications, Image Editor, etc.

    BVCP   10 *K*   Free   *Borland*

CLVB Digest April 1995 — Newsletter, in Windows HLP format, derived from the Internet with many articles relating to Visual Basic. April 1995 issue. Includes sample source code.

    CLBV9503   108 *K*   Free   *Faarvang, Jakob*

CLVB Digest February 1995 — Text newsletter, derived from the Internet, with many articles relating to Visual Basic. February 1995 issue. Includes sample source code.

    CLBV9501   56 *K*   Free   *Faarvang, Jakob*

CLVB Digest March 1995 — Newsletter, in Windows HLP format, derived from the Internet, with many articles relating to Visual Basic. March 1995 issue. Includes sample source code.

    CLBV9502   141 *K*   Free   *Faarvang, Jakob*

CLVB Digest May 1995 — Newsletter, in Windows HLP format, derived from the Internet, with many articles relating to Visual Basic. May 1995 issue. Includes sample source code.

    CLBV9504   119 *K*   Free   *Faarvang, Jakob*

Coding Standards Document — Document describes the benefits of using coding standards and code reviews, and describes a set of Visual Basic coding standards and extended GUI standards.

    STANDRDS   5 *K*   Free   *Computer Interface Design Inc.*

Companion Products Text — Microsoft's own listing of companion products and services for Visual Basic.

    VBADDONS   15 *K*   Free   *Microsoft*

Crystal Reports And Bound Repo — Word 6 document: Crystal Reports Pro 3.0: New Custom Control for Visual Basic". Explains the additional features of Crystal Reports Pro, which allows the new control to bind directly to a Visual Basic Data Control.

    BOUND   7 *K*   Free   *Crystal Services*

Crystal Reports Pro License — Word 6.0 document. "Crystal Reports Pro 4.0 Runtime Agreement and Files" lists the runtime files which licensed owners of Crystal Reports may distribute to end users.

    RUNTIM   12 *K*   Free   *Crystal Services*

Crystal Reports Runtime Doc — Word 2 format document: "Runtime Requirements for Crystal Reports for Visual Basic". Describes the files which make up the runtime requirements for applications including Crystal Reports.

    VBRUNT   4 *K*   Free   *Crystal Services*

Crystal Reports Technical Docs — Technical documents from Crystal Services about the most common questions, issues, and problems with Crystal Reports.

    CRTDOC   244 *K*   Free   *Crystal Services*

Desaware API Declarations — Declarations of constants and API functions for use in Visual Basic. From the book "PC Magazine Visual Basic Programmer's Guide To the Windows 3.1 API".

    DESADECS   39 *K*   Free   *Desaware*

Fast Track Disk — Declarations for the Windows API, with brief descriptions, data structures, and error codes in Windows Help Files. Registration gets a series of Visual Basic sample projects.

    WINDLL   117 *K* $29   *Wildcat Software*

Index For Data Access Guide — The index for the Data Access Guide in the Professional Features Book 2 that comes with Visual Basic 3.0 Professional Edition.

    DATIDX   21 *K*   Free   *Microsoft*

Jet Database Engine White Pape — Microsoft Word for Windows document covers the Microsoft Jet Database Engine and ODBC. Discusses how Microsoft Access and Visual Basic 3.0 interface to the jet engine.

    RJETWP   28 *K*   Free   *Microsoft*

KnowledgeBase 1/96 (Win95) — The complete Visual Basic 32-bit Knowledge Base in Windows 95 Help format. Requires Windows 95.

    VBKB32   1834 *K*   Free   *Microsoft*

KnowledgeBase 16-Bit 1/96 — The complete Visual Basic Knowledge Base for Visual Basic 1-3 and VB4/16-bit in Windows 3.x Help format.

    VBKB16   5672 *K*   Free   *Microsoft*

KnowledgeBase Win 3.X — The complete Visual Basic Knowledge Base in Windows 3.x Help format.

    VBKB_FT   1834 *K*   Free   *Microsoft*

KnowledgeBase Win 3.X — The complete Visual Basic Knowledge Base in Windows 3.x Help format.

    VBKB_FT3   4291 *K*   Free   *Microsoft*

PC Mag Guide To API Updates — Updates to the book "PC Magazine's Visual Basic Programmer's Guide to the Windows 3.1 API" covering Visual Basic 3.0.

    APIBK   18 *K*   Free   *Desaware*

Parameter Queries — Instructions on using Parameter Queries, an addition to the documentation in VB3 Professional Features Book 2 Page 97.

    QRYPRM   1 *K*   Free

Passing Selection Formulas-CRW — Word 6 document: "Passing Selection Formulas and Formulas at Runtime from VB (via VBX)". Describes allowing users to pass a record selection criteria from VB rather than having it hard-coded into the program.

    FORMLS   8 *K*   Free   *Crystal Services*

Q+E Database/VB Documentation — Windows Write format document for Pioneer Software's Q+E Database/VB commercial program. Detailed information about Q+E capabilities.

    QEVBWR   56 *K*   *Intersolv/Q+E Software*

Test Pentium — A small function to test your Pentium.
      PENTIU   1 *K*   Free

Using CTL3DV2.DLL — Information on using CTL3DV2.DLL, from the help file from Borland C++, translated for Visual Basic use.
      CTL3DV   1 *K*   Free

VB Documentation Errors — Microsoft's text file of documentation errors contained in the first printing of the Visual Basic manuals.
      VBDOCERR   4 *K*   Free   *Microsoft*

VB Quick Reference To Win API — Windows Help file companion to Daniel Appelman's book "Visual Basic Programmer's Guide to the Windows API" from Ziff-Davis Press. Not associated with Appelman or Ziff-Davis. This "preview" file follows odd-numbered chapters in the book.
      VBPQRWA   67 *K* $15   *Stillwater Systems*

VBBK08 Listing Of Books, Etc. — Listing of Visual Basic and Access books, publications, information services and conferences provided by Visual Basic Programmer's Journal. Microsoft Word 6.0 format.
      VBBK08   33 *K*   Free   *Visual Basic Programmer's Jrnl*

VBPJB2 VB And Access Books Etc — List of Visual Basic and Access books, publications, information services and conferences provided by Visual Basic Programmer's Journal magazine.
      VBPJB2   21 *K*   Free   *Fawcette Technical Publication*

Variable Naming And Coding Gui — Coding conventions guidelines document in Write format.
      CODEGU   8 *K*   Free

Visual Basic Backgrounder — Microsoft's original "Backgrounder" (press release) report on Visual Basic.
      VBASIC   5 *K*   Free   *Microsoft*

Visual Basic Conventions & Gd. — Complete document on naming conventions, coding style in VB, use of DLLs, and object-oriented tips and Access.
      NAMVB   12 *K*   Free   *Collier/Rother, Jim*

Visual Basic Office Descript. — Windows Help file describes Visual Basic Office in detail. See file VBOxxx.ZIP for shareware version.
      VBODES   39 *K*   Free   *Marquette Computer Consultants*

Windows 3.1 APIs — Windows 3.1 API declarations for Visual Basic. File with Const, Type, and Declare statements for all Windows 3.1 APIs.

    W31API   33 *K*   Free   *Microsoft*

Windows API Functions Cardfile — Windows Cardfile file containing a card for each Windows API function.

    APIFU   48 *K*   Free

Windows Online VB Column #16 — Article contains source code demonstrating how to create an 'owned window' which stays on top of other forms without blocking keyboard/mouse input.

    VB016E   13 *K*   Free   *Marquette Computer Consultants*

Windows Online VB Column #17 — Article contains source code demonstrating the use of API calls to move or limit the mouse cursor.

    VB017E   18 *K*   Free   *Marquette Computer Consultants*

Windows Online VB Column #18 — Article contains general tips about VB programming.

    VB018E   11 *K*   Free   *Marquette Computer Consultants*

Windows Online VB Column #19 — Article contains source code demonstrating how to get and set Windows System Colors.

    VB019E   25 *K*   Free   *Marquette Computer Consultants*

Windows Online VB Column #21 — Article reviews the book "Visual Basic How-To" by The Waite Group.

    VB021E   32 *K*   Free   *Marquette Computer Consultants*

Windows Online VB Column #22 — Article includes source code for a custom message box.

    VB022E   26 *K*   Free   *Marquette Computer Consultants*

48

RUN TIME LIBRARY

Updated VBRUN300.DLL (301) — Updated VBRUN300.DLL fixes bug when running on 286 machines and under Windows NT.

      VBRUN301   231 *K*   Free   *Microsoft*

VB Runtime Library Version — Reads the version numbers of VBRUN200.DLL and VBRUN300.DLL.

      VBVER   7 *K*   Free   *Germelmann, Christian*

Visual Basic 3.0 Runtime — Visual Basic 3.0 Runtime.

      VBRUN300   229 *K*   Free   *Microsoft*

Visual Basic 4.0 16-Bit Runtim — Visual Basic 4.0 16-bit runtime DLL.

      VB40016   472 *K*   Free   *Microsoft*

Visual Basic 4.0 32-Bit Runtim — Visual Basic 4.0 32-bit runtime DLL.

      VB40032   389 *K*   Free   *Microsoft*

Visual Basic 4.0a Runtime (16) — Updated 16-bit runtime file for Visual Basic 4.0a applications.

      VB4RUN16   1379 *K*   Free   *Microsoft*

Visual Basic 4.0a Runtime (32) — Updated 32-bit runtime file for Visual Basic 4.0a applications.

      VB4R32P   1245 *K*   Free   *Microsoft*

Visual Basic Run Time 1.0 — The run time library necessary to execute Visual Basic 1.0 programs. Some shareware and public domain files include this runtime file. To avoid needless duplication, it has been removed from those files which appear on this CD-ROM collection.

      VBRUN100   157 *K*   Free   *Microsoft*

Visual Basic Run Time 2.0 — The run time library necessary to execute Visual Basic 2.0 programs. See description for VBRUN100 also.

      VBRUN200   205 *K*   Free   *Microsoft*

49
SECURITY

Ctrl-Alt-Del Disable VBX — A VBX that disables Ctrl-Alt-Del. Keeps users from breaking out of applications accidentally or deliberately (for security). Includes a secure demo screen saver with system clock.

    NOCAD0   84 *K*   *Bowker, Bob*

MC Security 1.13 (16/32) — Set of serialization routines for developers to append a serial number and 50 characters of text information to a file. Allows tracing the registered owner of any copy of a file. VB4 source code and demo program included.

    MCSEC113   225 *K* $10SW   *Renard, Michael*

Offer Test Drives For VB — Allows you to create fully functioning demos of your application without having to create a seperate demo verison. Stops unauthorized use by relating a registration number to a specific machine. Allows you to specify how many times a demo may be used.

    OTDDEMO   554 *K* $59+   *Tabb, Marchan*

Register — Shareware registration program for VB.

    STRSZR10   144 *K*   *Kochaniak, Grzegorz*

Registration Key 3.1 — System to allow programmers to incorporate advanced registration key capabilities into programs written in C, C++, QuickBASIC, Visual Basic or Turbo Pascal.

    RKEY31VB   190 *K* $24+   *Pirie, Brian*

Shareware Registration Library — DLL contains functions to protect shareware against unauthorized use and registers/unlocks a program with a unique registration key. Demonstration version, sample VB source code included.

    RTREG   143 *K* $41   *Stanczak, Thomas*

50
SETUP

Compress Wizard — Uses WM_DROPFILES messages to let users drag and drop files from File Manager into the program's list box. The application will then compress the files using Microsoft's COMPRESS.EXE program.

COMPWIZ   266 *K* $12   *Simmons, Paul*

Easy SFX Self Extract Install — Utility creates a unique self extracting and installing file. Allows user to choose target drive and directory. Displays a README file after extraction and optionally starts the installed program.

EZSFX   260 *K* $40   *Easy Software*

Eschalon Setup Pro Trial — Installation utility provides a graphical way to create your installation. Use its Setup Expert to specify details of the installation, organize your files, test and verify setup files, and build the setup disks.

ESETUP   558 *K* $100   *Eschalon Development, Inc.*

Fix SetupWizard's Lists (VB4) — Utility makes it possible for a developer using Windows 95 to produce distribution disks with Setup Wizard what will install correctly on either Windows 3.1 or Windows 95 target systems.

FIXSETUP   44 *K*   Free   *Cilwa, Paul A.*

Freeman Installer 2.2 — Installation utility. Visual IDE. Automatic test, run, make, build, and disk set building. One-mouse-click multilingual support. Built-in compression. Uninstall. Can modify AUTOEXEC and CONFIG.SYS. Displays 256-color bitmaps in custom dialogs.

FINST22   1332 *K* $30   *Freeman-Teresa Software*

Initialization Monitor 1.0 — Automatic INI file comparisons. Lets you verify that INI files are being written correctly. Lets you inspect changes to INI files.

INIMON   35 *K* $5   *Simple Software (Bigford)*

Install Master (DEMO) — Install/uninstall Windows apps without learning scripts. Includes compression. Add graphics, percent bars, and special effects. Click to select your installation preferences: full/partial install, upgrade, user system info, etc. DEMO does not install.

    VBIMDEMO   1288 *K* $99   *Poseidon Software, Ltd.*

Installigence Demo — DEMO of a complete Setup/Install utility. Installation Factory is a visual environment to design your setup. The Installation Engine executes the setup. Can serialize each copy of your program.

    IGDEMO   1091 *K* $295   *Instance Corporation*

K-Install 2.7 — Powerful, robust installation program for DOS and Windows software. Handles multi disk and partial installs, archive unpacking, replace or append to files, AUTOEXEC.BAT, CONFIG.SYS, INI file and Program Manager updating, and more.

    KINSTWIN   120 *K* $125   *Ark Angels*

Register Management — Sample application shows how to add Registration Management to your application. Source code included and fully commented.

    REGIST   100 *K*   Free

Registration Module — VB3 source code that autodetects Win 3.x/Win95 and registers accordingly. Using a workaround, it is able to add your 16-bit VB3 program to the add/remove applet of Win95.

    REGDATA   9 *K*   Free   *Bamber, Gordon*

SHARE Install During Setup — File replaces the ADDSHAREIFNEEDED in SETUP1.BAS included with Visual Basic; to automatically insert SHARE.EXE into AUTOEXEC.BAT during Setup.

    SHARE   2 *K*   Free   *Snyder, James Wj*

Serialization — Routines and utility program intended for developers to append a serial number or other identifier to the end of an EXE, DLL, or other static size files. English and French prompts. Full source code.

    SERIAL   105 *K*   Free

Setup Builder 1.07 — Windows 3.1 utility to create professional lokingf installation procedures. Handles multiple disks, compression, version/overwrite checking, backdrops, 3D look, branding, PM groups and icons, registry, and uninstall.

    SB   404 *K* $80   *Plowman, Graham*

Setup Professional 5.0 — Setup bootstrap alternative to VB's SETUP. Full dialog box and error message customization, Windows file version checking, setup log, and temp directory use. Includes Help file. C source available. Supports VB4.

    PSETUPMC   149 *K* $15   *Chapman, Mike*

Setup Standard Edition 4.7 — Setup bootstrap alternative to VB's SETUP. Full dialog box and error message customization, Windows file version checking, setup log, and temp directory use. Includes Help file. C source available.

    ASETUP   112 *K*   Free   *Chapman, Mike*

Visible Serialization (tm) 1.1 — Utilities for appending a serial number or other identifiers to an EXE file.

    VSER11   47 *K* $19.95   *RCCO Research Associates*

WISE Installation System DEMO — Creates professional setup programs. Create installations via drag'n'drop without writing a single line of code. Wise scans your programs for VBX/DLL references. Automatically compresses files. Includes UNINSTALL prg. 16 and 32 bit versions. 30-day demo.

    WISESW   1333 *K* $199   *Great Lakes Business Solutions*

Wright Registry Control 1.06 — OCX. Lets Visual Basic 4 and Access95 applications easily interact with the Win95/WinNT registry using properties, methods, and collections.

    WREG   1214 *K* $20   *Wright Futures, Inc.*

51
SOUND

CD Audio — Source code for a simple CD audio disc player.
    CDAUD3   27 *K*   Free

CD Audio Player — CD audio player. Includes full source code and VB4/16 executable. Features: plays tracks randomly; shuffle-play; programmed play; repeat; seek; skip.
    CDPLAY   27 *K*   *Smith, Derek*

FBIFile WAV Player Demo — Source code demonstrates how to incorporate WAV sound files in VB programs.
    FBIFILE   181 *K*   Free   *Davis, Mike*

MCI Command Strings — Use the API and MCI to program multimedia applications. Pure VB source code demo file and extensive Windows Help file. Covers animation, CD Audio, MIDI Sequencer, Videodisc, video overlay, and waveform commands.
    MCIHELP   53 *K*   Free   *XFrench*

MIDI For Visual Basic — Visual Basic source code modules can be the heart of any Visual Basic MIDI project. Open and close MIDI devices, MIDI in and out, sync to MIDI time code, generate it at any rate, save configuration to an INI file, etc. A functional sequencer prg is incl.
    VBMIDI   44 *K*   Free   *Mainat, Josep M.*

MediaPlayer — MediaPlayer plays WAV and AVI files using Windows File Manger Common Dialog. Includes sample multimedia files. Source code available with registration.
    MEDIA   255 *K* $15   *Mundy, Ward*

Mergewav — DLL module to merge WAV files on the fly. Source in VB3 as function or C++ for DLL available with tutorial. Extremely fast, using global memory and low level MMSYSTEM APIs. Special conditions for commercial use.

MERGEC   166 K $25   *Thomas, Neville W.*

Midi MPU-401 Music Demo — No longer supported. MPU-401 midi card demo and source routines.

VBMPU   10 K   *Graves, Michael Love*

Midi Time Code Read/Write — EXE, VBX and source to read MTC from any MIDI device and to send MTC at any rate: 24, 25, 30 (drop/nondrop frame) 3D look. Source code provides all declarations and procedures for selecting MIDI devices and read/write buffered MIDI with low level calls.

MTC   60 K   Free   *Mainat, Joseph M.*

One Note Midi — Sample source code which shows how to access the low level midi capabilities of Windows using VB.

ONENOT   25 K   Free   *Artic Software*

PSound — A routine with a sound driver library to demonstrate how to place sounds into programs. Source code is included but a Sound Blaster compatible music card is required.

PSOUND   36 K

Play WAV Files — Source code and samples demonstrate how to play WAV sound files in Visual Basic.

WAVEPLAY   358 K   Free   *Lehman, Jeff*

Sndbite Wave Embedding CC — Custom control allows the embedding of WAV files in your VB application. Multiple WAV files may be used in your application without shipping the individual WAV files. Includes VB example talking clock.

SNDBIT   123 K $28SW   *Maplerow Brothers Software*

Sound — Two source code subroutines and the necessary API calls to output different sounds to the PC speaker.

SOUND   2 K   Free

Soundex Source Code — Source code for the SOUNDEX algorithm.

SOUNDEX   3 K   Free

SpSound Routines — DLL and sample source code provide low level I/O port based sound routines.

SPSOUN   9 K   Free   *Giordano, Alfred J.*

StarBar For Windows — Displays the time normally or as "Starfleet" time; plays a selection of "Star Trek" related sounds, programmable to play on the hour, on the half-hour, or none.

    STRBAR14   80 *K*   *Gerton, David*

System Sound Shuffler Part One — Lets you designate multiple sound files for each system event and "shuffle" them. Source code included, requires the Professional Toolkit. See file SHUFL2.

    SHUFL1   7 *K*   Free   *Stine, Brian D.*

System Sound Shuffler Part Two — Compiled program (see file SHUFL1) for users without VB Pro.

    SHUFL2   19 *K*   Free   *Stine, Brian D.*

VB MIDI Piano Demo — Develop Multimedia/MIDI applications using VB and these 8 custom controls. MIDI In with high res time stamp; MIDI Out with time queue; MIDI file read/write; VU meters; mixer faders, stereo knobs, and sample code.

    VBPIAN2   28 *K* $99   *Artic Software*

VBVoice DEMO — VBX adds graphical voice design system. High level controls allow you to: access your databases via telephone; dial out and deliver voice information; add voice mail and faxback to your application; take messages and store in a database.

    VBVOIC   740 *K* $395+   *Pronexus*

WAV Files From PC Speaker — Plays Windows WAV files through the normal PC speaker (no sound board required.) Partial source code included.

    VBWAV   2 *K*   Free   *VideoSoft*

WAV Playing/Info VBX — Makes it easy to play and get information about WAV files. PLay WAV files in the background as your program performs other tasks; add recorded speech to your applications; put beeps, whistles, and other sounds into your games.

    WAVE10   43 *K* $15   *Mabry Software*

WavPlus 2.0 — Adds expanded WAV and MID file playback and recording for VB, especially VB standard version. Dozens of new commands. Easy command interface.

    WAVPL2   455 *K* $10 SW   *Digital PowerTOOLS*

Wave After Wave 2.01 — Lets you load and access up to 12 WAV files at one time. Source code available with registration.

    WAW   22 *K* $5 SW   *Iyer, Sunil*

Wave Sound Control — Control provides sound via WAV files.

    VBWAVE   20 *K*   Free   *Gamber, Mark*

WavePlayer — A fast WAV player. Source code included, demonstrating the use of the sndPlaySound multimedia call.

    WAVPLY   117 *K*   Free   *Asensio, Pete*

Waveform Spectrum Plot — Source code allows VB programmers to plot waveform files (WAV) in their multimedia applications. This sample application will load most WAV files and plot a static representation of the wave in a picture box.

    WAVEPL   56 *K*   Free

52
SPECIAL

AVI Files In Window — Simple source code to play an AVI file in any window you choose instead of the default window.

    AVIWI   9 K   Free   *Mathison, Rolf*

AVI Viewer — Demonstrates how to play AVI files through a custom window rather than the default window. Source code included.

    AVIWIN   5 K   Free

Array Sequence — This simple program will re-sequence the numbering of an array's code, if copied to the Clipboard, and then copies the renumbered code back to the Clipboard. Full source code.

    ARRSEQ   5 K   Free   *Eke, Richard*

Autonum 1.02 — Generates sequences of numbers to the clipboard for use in documents, etc.

    ANV10   67 K   Free

Books — Text file listing 22 Visual Basic books, by author and title.

    BOOKS_VB   2 K   Free   *Book Stacks BBS*

Convert MBF Format Numbers — Assists Visual Basic programmers who need a way to access or convert the numerical data in Microsoft Binary Format created by older programs written with GW-BASIC or QuickBasic 3.0 and earlier, and also Turbo Pascal 6-byte Real numbers..

    CVDMBF   10 K   Free   *Carr, J. Frank*

Encrypt/Decrypt — Simple Encryption/Decryption function written in VB. All source code. Includes a form to show an example of its use.

    ENCRYP   3 K   Free

Joystick Status — Everything needed for joystick support in Visual Basic. See file JOYSTA.ZIP for VB source code.

    JOYSTF   232 K   Free   *Six, Raymond W.*

Joystick Status Source Code — Source code for the joystick status application, file JOYSTF.ZIP.

    JOYSTA   4 *K*   Free   *Six, Raymond W.*

Joystick.VBX — Custom control to detect and use a joystick within VB. Joystick driver, control-panel applet, and sample source code included.

    JOYSTI   26 *K*   Free   *Thomas, Zane*

Microsoft Word 6.0 Viewer — Free viewer program for Microsoft Word 6.0 (and previous version) documents. Opens, views, and prints Word documents. Supports copy and paste from an open document. Not supported by Microsoft.

    WORDVU   1427 *K*   Free   *Microsoft Product Support*

Microsoft Word 7 Viewer (Win95 — Free viewer program for Microsoft Word 7.0 (and previous version) documents. Opens, views, and prints Word documents. Supports copy and paste from an open document. Not supported by Microsoft. Requires Windows 95.

    WD95VIEW   1673 *K*   Free   *Microsoft Product Support*

Screen Saver Launcher — Demonstrates the use of SendMessage API function. Launches your screen saver at the touch of a button. Source code included.

    SCRSAV   4 *K*   Free   *Coope, Geoff*

Sort Demonstration — Demonstrates bubble sort, DF sort, GK sort, heap sort, insertion sort, quick sort, selective sort, shell sort. Source code included.

    SORTS2   15 *K*   Free

Spell Checker API Sample — Sample source code for accessing MSSPELL.DLL from Visual Basic for spell checking.

    CSAPI   8 *K*   Free

VB Tech Journal Writer's Guide — Writer's guidelines for the magazine VB Tech Journal published by Oakley Publishing Company. Windows Help file contains contact persons, publishing schedule for 1995, outlines for article formats.

    VBTECH   20 *K*   Free   *VB Tech Journal*

53
SPELLCHECK

Spell Checker For Edit Boxes — DLLs to provide spell check facilities to any application that uses the standard edit control or which can export text via the clipboard. Free for personal or shareware program use.

      SPELL30   945 *K* $30   *Quinion, Brian*

Steve's VB Spell — Spellcheck() function to which you can pass any VB Textbox. Function uses OLE 2.0 automation to have Excel 5.0 spell checker verify the spelling of the text in the box. Requires VB 3.0 and Excel 5.0.

      SPELL   7 *K*   Free   *Peschka, Steve*

54
System Utility

AIGZIT - Exit Windows Fast — Utility provides a fast, easy way to exit Windows - just click the icon to exit Windows. VB source code is included in a Windows Write file.

> AIGZIT   35 *K*   Free   *Heydman, Matthew*

ALT-PAD Entry Test — Small utility shows what is actually received by Windows (and Visual Basic) when characters are entered using an ALT-number combination. (For example, try ALT-0215 versus ALT-215.)

> ALTPAD   4 *K*   Free

About Box VB4 — VB4 sample code for a generic About box that uses the information stored in File/Make/Options.

> VBABOUT   8 *K*   Free   *MMC Software*

Access Company And User Name — Source code and demo shows how to access the User Name and Company Name and true Windows version stored in Windows.

> WUSER   19 *K*   Free   *Germelmann, Christian*

Access Windows Registration DB — VB3 source code for accessing the Windows registration database. From the "OLE Expert" column in the April/May 1994 issue of Visual Basic Programmer's Journal.

> REGDB   2 *K*   Free   *Pleas, Keith R.*

Analyzer — A utility which measures and displays a constant update of CPU speed. The readout is numeric in a window or displayed graphically while iconized.

> ANALYZER   3 *K*   Free   *Brody, Evan*

Assoc — Not actively supported. A facility to provide a list of associations currently in effect between file extensions and applications. Permits modification of associations without accessing the Program Manager or WIN.INI.

> ASSOC   10 *K*   Free   *SP Services*

DG Status — Movable status line, displays mode (Standard or Enhanced), day of week and date, and how much memory remains.

    DGSTAT   4 *K*   Free   *Goldfarb, David*

Detour 1.2 — A program selection utility allowing one extension to be associated with several programs. Simple setup with its own configuration utility. Easy to choose the preferred application through its pushbutton interface.

    DETOUR   20 *K*   Free   *Bolin, Christopher*

DiskStat — Provides report on the percentage of free space on all non-removable storage devices.

    DISKSTAT   15 *K*   Free   *Wykes, Harry*

DosButton — This simple utility displays a window with a button that takes you to DOS. A one line program which shows the power of VB. Source code included.

    DOSBUT   2 *K*   Free

Easy Registration32 — DLL to easily manipulate the Registry.

    EASYRG   11 *K* $30   *Williams, Cris*

ExitWin - Exit Windows — Source code to exit windows immediately, restart Windows, or reboot computer.

    EXITWI   9 *K*   Free   *Moyle, Greg*

File Open/Save (VB4) — VB4 sample code for accessing the File Open and File Save dialogs using the Win32 API.

    FDLG32   9 *K*   Free   *MMC Software*

FileMaster — A smooth file launcher and viewer.

    FMSTRV1   17 *K*   Free   *VisualSoft*

FileVersionInfo (VB4) — VB4 sample code for retrieving FileVersionInfo using Win32 API calls.

    FVER32   6 *K*   Free   *MMC Software*

Hotkey — This program allows you to assign "hot-keys" to your applications for quick access to frequently used programs, data, or functions. Source code, a DLL, and an executable example are included. See VBZ01.ZIP.

    HOTKEY   11 *K*   *User Friendly, Inc.*

InfSpy 2.10 — Windows environment viewer allowing you to view Tasks, Windows, Classes, Heap, Modules, File Handles, DOS and Memory information. You can trace messages, stack and set up automatic timers to provide real-time tracing on every aspect of Windows.

SPY210 291 *K* $10SW *Dean Software Design*

KeyState (CapsLock And NumLock — Source code to set the status of the Caps Lock and Num Lock keys on a status bar. A workaround for a bug described in a Microsoft KnowledgeBase article.

KEYSTA 4 *K* Free *Bridge, Inc.*

Lock - Disable Task-Switching — Full source code demonstrates how to disable task-switching from within a Visual Basic program.

LOCK 5 *K* Free *Hengelhaupt, Thomas*

Module API Functions — Example shows how to change task list entry, find the hInstance count, find the next instance of the application. Full source code.

MODULEAP 7 *K* Free

Modules, Tasks, And Classes — Example of using the TOOLHELP module with VB. Displays found modules, tasks, and classes. double-clicking a module will display more information. Full source code included.

MTCU 14 *K* Free

MultiFSR Meter 1.0 — DEMO of pure source code for making a Free System Resources meter without any VBX controls. Registration unencrypts the supplied source code.

MULTI 16 *K* $12 *Griffith, Matthew W.*

NOBOOT - Ctrl-Alt-Del Disable — Custom control allows the programmer to disable the Ctrl-Alt-Del sequence from Visual Basic. Sample source code included.

NOBOOT10 42 *K* Free *Mabry Software*

Newstart — A utility designed to change your startup RLE file from Microsoft's to one of your choice. Source code included.

NST14S 54 *K* Free *Elkins, Jeff*

Peeper 1.25 Version Info — Extract version, identification info from Windows DLLs and EXEs. Also displays imported modules. Version info can be printed for a single file or all files in the directory.

PEEPER 604 *K* $23 SW *Fineware Systems*

Print Manager Switch 1.3 — Utility displays status of Print Manager and allows you to enable or disable it. Source code included.

    PMS3   12 K   Free   *Morris, Jeffrey*

QuitWin — A utility for a quick and orderly exit from Windows 3.0. Registration will get you the source code. (Previous version called EXITWI.ZIP)

    QUITWIN   5 K $9 SW   *MarilynSoft*

Read/Write INI Sample (32-Bit) — Source code for a utility to read and write INI files easily and quickly.

    RWINI32   8 K   Free   *Csefai, George*

Retrieve Messagebox Info Win95 — Code snippet demonstrates using API SystemParametersInfo to retrieve Win95 MessageBox information. Also demonstrates passing a byte structure to an API. Requires 32-bit VB4.

    DMOFNT95   4 K   Free   *Bridge, Inc.*

Shell — Example source code to shell to a Windows application and to have the file of your choice loaded.

    SHELLDM   3 K   Free   *Odom, Ronnie*

Shell And Wait — VB4 32-bit source code to shell to another application, wait for it to finish, and return.

    SHELL   2 K   Free   *Jackson, Bruce*

Show Environment — Creates a text window showing all currently set environment variables.

    ENV100   8 K $10SW   *Allen, Phil*

Steve's OLE 2.0 ProgMan — Inventories your desktop configuration - groups, icons, and properties for each icon. Collected info is presented in outline format with an option to save to Word, starting Word via OLE 2.0. Source included. Requires VB 3.0 and Word 6.0a (6.0 may GPF).

    PMINFO   43 K   Free   *Peschka, Steve*

Stoplite 1.1 — System resource monitor for Windows. Shows a green light when resources are about 60%, yellow when resources are between 30 and 60%, red when resources are below 30%. Source code available at extra charge.

    STOPLITE   20 K $7   *Anno Domini, Inc.*

System Info — Demonstrates a technique for extracting various system information using Visual Basic 3.0. Also demonstrates how to play WAV sound files using a sound card or PC speaker driver. Source code available on registration.

    SYSINF   26 K $10   *Mundy, Ward*

Tasklist 1.0 Revised — Sample program for displaying a task list (like Windows TASKMAN) or a module list within Visual Basic. Full source code. Author cautions this is not a fully tested application.

    TASKV1   49 *K*   Free   *De Bruijn, Michiel*

Utility Custom Control — Custom control provides easy access to the Windows resources, diskspace and memory. Any time GDI or USER resources drop or raise an event is fired. When diskspace or memory change an event is fired. Sample source code included.

    UTIL   23 *K*   Free   *Venugopalan, Vivek*

VBDOS5 — A floppy disk formatter which takes advantage of the formatting features of MS-DOS 5.0. There is also a button which emulates the MEM command to show upper and lower memory usage. Source code is included.

    VBDOS5   9 *K*

Wemory 1.0 — This program displays a small window showing free system RAM and updates it continuously. Optionally, it shows the time and date in another small window.

    WEMORY   8 *K* $5SW   *Porcaro, Jeff*

Win32 System Info Calls — Sample code for several Win32 API calls in VB4. Includes GetSystemInfo, GetVersionEx, GetLogicalDriveString, GetDriveType, GetComputerName, GetUserName, GetDiskFreeSpace and more.

    VBVER32   7 *K*   Free   *MMC Software*

WinExit — Utility to exit Windows, restart Windows, or return to DOS. Sends message to notify all applications to terminate. Source code not included but available with registration.

    WINEXIT   5 *K* $13   *Shender, Alexander*

WinIO.dll 1.4 — DLL to perform very low level i/o functions which Windows normally locks out. Lets VB programs write to physical parts of the PC.

    WINIO   23 *K*   PD   *Himpe, Vincent*

WinLock — A simple Windows security system. It will allow a single letter or digit password. Once locked all windows are frozen except the password window. If the incorrect letter or digit is entered, the system locks. A curio.

    WINLOCK1   5 *K*   Free   *Zeitman, Dan*

Windows Process Status — Replacement for WPS.EXE (Windows Process Status) included with Visual Basic. Full source code included.

    MODULE   186 *K*   Free

Wingine — Search a file or files for text contain within. Up to 25 AND, plus 25 OR and NOT comparisons can be entered.

WINGINE   34 *K* $15 CR   *Software Shop*

Adding 3D Effects To Controls — Windows Help file. Windows 3.1 adds 3D support for pushbuttons, but all other controls appear 2D by default. This file describes how to give a 3D effect to any control. Extensively illustrated.

    104   30 *K*   Free   *Microsoft*

Big Text View — A Text Viewer that exceeds the 32K limit of the standard VB Text Box. Source code included.

    BIGTEXT   8 *K*   Free   *Hipp, Frank*

Cliptest — Source code illustrates how to copy, cut, and paste text from one form to another via a menu located on a third form.

    CLPDEM   3 *K*   Free

Crystal Reports 3.0 Announceme — Announcement of Crystal Reports 3.0 and Crystal Reports Server. New features and upgrade paths and costs for Visual Basic owners are covered.

    CRW3IN   8 *K*   Free   *Crystal Services*

Detecting End Of Drag'n'drop — Text shows how to detect a Mouse_up event at the end of a Drag Sequence. The technique uses one API call and a VB Timer to generate the event when the operator releases the mouse button.

    DRAGDR   2 *K*   Free   *Strathman, Michael D.*

Early Morning Editor Control — Text editor control. Handles lines up to 64K; handles over 2 billion lines; supports line and column blocks as well as stream blocks; supports fixed and proportional fonts; can load and save whole files. Supports VB 2.0 and greater. Requires VBRUN300.DLL

    EMEDIT20   318 *K* $30 SW   *Early Morning Software*

FAQ 04/95 — Frequently Asked Questions concerning Visual Basic from the Internet. April, 1995 edition. Plain text format.

    FAQ0495   81 *K*   Free   *Haugland, Jan Steiner*

FAQ 11/94 — Frequently Asked Questions concerning Visual Basic from the Internet. November, 1994 edition. Plain text format.

    FAQ1194   *40 K*   Free   *Haugland, Jan Steiner*

FAQ 12/94 — Frequently Asked Questions concerning Visual Basic from the Internet. December, 1994 edition. Windows Help format.

    FAQ1294   *100 K*   Free   *Haugland, Jan Steiner*

Force Upper Or Lower Case — Functions to force upper or lower case within a textbox. Full source code.

    UPPLOW   *4 K*   Free   *Bridge, Inc.*

Frequently Asked Questions — Excerpts from four Frequently Asked Questions lists that circulate on the Internet. Includes VB/Win and VB/Dos. See files FAQxxxx for newer versions with additional topics.

    FAQ   *66 K*   Free   *Willits, Don*

HiLight, ChgCase — Two subroutines: HiLight-highlights the contents of a TextBox with focus; ChgCase-reformats a textbox to upper and lower case when the textbox loses focus.

    CMSUBS   *3 K*

HighEdit 3.0 DEMO — Fully integrated, programmable, word processing component. Supports documents larger than 64K. Advanced form letter and mail merge features. Supports several graphic formats, including BMP, PCX, TIF, GIF, TGA, WMF. Offers table functions. Print preview.

    HE30VB   *718 K* $299   *BeCubed Software Inc.*

HyperVB Multifont Text DEMO — Collection of Visual Basic form and code modules that enable the creation of multi-font formatted text controls and hypertext links within VB programs. Built from pure VB source code, no VBXs or DLLs.

    HYPERV   *86 K* $70   *Data Preference*

Improved Notepad With Macros — Improved Notepad with macro capability, ability to choose different fonts, runs with word-wrap on at all times. Source code included.

    INPV10   *97 K*   Free   *Gordon*

Jet 2.0/VB 3.0 Compat. Notes — Windows Write and Word for Windows documents discussing the Jet 2.0/Visual Basic 3.0 Compatibility Layer which allows VB 3 to access Jet 2.0 format database files.

    JET_VB   *76 K*   Free   *Microsoft*

Jet Inspector Benchmark Data — Text file describing a JET Inspector analysis of the JET engine using the VBench Data Access Benchmark Program. Shows an analysis of five different methods of accessing the JET engine.

    JETPER   38 *K*   Free   *Blue Lagoon Software*

LRPAD String Padding — Source code; simple function to pad a string to a given length.

    LRPAD   2 *K*   Free   *Harbolt, Martin L.*

Liberty Basic Document — A beginning tutorial for using Liberty BASIC (file LB09C).

    KLUTZ1   26 *K*   Free   *Shoptalk Systems*

MC String 3.40 — DLL library of 66 string routines for VB 4.0 (32 bit) developers using Windows 95/NT.

    MCSTR340   323 *K* $10SW   *Renard, Michael*

Mabry Software Info And Produc — Contact information and a complete list of Mabry Software products, in Windows Help file format. Current as of October 3, 1994.

    MABRY   21 *K*   Free   *Mabry Software*

Microsoft Jet Engine 2.0 Overv — Introduction to the Microsoft Jet Database Engine built into Microsoft Access and Visual Basic. Word for Windows document. For the Access/VB user who wishes to understand how data is managed in the products.

    JETWP   94 *K*   Free   *Microsoft*

Microsoft Support Services 2.2 — Windows Help file contains information on support services offered by Microsoft.

    MSSUPP22   17 *K*   Free   *JSH Scientific*

MultiText 1.30 — VBX non-editable textbox allowing multiple fonts, font styles, colors, and hyperlinks. Text may be selected with cursor and copied to clipboard. Text can be loaded directly from disk. Includes an RTF import facility.

    MTEXT130   39 *K* $25SW   *Bannister, Steve*

NParse32 — 32 bit OCX that enables Visual Basic Programmers to easily add text file and string parsing capabilities to their Windows 95 and NT applications. When used on a file, it parses each line and returns each field, the record number, the number of fields,etc

    NPARSE32   979 *K* $35   *Nanoware*

Naming Conventions — Programming guidelines for: variables and constants; and controls. Intended so multiple programmers can instantly tell which controls are involved and the data type and scope of any variable. Word for Windows text file.

    CONVEN   4 *K*   Free   *Dolson, Jim*

Parse Demo Project 2.0 — Demonstrates routines that can be efficiently used to parse a string into its elements. They can be used to return the word count and line count in a textbox. A single or variable length delimited may be used. Source code included.

    PARSED   16 *K*   Free   *Reynolds, Paul*

Pretty Printer Notes — Description and notes about Pretty Printer from Aardvark Software (see file VBPPxx). Useful note about documenting source code and communicating with non-programmers even if the product is not used.

    VBPPNOTE   7 *K*   *Aardvark Software Inc.*

Sheridan Datagrid Cut/Copy — Source code example routine to allow cut, copy, and paste to users of DataGrid by Sheridan.

    DGRIDTXT   2 *K*   Free

Soundex And Metaphone CC 1.4 — Gives your program Soundex, Extended Soundex, and Metaphone information. These algorithms translate words (names) into codes that can be used to find like-sounding words. Source code available for $25.

    SOUNDX   182 *K* $10   *Mabry Software*

Spelmate Spell Checker 1.2 — Spell checker DLL for Visual Basic as well as C++ and Pascal. Sample source code included.

    SPMATE12   437 *K* $50 SW   *Herron, James*

Steve's Find And Replace — Extensively commented source code demonstrates how to apply "find and replace" to a text string.

    SEARCHST   10 *K*   Free

Uneditable Text Box Pict. Box — Example of using a picture box as an uneditable text box that can still scroll horizontally and vertically. Can handle huge files.

    TEXT2   9 *K*   Free   *Gradowski, Mark D.*

Using True DBGrid Unbound — Word document of the DBGrid unbound mode. Includes sample code and descriptions of the RowBuffer object and the four unbound events.

    DBGRIDUB   31 *K*   *Apex Software Corporation*

VbWin Programmer Magazine #10 — Windows Help file contains over 2400 topics on Visual Basic programming, mostly from Internet postings. October 1994 issue.

    VBWM10   629 *K*   Free   *Schoonover, Mark*

VbWin Programmer Magazine #11 — Windows Help file contains over 2400 topics on Visual Basic programming, mostly from Internet postings. November 1994 issue.

    VBWM9411   910 *K*   Free   *Schoonover, Mark*

VbWin Programmer Magazine #12 — Windows Help file contains over 2400 topics on Visual Basic programming, mostly from Internet postings. December 1994 issue.

    VBWM9412   926 *K*   Free   *Schoonover, Mark*

VbWin Programmer Magazine #8 — Over 2400 topics on Visual Basic programming, mostly from Internet postings. August 1994 issue. Postscript print format.

    VBWM9408   376 *K*   Free   *Schoonover, Mark*

VbWin Programmer Magazine #9 — Windows Help file contains over 2400 topics on Visual Basic programming, mostly from Internet postings. September 1994 issue.

    VBWM09   732 *K*   Free   *Schoonover, Mark*

VbWin Programmer Magazine 1/95 — Windows Help file contains over 2400 topics on Visual Basic programming, mostly from Internet postings. January 1995 issue. Contains listings of user groups, article "Dynamic Table Attaching", and more.

    VBWM9501   1078 *K*   Free   *Schoonover, Mark*

VbWin Programmer Magazine 2/95 — Windows Help file contains over 2400 topics on Visual Basic programming, mostly from Internet postings. February 1995 issue. Contains listings of user groups, Internet sites relating to Visual Basic, and more.

    VBWM9502   743 *K*   Free   *Schoonover, Mark*

Visual Basic For Apps Tips — Microsoft KnowledgeBase concerning Visual Basic for Applications as of 5/9/1994.

    VBAPP   485 *K*   Free   *Microsoft*

Visual Basic Naming Convention — Naming conventions provided as guidelines for programmers to standardize and decode the structure and logic of an application, to provide readable and unambiguous variable names, and to be consistent with other language conventions.

    NAMING   3 *K*   Free   *Brewer, Dirk*

Visual Basic Shareware Rev. #2 — Windows Help file reviews several shareware products for Visual Basic: INFSPY.EXE, VBMSGR.VBX, PROBE.VBX.
    VBSR02   35 *K*   Free   *TANSTAAFL Software*

Visual Basic Shareware Review — Windows Help file reviews several shareware products for Visual Basic: TITLESPY.VBX, CANIMATE.VBX, VB2DOC6.VBX, VBASM.DLL, VBVALET.DOT.
    VBSR01   74 *K*   Free   *TANSTAAFL Software*

Visual Basic To Document — This Word for Windows template will ask you to select a Visual Basic MAK file and will then create a document based on the FRM and BAS files contained within. Creates table of contents, referencing all FUNCTIONs, SUBs, and count of each Sub/function use.
    VB2DOC   92 *K* $25   *Juden, Eddie V.*

Visual Basic Vs. PowerBuilder — Word for Windows document. A comparison of Microsoft's Visual Basic 3.0 vs. Powersoft's PowerBuilder.
    VBPB   12 *K*   Free   *Green, William*

56
TIMER

High Res Timer DLL — DLL that can time events down to .838 microseconds. Times functions or loops. Sample source code included.

> FASTTIME   9 *K*   Free   *Gradowski, Mark D.*

High Resolution Timer VBX — High resolution timer custom control for Visual Basic. Lets you monitor events to nearly a millisecond, instead of the 55ms of the standard VB timer control.

> HITIME   160 *K* $20+SW   *Mabry Software*

A.F. Street Consulting
Att: Bud Street
R.R. #1
Peterborough, ON K9J 6X2
CANADA
705-292-5502
CIS:72152,333

AA-Software International
ATT:C. Scott Willy
12 Ter Domaine Du Bois
Joli
06330 Roquefort-Les-Pins
FRANCE
+33-93-77-50-47
Fax:+33-93-77-19-78
CIS:100343,2570
cswilly@acm.org

ABC Software
31 Magdalen Way
Worle Weston Super Mare
ENGLAND
+01-934-516714
CIS:100342,1207

AFD Computers
51 Meadowfoot Road
West Kilbride, KA23 9BU
UNITED KINGDOM
+44-1294-823221
Fax:+44-1294-822905
Postcode@afd.co.uk

AJS Publishing
P.O. Box 83220
Los Angeles, CA 90083
800-992-3383
310-215-9145
Fax:310-215-9135

Aaerdeus, Inc.
302 College Avenue
Palo Alto CA 94306
415-325-7529

Aardvark Software Inc.
Att: Martin Tillinger
972 Sheffield Rd.
Teaneck, NJ 07666
201-833-4355
800-482-2742
Fax:201-833-1216
CIS:70544,1372

Aardvark Software
972 Sheffield Rd.
Teaneck, NJ 07666
800-482-2742
201-833-4355
Fax:210-833-1216

Abajain, Tony
CIS:75332,273

Abel, Todd J.
2585 Cooley Road
Canandaigua, New York
14425
CIS:73611,1023

Abri Technologies Inc.
HC 62, Box 100K
Great Capacon WV 25422
304-947-7129
CIS:72345,1623

Activ Software
Att: David Wogan
122 Chadwin Road
London E13 8NF
UNITED KINGDOM
+44-171-473-5394
CIS:100525,3235

AddSoft Inc.
11850 Nicholas St. Ste. 120
Omaha, NE 68154
402-491-4141
Fax:402-491-4152
800-229-0559

Advance Animation Systems
Canyon Crest CA
909-780-1508
Orders:800-780-1508
CIS:72643,3042

Advance Automation Systems
Visual Approach
2930 W. 235th St. #4
Torrance CA 90505
310-530-3938

Advanced Applications
6700 North Tryon Street
Box 560991
Charlotte NC 28256-0991
704-597-3948
CIS:72713,2106

Advanced Support Group
11900 Grant Place
Des Peres MO 63131-4512
314-965-5630
Fax:314-966-1833
CIS:70304,3642

Advice Press
366 Cambridge Avenue
Palo Alto, CA 94306
415-321-2198
Fax: 415-321-2199
info@advice.com
orders@advice.com

AeroData
2024 Maple Park Drive
Ann Arbor MI 48108
rander1040@aol.com

Albrecht, Karl D.
P.O. Box 478
San Lorenzo CA 94580-0478
Karl25@aol.com

Alcott, Glenn
86-22 60th Road
Elmhurst NY 11373
CIS:76044,747

Allcock, Alun
CIS:100255,1506

Allen, Phil
2161 Fawnwood Drive S.E.
Kentwood, MI 49508
CIS:72047,2134
GENIE:P.ALLEN8

Alliance Software Specialists
7911-30th Avenue Suite 3A
Kenosha, WI 53142-4611
414-859-2124
AllianceSS@aol.com

Allman, Gary
2040 Building #1892
Midland MI 48640
CIS:73742,3312

Altwies, Tony
CIS:75443,134

Amans, Robert L.
3242 Salen Drive
Rochster Hills MI 48306
313-373-7904
CIS:72716,1522

American Computer Consultants
1028 Old Mill Rd.
Lake Forest IL 60045
708-295-8490
Fax:708-295-8490x33

Anderle, Michael T.
manderle2@aol.com

Anderson, Tim
CIS:100023,3154
freer@cix.compulink.co.uk

AndyD
AndyD@Pragmatix.com

Anet Inc.
1070 Quartermaster Canyon
San Ramon CA 94583
510-735-1173
800-434-3439
Fax:510-743-1687
CIS:70651,1125

Anno Domini, Inc.
4513-B Lawndale Drive
Greensboro NC 27455
CIS:76531,2651
Keystone95@aol.com

Ansuini, Doug
PO Box 101
Albion RI 02802-0101
CIS:74012.2555

Anton Software Limited
40 Midfield Way
Orpington
Kent BR5 2QJ
UNITED KINGDOM
+44-0-1689-812001
CIS:100265,2172
tonys@dpr.co.uk

Antony, P. Scott
P.O. Box 11047
Milwaukee WI 53211
CIS:74002,2373
PSAntony@aol.com

Apex Software Corporation
4516 Henry Street, Ste. 202
Pittsburgh PA 15213-3785
412-681-4343
800-858-2739
Fax:412-681-4384
truegrid@apexsc.com

Ark Angels
P.O. Box 190
Hazelbrook NSW 2779
AUSTRALIA
+61-47-588-100
Fax:+61-47-588-638
CIS:100237,141

Arnote, Paul
1208 Randolph
Leavenworth, KS 66048
aerosolman@aol.om

Artic Software
Att: Arthur Edstrom
P.O. Box 28
Waterford WI 53185-0028
800-892-0677 414-534-4309 CIS:75410,2203

Asensio, Pete
Atlantic Microsystems
110 Fishing Brook Road
Westbrook, CT 06498
CIS:70143,467

Asgard Software
PO Box 624Road
Oxford OX4 3BL
UK
+44-865-772160
Fax:771461
CIS:100113,431

Ashton Information Services
28, Dragon View
Harrogate, North Yorkshire
HG1 4DG
UK

Asik, Adil
AdilAsik@aol.com

Averbuch, Michael
2116 S. Plymouth Drive
Champaign IL 61821

Axiomatic Software
Att: Andrew Cheshire
113 Josiah Road, Northfield
Birmingham B31 5DG
UK
+44-21-477-9913
CIS:100273,1543

Axtel, Inc.
18255 Mt. Baldy Circle
Fountain Valley CA 92708
714-964-6666
CIS:75720,2412
www.adnc.com/axtel

Aziz, Atif
7 Chemin de la Tour de
Champel
1206 Geneva
SWITZERLAND
+41-22-3468028
CIS:72644,3306

BC Soft AB
Box 34175
S-100 26 Stockholm
SWEDEN
+46-8-657-91-90
Fax:+46-8-656-67-72
CIS:70630,1337

BKMA Inc.
POBox 170
Kingston, WA 98346-0170
Fax:206-779-7747
CIS:71251,1771

BMH Software
C/O Ross Henning
124 Guinevere
Victoria, TX 77904
512-578-9100

Bacon, Royce D.
RDB Systems
8942 W. Lawrence Ave.
Milwaukee, WI 53225
414-462-3418
CIS:70042,1001

Bainbridge Knowledge Mngt Arts
PO Box 170
Kensington, WA 98346-0170
206-972-0321
Fax:206-779-9713
CIS:71251,1771
bkma@folkarts.com

Bamber, Gordon
11 Helena Road
Brighton E. Sussex
BN2 6BS
ENGLAND
CIS:74437,672

Bannister, Steve
41 Milton Street
Northampton NN2 7JG
ENGLAND
+44-01604-719413
s.bannister@open.ac.uk

Barber, Jim
Crystal Linen
CIS:75230,3644
Jlbarber@Wolfe.Net

Barlow, Chris
CIS:76440,1370

Barnes, I. D.
10 Birdwood Ave.
Springwood 2777 NSW
AUSTRALIA
+61-47-54-3266
Fax:+61-47-51-5946

Barnes, Nic
CHC Software
27 West Park
London SE9 4RZ
ENGLAND
+44-81-694-0110
Fax:+44-81-692-3555
CIS:100111,3452

Barrett, David
UK
CIS:100010,2171 .

Barrett, Jim
CIS:72417,627

Barrett, Simon
The Barn, Cwm Camlais
recon, Powys, LD3 8TD
UNITED KINGDOM
44-0-874-636835
CIS:100102,1247

Basic Code Cache
P.O. Box 507
Sandy Hook CT 06482

Basically Visual Magazine
P.O.Box 1214
York, PA 17405-1214

Bassal, Thomas
Bavariaring 41
80336 Muenchen
GERMANY
+49-89-772291
Fax:+49-89-772291
CIS:100276,1324

BeCubed Software Inc.
1750 Marietta Hwy Ste. 240
Canton GA 30114
770-720-1077
Fax:770-720-1078
bill@becubed.com

Beach, Chris
CIS:100436,172

Bear Hug, The
1031 Waltway
Houston, Texas 77008

Bebber, Douglas A.
2420 Briar Oak Circle
Sarasota, FL 34232
941-377-4705
CIS:72123,3661
dbtech@ibm.net

Becker, Jeff
4880-8 Dorsey Hall Drive
Ellicott City MD 21042

Becker, Thomas
CIS:73473,1363

Beekes, Bernd
Eugen Haas GmbH & Co.
KG
Gummersbacher Str. 44-48
D 5270 Gummersbach
GERMANY
CIS:100031,2063
49-2261-55369

Behling, Jutta
CIS:100524,3121

Bencivengo, Nicholas Jr.
Simple Solutions, Inc.
10 Older Orchard Road
Clinton CT 06413
CIS:71344,2415

Benedict, Chuck
1503 Clear Valley
Houston TX 77014
CIS:73672,1662

Benignitas
Benignitas@aol.com

Benito, Daniel
Soto Hidalgo, 8
28042 Madrid
SPAIN
CIS:100022,141

**Bennet-Tec Information
Serv.**
10 Steuben Drive
Jericho, NY 11753
516-433-6283
Fax:516-822-2679
CIS:71201,1075

Bennis, Robert G.
rgb7795@aol.com

Bercik, Bill
Snooky@aol.com

Bergmann, Ken
B Elegant Software
P.O. Box 264
Issaquah WA 98027
206-557-4279
CIS:74441,163

Bergmann-Terrell, Eric
CIS:73667,3517

Besset, Mark
CIS:72370,1773

Beyer, Wolfgang
Beyer@Lrz-Muenchen.De

Big Dog Software
Att: Daniel Rogers
25 Shirley Parkway
Piscataway NJ 08854
908-885-1513
CIS:70744,1624

Biggins, Aidan
CIS:100010,1257

BillT121
BillT121@aol.com

Biney, Dr. B
12 Birling Road
Ashford, Kent
TN24 8BB
GREAT BRITAIN
CIS:100111,2330

Bish Programming
5725 San Gabriel Court
Sacramento CA 95842

Bishop, Shawn
Shortdog Inc.
241 Eversole St.
Hazard, KY 41701
606-439-0609

Bits & Bytes Solutions
615 Bellevue Avenue East
#102
Seattle, WA 98102
206-328-1523
Fax:206-328-1523
CIS:72603,1674

Blaum, Greg
CIS:71212,1763

Blaylock, Don
CIS:73132,1073

Blessing, John
Leigh Business Enterprises
CIS:100444,623

Bliss, Steve
CIS:75620,47

Blue Lagoon Software
6047 Tampa Ave., Suite 209
Tarzana CA 91356
818-345-2200
Fax:818-345-8905
BBS:818-343-8433
CIS:70152,1601

Blue Sky Software
7486 La Jolla Blvd., Ste. 3
La Jolla, CA 92037
619-459-6365
800-677-4946
Fax:619-459-6366

Bokai Corporation
1221 Dundix Rd. #106
Mississauga ON L4Y 3Y9
CANADA
CIS:75333,1235

Bonincontri, Michael
Mboninco@aol.com

Bonner, Paul
C/O PC/Computing
Magazine
950 Tower Lane 20th Floor
Foster City CA 94404
CIS:76000,13

Book Stacks BBS
BBS:216-861-0469

Borland
100 Borland Way
Scotts Valley CA 95066
408-431-1000 800-331-0877
Fax:408-439-9119
BBS:408-439-9096

Bostwick, Marshall
927 East Smith Road
Medina, OH 44256
216-864-1778
CIS:76646,2552

Bourderson, Benjamin
9, Rue Magenta
69100 Villeurbanne
FRANCE

Bowker, Bob
2811 La Cuesta Drive
Los Angeles CA 90046
213-851-5298
CIS:70250,306

Braeuchi, Jakob
Bottigenstr. 102
CH-3018 Bern
SWITZERLAND
+31-3331254
CIS:100014,567

Bragg, Gregory
#1208, 35 Esterbrooke Ave.
Willowdale
Toronto ON M2J 2C6
416-399-0995
Fax:416-497-9314
CIS:75027,2674

Brant, Kyle
5441 Fenmore Road
Indianapolis, IN 46208
317-297-9801
CIS:74220,2420

Bridge, Inc.
Att: Larry Rebich
913 Hacienda Way
Millbrae, CA 94030
415-737-0870
Fax:415-737-0871
CIS:71662,205

Bridges, Steve
76 Nash Street
New Haven CT 06511
CIS:71507,1033

Briggs, Ryan
433 E. Deepdale Rd.
Phoenix AZ 85022
pryan@netcom.com

Broeze, Arjen
SheAr Software
Gronausevoetpad 104
7511 BN Enschede
HOLLAND
Vbx_Dev@Shear.Iaf.Nl

Brown, Jon
CIS:100433,2770

Brown, Martin
Amersham UK
UK
CIS:100014,1354

Brown, Matthew
CIS:73134,2147
Matth20005@aol.com

Brown, Richard
1943 Fowl Rd. Apt. C-5
Elyria OH 44035
CIS:70674,1227

Brown, Tim
CSO
13715 NE 36th Place
Bellevue WA 98005
CIS:73557,3461

Bryte Ideas Software
18557 Caminito Pasadero
Suite 388
San Diego CA 92128

Buchholz, Elliot C.
CIS:71034,2464

Buhrer, Richard
CIS:70671,1501

Bunton, Vernon
263 San Jose Drive
Novato CA 94949
415-883-1503

Burgess, Mike
287 S. Chadwick Cirle
American Fork UT 84003
MikeB41@aol.com

Burke, Eric
1617 Oakland Ave.
Mt. Vernon IL 62864
Ericburke@aol.com

Burnham, Gordon
631 Iroquois Avenue
Louisville KY 40214-1226
502-363-5136

Bystrom, Dan
+46-708-68-65-78
Fax:+46-457-274-81

Bytech Business Systems, Inc.
5C Medical Park Dr.
Pomona, NY 10970
914-354-8666

Bytes & Letters
Hilger Software Technology
Postfach 16 27
66716 Saarlouis
GERMANY
+49-6831-506534
Fax:+49-6831-506634
CIS:100275,3554

CC Advies
PO Box 351
3940 AL DOORN
NETHERLANDS

CMC Systems
CIS:73577,1416

CRA
9814 Indian Qn Pt. Rd.
Ft. Washington MD 20744
CIS: 102136.3077

Cactus Development Inc.
7113 Burnet Road Suite 214
Austin, TX 78757-2216
Orders:800-336-9444
512-453-2244
Fax:512-453-3757
CIS:72662,1356

Caladonia Systems, Inc.
P.O. Box 1954
Tacoma WA 98401-1954
306-468-4700 800-650-4116
Fax:306-468-4717
info@caladonia.com

Camarillo Technology
CIS:102425,2531

Campbell, George
1472 Sixth St.
Los Osos CA 93402
CIS:71571,222 BBS:805-528-3753

Carr, J. Frank
685 Kenneth Lane
Norcross, GA 30093
404-880-5762 CIS:
75120,2420

Carter, Ian
Timeamber Limited
34 Park View
Sheffield S31 8SE
ENGLAND
+44=0=1909-773689
CIS:100435,3040

Catalyst Software
56925 Yucca Trail #254ucca
Valley CA 92284
619-228-9653
Fax:619-369-1185
CIS:72202,1427
cary@catsoft.com

Cath, Jeremy E.
Stoke Cottage, Marsh Lane
Taplow, Maidenhead
Berkshire, SL6 0DF
UK
+44-628-789229
CIS:100315,521

Caughran, Mike
Cedar Island Software
9018 Division St.
Juneau Alaska 99801
CIS:71034,2371

CenterView Software
651 Gateway Boulevard
S.1050
South San Francisco CA
94080
415-266-7060
800-4-CHOREO
Fax:415-266-7065
CIS:74504,2530

Chambers, Lennox
#61 - 10111 Swinton Cres.
Richmond BC V7A 3S9
CANADA

Chameleon Group
2335 Hazy Creek
Houston TX 77084
713-647-6539
Fax:713-647-6295
TheGroup@aol.com

Chapman, Mike
Chapter One / TechDesign
27 Gorse Drive
Smallfield, Surrey, RH6 9GJ
ENGLAND
CIS:100030,351
Fax:+44-1342-844507

Chavez, Steven R.
706 Spinnaker Drive
Perris, CA 92571

Chevron, Denis
102 Rue De Maubeuge
75010 Paris
FRANCE
+33-1-40726483
CIS:100333,27

Chiselbrook, Craig
5 Cliff Drive
Avon CT 06001-3413
CIS:74650,3571
CraigC@ziplink.net

Chiselbrook, Craig
5 Cliff Drive
Avon CT 06001-3413
CIS:74650,3571
craigchis@aol.com

Cilwa, Paul A.
CIS:74362,2653

Clark Software
P.O. Box 1458
Gig Harbor WA 98335
206-858-8362
Fax:206-858-2977

Clark, Jim
1468 Woodland Ave.
Woodburn OR 97071
abracadab@aol.com

Clark, Paul
CIS:73123,1700

Clarkson, Charles K.
CIS:76744,466

Clay, Jason
C/O Innovative Tech Inc.
4108 Dilts Lane
Bridgewater NJ 08807
CIS: 75453.3331

Coggin, Daniel
RR1 Box 3455
Ft. White FL 32038
Chrome451@aol.com

Collado, Louis
3616 Willow Lake Court
St. Cloud, FL 34769-6506

Collier/Rother, Jim
CIS:71064,130

Colton, J. E.
2 Lessingham Road
Widnes
Cheshire WA8 9FU
ENGLAND

Componere Software
1381 Kildaire Farm Rd.
#119
Cary NC 27511-5525
componere@aol.com

Computer Interface Design

Inc.
C/O Harry Stinson
2302 Fix Fire Ct.
Reston VA 22091-4605
703-264-7869 800-663-
2401

Computer Mindware Corp.
36 Trinity Place
E. Hanover, NJ 07936
201-884-1123
CIS:76615,2564

**Computer Technologies,
Inc.**
PO Box 8927
Greensboro NC 27419-0927
704-634-1766
Fax:704-634-1772
CIS:71163,2657

Cornish, Randy
847-843-8870
CIS:74124,2050

Covell, Stephen E.
CIS:75010,3700

Cramp, Stephen
Dolphin Systems
13584 Kennedy Rd. N.
Inglewood Ontario
L0N 1K0
CANADA
905-838-2896
Fax:905-838-0649
CIS:70471,137
Stephenc@Idirect.com

Crawford, Ross
3/73 Ripley Road
West Monnah 7009
AUSTRALIA
CIS:100354,677

Crazy Rides
Gerry Kichok
60 Bristol Road East
Suite 221
Mississauga ON L4Z 3K8
CANADA
905-712-9824
Fax:905-712-9824
CIS:74072,3600

Creativision Graphics
David Balmer
817-656-5970
Fax:817-656-7794
CIS:70404,3014
CVPsupport@aol.com

Crescent Software Inc.
11 Bailey Avenue
Ridgefield CT 06877
203-438-5300 800-35-
BASIC
Fax:203-431-4626
CIS:72657,3070

Crouse, Aaron P.
422 S. Weyant Ave.
Columbus OH 43213
614-235-5341
CIS:72123,1243
aaroncr@aol.com

Crygier, Ed
1010 W. Firestone Dr.
Hoffman Estates, IL 60195

Crystal Services
Suite 2200
1050 West Pender Street
Vancouver BC V6E 3S7
CANADA
604-681-3435
604-681-2934
800-877-2340
CIS:71035,2430

Cunday, Richard
Colorado Information Eng.
CIS:72520,3711

Curran, James M.
18 John St. #2-B
Bloomfield NJ 07003-5149
CIS:72261,655

Curtram Consulting
200 Yorkland Blvd.
Suite 801
Toronto Ontario M2J 5C1
CANADA
416-502-1311
Fax:416-502-1345

Curzon, Richard
9 Manser Court
Ajax, Ontario
L1T 3C5
CANADA
CIS:71371,2521

Cutting Edge Consulting Inc.
317 Bennington Hills Ct.
West Henrietta NY 14586
716-271-6391
CIS:74362,2163

Cycloid Software
371 Elan Village Lane
Suite 408
San Jose CA 95134
Fax:408-432-7423
sales@cycloid.com

Cz Software Corporation
Deerr-Lord, Jacque
7276 NE 122nd Street
Kirkland WA 98034
206-820-6107
Fax:206-814-2980
CIS:75260,732
Czsoft@Halcyon.com

DB Technologies
Attn: Douglas A. Bebber
2420 Briar Oak Circle
Sarasota FL 34232
813-378-3760 expired
CIS:72123,3661

Dacon, Tom
CIS:71062,426

Dameware Development
1024 Live Oak Loop
Mandeville LA 70448
504-626-7545
Fax:504-626-1189
dameware@ni-inc.com

Darlington, Stephen
5 Clowser Close
Wintergardens Sutton
Surrey
SM1 4TP
UNITED KINGDOM
+44-0181-643-8078
Fax:+44-0181-770-3644
tcrstephen@epidem.icr.ac.uk

Dart Communications
6647 Old Thompson Rd.
Syracuse NY 13211
315-431-1024
Fax:315-431-1025
sales@dart.com

Dass, Beena
Graphic Solutions
P.O. Box 784
Westport CT 06881-0784

Data Preference
27226 Lawrence Drive
Dearborn Heights MI 48127
313-278-4187
CIS:70162,1037

DataObjects Inc.
2975 Valley Creek Rd.
Culleoka TN 38451
615-987-0421
Fax:615-987-0421

DataSys Pty Ltd
GPO Box 9635
HONG KONG
+852-2987-4914
CIS:100452,472

DataTools
800-987-0421
615-987-0421

Davidsaver, Mark
213 S. Park Street
Bishop Hill, IL 61419

Davis, Mike
CIS:73122,1474
VDGMike@aol.com

De Bruijn, Michiel
P.O. Box 22396
NL-3003 DL
ROTTERDAM
NETHERLANDS
CIS:100021,1061
Mdb@Vbd.Nl

De Herrera, Felix
13215-C8 SE Mill Plain
Suite 186
Vancouver WA 98684
felixd@teleport.com

De Palma, John R
CIS:76076,571

DeBacker, Greg
CIS:71042,36

Dean Software Design
P.O. Box 2331
Everett WA 98203-0331

Dean, Andrew S.
946 Glen Arden Way, NE
Atlanta, GA 30306
404-874-6938
Fax:404-872-2980
CIS:71233,1412

Decker, Mike
CIS:70651,50

Deleau, Jean-Marie
92 rue En Bois
4000 - LIEGE
BELGIUM
djm@infoboard.be

Delta Soft Inc.
12 Danton Court
Ajax, Ontario L1S 3G1
CANADA
416-619-2018
CIS:70404,655

Denenberg, Steve
CIS:71630,1265

Denicomp Systems
P.O. Box 731
Exton PA 19341
CIS:71612,2333

Denihan, Timothy J.
3721 LAkecrest Dr.
Grapevine TX 76051
817-488-7630
Fax:817-640-7426
CIS:70600,745
tdenihan@mail.gte.net

Desaware
1100 E. Campbell
Campbell CA 95008
408-377-4770
Fax:408-371-3530
CIS:74431,3535
support@desaware.com

Deutch, Jim
CIS:73313,2327

DevSoft Inc.
P.O. Box 13821
Research Triangle Pk NC
27709
Fax:919-493-5805
CIS:75244,2736
Devsoft@aol.com

Dexter, Matthew
dexter@chem.surrey.ac.uk

Dexter, Walter F.
2530 Westlake Ave.
Peoria IL 61615
CIS:76450,663
wfd@prairienet.org

Di Bacco, Daniel
Huttenstr. 12
97072 Wirtzburg
GERMANY
CIS:100140,1156

DiBiasio, Mark
C/O Software City
15958-B Shady Grove Road
Gaithersburg, MD 20877
301-670-0818
Fax:301-330-5087

Dickinson, Don
5229 6th St. NE
Minneapolis MN 55421
CIS:72762,645

Dickson, David
CIS:73477,221

Diettrich, Dr. Hans-Peter
Weissenuburgster. 2 C
D-70018 Stuttgart
GERMANY

Digital PowerTOOLS
P.O. Box 97794
Jackson, MS 39288-7794
601-932-5931
CIS:74547,23
Vernon486@aol.com

Dilley, John J., CCP
26210 Pacific Highway
South
Kent, WA 98032

Dirigible Software
310-614-9466
PROGRAM396@aol.com

Disk And Desk Software
C/O Richard Ratayczak
3360 South 12th Street
Milwaukee, WI 53215
414-483-7702
CIS:71524,2416 BBS:414-
242-2329 rickr@execpc.com

Dolan, Bob
P.O. Box 16514
Rochester, NY 14616-0514
716-865-8248
CIS:71075,3256
bdolan@Rochgte.fidonet.org

Dombroski, Bob
215-287-6484

Dompier, Jim
CIS:73501,445

Dompier, Jim
IslandSoft
5333 Likini St. #1906
Honolulu HI 96818
Fax:808-836-3304
CIS:73501,445
Islesoft@Lava.Net

Dooley, Sharon F.
CIS:70740,2330

Dovcom
P.O. Box 580
Provo UT 84603-0580
801-221-4527
CIS:74552,1027

Dover, Bob
Visual Developers Group
CIS:73302,1357

Dragon Software
P.O. Box 299
Lumberport WV 26386
304-584-4143 BBS:304-
363-2252
dsoftware@aol.com

Duhamel, Guy
CIS:100334,2130

Durocher, James
5140 Farm Ridge Place
Colorado Springs CO 80917
CIS:76061,3515
JDurocher@aol.com

E & B Systems
957 Johnson Street
Elmira NY 14901
Mikepark@Ix.Netcom.com

ETN Corporation
RD4 Box 659
Montoursville PA 17754
717-435-2202
Fax:717-435-2802

Early Morning Software
Attn: Ted Stockwell
3544 W. 83rd Pl.
Chicago, IL 60652
312-925-1628
CIS:74454,1002

Eastern Digital Resources
P.O. Box 1451
Clearwater SC 29822-1451
706-855-2397
Fax:706-737-2336
JohnR238@aol.com

Easy Software
3 Brookside Court
Prestbury Road
Macclesfield SK10 3BR
UNITED KINGDOM
+44-1625-614669
CIS:100410,717

Eclipse Software

Programming
1108B Waverly St.
Framingham MA 01701
508-620-2831
Fax:508-620-2831
paulw@tiac.net

Educational & Business Systems
957 Johnson Street
Elmira NY 14901
CIS:71003,1670
Mikepark@Ix.Netcom.com

Eibl, Gunter
BUG Basic User Group
Feldstrasse 18
D-8012 Ottobrunn /
Munich
GERMANY
+011-49-89-609-7046
Fax:+011-49-89-609-8229
CIS:10012,1323

Eisenberg, David F.
CIS:71662,47

Eka
CIS:72560,1630

Eke, Richard
CIS:100031,233

Elkins, Jeff
3651 Greenbriar Drive
Columbia, SC 29206
GEnie:J.ELKINS1

Embrey, Leland E.
Lemming Labs
26910 Glen Place
Carmel, CA 93923
408-595-6353
CIS:73131,50

Emke, Aaron
CIS:76065,3376

Endorphin Software
65 Uplands
Brecon, Powys LD3 9HS
UNITED KINGDOM
davegizmo@aol.com

English, Donald R.
5526 North Salina
Wichita, Kansas 67204
CIS:70724,2576

Enterprise Software
3930 Turnbridge Ct. Suite 203
Brunswick OH 44212
EnterSware@aol.com

Esanbock, Douglas
PO Box 395
Spring Valley WI 54767
esanbock@slip.net

Eschalon Development Inc.
110-2 Renaissance Sq.
New Westminster BC
V3M 6K3
CANADA
604-520-1543
CIS:76625,1320

Eschalon Development, Inc.
24-2979 Panorama Drive
Coquitlam BC V3E 2W8
CANADA
604-945-3198
CIS:76625,1320

Esterling, Rick
Three Cruse Alley
Huntsville, AL 35801
CIS:73322,702

European Software Connection
P.O. Box 1982
Lawrence, KS 66044-1982
913-832-2070
Fax:913-832-8787

Evers, Dave
500 Larch Rd. #58
Quincy, IL 2301
217-224-3615
M

Exile Software
CIS:100267,546
Scling@Hk.Super.Net

Extreme Software
15059 North 59th Way
Scottsdale AZ 85254-2397
602-996-9773
extremesoft@aol.com

Eye Can Publishing
Bob Parsons, PO Box 501
Dee Why Beach
Sydney 2099
AUSTRALIA
+61-02-9982-5750
Fax:+61-02-439-2379
CIS:100017,222

FAR, Inc.
Attn: John Fleming
P.O. Box 202
Oak Forest, IL 60452
CIS:70043,1652

FMS, Inc.
8027 Leesburg Pike
Suite 410
Vienna, VA 22182
703-356-4700
Fax:703-448-3861
CIS:73710,463

Faarvang, Jakob
Kirkebjerg 2
5690 Tommerup
DENMARK
jakobf@colossus.ping.dk

Falconer, Jay J.
Bitwise Software
International
CIS:72074,2677

FarPoint Technologies, Inc.
133 Southcenter Court, #100
Morrisville NC 27560
919-460-1887 800-645-5913
Fax:919-460-7606
BBS:919-460-5771

Farber, Ryan
ragna@aol.com

Fashenpour, Dave
Entity Master Systems
714 Regency Court
Friendswood TX 77546
713-996-0819
CIS:76461,241

Fawcette Technical Publication
280 Second St. #200
Los Altos CA 94022-3603
415-917-7650
Fax:415-688-1812

Febish, George J.
ObjectSoft Corporation
201-816-8900

Federal Hill Software
Attn: Mike Himowitz
P.O.Box 765
Owings Mills MD 21117
800-846-4319 410-356-5592 CIS:71655,1327

Fehr, Andreas
Neudoftstr. 15
8810 Horgen
SWITZERLAND
CIS:100042,2070
afehr@itr.ch

Feller, Bob
Robert.Feller@MCI.com

Fenestra Software L.L.C.
P.O. Box 87347
Phoenix AZ 85080-7347
CIS:70176,264
jcs@primenest.com

Ferguson, Jim
5016-4 Hunt Club Road
Wilmington NC 28403
919-799-4396
CIS:71477,2345

Fillion, Pierre
8460 Perras Apt. #1
Montreal, Quebec
H1A 5C7
CANADA
CIS:71162,51

Fineware Systems
P.O. Box 75776
Oklahoma City OK 73147
CIS:70650,2022
Prodigy:BBTK05A
vbal@aol.com

Fishinghawk, James
2922 W Evergreen
Visalia, CA 93277
jhawk@psnw.com
jhawk@edstar.gse.ucsb.edu

Fletcher, David
P.O. Box 12041
Shawnee Mission KS
66282-2041

Forbes, Garry
P.O. Box 60096
Sunnyvale, CA 94088-0096
CIS:76207,333

Force 12
78 Broad Street
New London, CT 06320
203-444-7954
Fax:203-437-8242
CIS:70740,2472

Ford, Nelson
PO Box 35705
Houston TX 77235-5705
CIS:71355,470

Foster, Brett
RR #2
Almonte, Ontario
K0A 1A0
CANADA

Four Lakes Computing
Attn. Eugene Nelson
1238 Williamson #2
Madison WI 53703
608-256-3382
CIS:70662,2501

Fox, Peter
2 Tees Close
Witham, Essex CM8 1LG
ENGLAND
+44-376-517-206
CIS:100116,1031
peter@pfox.demon.co.uk

Franklin, Carl
Visual Basic Programmers
299 California Ave. #120
Palo Alto, CA 94306-1912

Freel, Fred
CIS:70642,673

Freeman-Teresa Software
GPO Box 712
Broadway NSW 2007
AUSTRALIA
+61-2-2116314
CIS:100351,3364
tongk@arch.su.edu.au

Friend, Jonathan
CIS:101331,3160

Fry, Brian W.
213 Fox Run
Huntington, CT 06484
203-571-5206
CIS:70732,1327

Full Sail Software
6324 Canyon Circle
Ft. Worth, TX 76133
817-292-1852
Fax:817-292-1176
CIS:73521,3353
carlp12@aol.com

Fundamental Objects Inc.
www.software.net

Funk, Keith B.
CIS:72240,2020

GC Consulting Services Ltd.
Fellsgarth House
Hognaston, Ashbourne,
Derbyshire, DE6 1PR
ENGLAND
+44-335-370562
Fax:370562
CIS:100113,2774

GRAFtech Devel. Corp.
PO Box 851228
Westland MI 48185
517-487-2780
Fax:313-595-3180
CIS:75210,3335

Gagliano, Jim
Rochester NY
CIS:74017,3342

Galaxy Software
7044 St. Joe Road
Fort Wayne IN 46835
Galaxysoft@Msn.com
CIS:102167,2656

Gallino, Jeff
3306 Lagoon Ave.
Atwater CA 95301

Gamber, Mark
18 Village Dr.
Lancaster PA 17601
CIS:76450,2754 expired

Gamesman Inc.
1161 McMillan Avenue
Winnipeg MT R3M 0T7
CANADA
204-475-7903
Fax:204-284-3307
CIS:75201,3524

Gan Hui Mei
445 Xun Yang New
Shanghai 200061
CHINA

Gandolf Development
205-991-5920
CIS:74551,1345

Garrison, Gary P.
Software Assist Corporation
75 Maryland Ave. South
Golden Valley MN
55426-1544
612-541-0144
CIS:76400,3555

Gatti, Alessandro
2515 Scott Street
San Francisco, CA
94115-1149
415-567-6659
Fax:415-567-1362
CIS:71564,1470

Gaughan, John
John456@aol.com

Genesis Software
C/O Rob Jones
2709 Penny Lane
McKinney TX 75070
CIS:75070,2615

Gentils, David M.
D & L Tech Services
239 William Street
West Haven CT 06516
CIS:75543,1402

GeoDuck Systems
Att: Richard Buhrer
1202 East Pike St. Suite 665
Seattle WA 98122
206-324-9024
CIS:70671,1501

Germelmann, Christian
Am Glaskopf 26
D-35039 Marburg/Lahn
GERMANY
+49-6421-45457
CIS:100520,2644

Gernaey, Michael
gernaeym@mailhost.gate.net

Gerton, David
#8 Willowmere Road
Danville CA 94526

Gigasoft, Inc.
696 Lantana
Keller, TX 76248
817-431-8470
Fax:817-431-9860

Giordano, Alfred J.
One Freeland Street
Monroe NY 10950
914-783-2526
CIS:76407,143

Giovine, Gabriele del
CIS:72660,1344

Global Majik Software
P.O. Box 322
Madison AL 35758
205-864-0708
Fax:205-864-0708
CIS:73261,3642
gms@globalmajic.com

Goldfarb, David
3595 Tilden Avenue
Los Angeles CA 90034

Gordon
CIS:72567,3416

Gorman, Robert
CIS:75010,754

Gottlieb, Daniel
1262 Bramble Road
Atlanta GA 30329
CIS:73552,1460

Gottschalk, Jeff
02065 Minster-Egypt Road
Minster, Ohio 45365
CIS:72322,1741

Gotz, Steven
CIS:70563,207

Gouge, David W.
Rt. 2 Box 22209
Show Low AZ 85901
daveg@whitemtns.com

Gower, Mathew W.
P.O. Box 824
Ridgely MD 21660

Grabe, Marcus O. M.
Grabe Info-Tech
Artur-Kutscher-Platz 3
80802 Muenchen
GERMANY
+49-89-346916
Fax:+49-89-346918
CIS:100120,1405

Gradowski, Mark D.
CIS:73013,244

Graff, George W.
121 Easy Hammaker Street
Thurmont MD 21788
Vbgeorge@Paonline.com

Graham, Glenn
CIS:72662,2733

Graphical Bytes
P.O. Box 2
Southampton, NY 11969-0002
516-283-4473

Graves, Michael Love
CIS:72240,1123

Great Lakes Business Solutions
39905 Lotzford, Suite 200
Canton MI 48187
313-981-4970
Fax:313-981-9746
BBS:810-363-6418
CIS:75111,606

Green, William
CIS:71203,1414

GreenTree Technologies
25 Voorhis Dr.
Old Bethpage NY 11804
CIS:71222,3352

Greenleaf Software, Inc.
16479 Dallas Parkway
Suite 570
Dallas TX 75248
214-248-2561 800-523-9830 BBS:250-3778
Fax:214-248-7830
info@gleaf.com

Grey Parrot Software
Att: Kenneth G. Long
7602-D Pinery Way
Tampa FL 33615
CIS:74452,263

Grier, Dick
CIS:76244,1145

Griffith, Matthew W.
CIS:76531,2651

Group Benefits Shoppers
2500 Central Ave. Suite G
Boulder CO 80303
303-449-4897
Fax:303-449-0797
CIS:70632,1264
gbs@rmii.com

Guardalben, Giovanni
Hi.T Srl
Via Carlo Steeb, 7
37122 Verona
ITALY
+39-45-592966

Guimond, Stephen C.
CIS:70253,502

Guttilia, Brad
4718 Hummingbird Dr.
Waldorf MD 20603
CIS:73051,1761

Guttilla, Brad
4718 Hummingbird Dr.
Waldorf MD 20603
CIS:73051,1761
bfguttilla@aol.com
bfgut@ix.netcom.com

Guy, Edward
1752 Duchess Avenue
West Vancouver
British Columbia V7V 1P9
CANADA
604-926-1370
CIS:71750,1036

HDC Computer Corporation
6742 185th Avenue NE
Redmond, WA 98052
206-885-5550
Fax:206-881-9770

HELP Software
PO Box 1423
Raymore, MO 64083
816-331-5809
CIS:73720,2530

HSC Software Developers
317 Highway C
Chesterfield MO 63005
314-530-7647

Haduch, Robert Wydler
Friedheimstr. 24
CH-8057 Zurich
SWITZERLAND
+41-01-3121062
CIS:100116,3443

Hamilton, Peter
CIS:73774,3661

Hampshire Software
300 Washington Street #216
North Pembroke MA 02358
800-NetSoft
617-826-4208
Fax:617-826-4692
CIS:72607,3042

Hanlin III, Thomas G.
3544 E. Southern Ave #104
Mesa AZ 85204

Hansen, Mogens
Blogordsgade 14, 2 Th.
DK-2200 Copenhagen N
DENMARK
CIS:100277,2536

Hanson, Mark
PO Box 10154
Rochester, NY 14610-0154
CIS:72773,71

Hanson, Michael E.
CIS:75143,126

Harbolt, Martin L.
MartyDarts@aol.com

Harper, Thomas
33776 Robles Dr. Apt. A
Dana Point CA 92629
CIS:73122,2714
IMProg@aol.com

Harrich, Jack
CIS:76741,163

Harris, Dave
PO Box 27681
Fresno CA 93729

Haugland, Jan Steiner
Jan.Haugland@Uib.No

Hawkes, Peter R.
4 Highdown Drive
Littlehampton
BN17 6HJ
ENGLAND

Hayes, Brain C.
CIS:74653,1760

Haynes, Chris
1099 Mason Rd.
Ashby MA 01431
CIS:73642,3626

Hayward, John
CIS:100034,320

Hedtke, Lee
CIS:76323,1443

Hegerty, Chad
CIS:71212,1045
MSN:HegertyC

Hengelhaupt, Thomas
CIS:100120,115

Heritage Technology Solutions
1210 Goodman Ave.
Redondo Beach CA 90277
310-374-7748
Fax:310-372-5808
Joelyons@Netcom.com

Hernandez, J. M.
CIS:70323,1772

Herron, James
29 Duncryne Place
Bishopbriggs, Glasgow
G64 2DP
Scotland
UNITED KINGDOM
+44-41-762-0967
herron@comms.eee.strathcly
de.ac.uk

Heydman, Matthew
TheBigShoe@aol.com

Highsmith, J
Softcare Corp
Griffin, GA
404-412-0827
Fax:404-412-0827

Hilgart, John
29W527 Winchester #4
Warrenville, IL 60555

Himmer, Eric F.
CIS:75540,1770

Himpe, Vincent
A.Detayelaan 12
8792 Desselgem
BELGIUM
vi_himpe@mietec.be
vincent.himpe@ping.be

Hipp, Frank
Fhipp@aol.com

Hipp, Frank
fhipp@aol.com

Hite, David
CIS:72130,2400

Hoag, Steve
CIS:74514,1705

Hocker, Paul
CIS:73521,2055

Hoeltge, Chris
Greenwich Financial
Modeling
55 Broad St. 14th Floor
New York, NY 10004

Hohl, Alfred
CIS:100601,1404

Holland, Sarah
3 - 2176 West 13th Avenue
Vancouver, B.C.
V6K 2S1
CANADA
CIS:70620,1425

Holupka, Andrew P.
4850 White Cloud Rd.
Leechburg, PA 15656
aph@slip.net

Homegrown Software
Attn: Marshall Bostwick
1601 West 350 North, #3
West Lafayette, IN 47906
CIS:76646,2552

Hopkins, Geoff
6 School Road
Upper Beeding
Steyning, West Sussex
BN44 EHY
ENGLAND
CIS:100064,3722

Hot Chilli Software
CIS:100035,3510

Houtari, Scott
scotth@wagged.com

Hudson, James A.
12721 S.E. 172 St.
Renton WA 98058
CIS:75317,232
JHoudini@aol.com

Hunt, Rick
CIS:100307,2062

Huntington Software
9152 Brabham Drive
Huntington Beach CA
92646
CIS:72040,1640

Huon, Benoit
38 Rue De Guy Bres
B-7000 MONS
BELGIUM

Hutchings, Donathan
Hutchings Computer
Consulting
105 Scarborough Circle
New Market AL 35761

Hutmacher, Dave Th.
Zurich
SWITZERLAND
CIS:100012,74

Hyperion Microsystems
P.O. Box 243
Edmonds, WA 98020
CIS:76370,3353

I.I.G. Development Ltd.
Suite 701, 1633 West 10th
Ave.
Vancouver BC V6J 2A2
CANADA

IRIS Media Systems
1684 Locust St. Suite #125
Walnut Creek, CA
510-256-4673
Fax:510-256-6353

ISES, Inc.
102 Sunrise Drive
Gillette NJ 07933
Fax:908-580-1008
CIS:72417,627

ISNT Limited
104 Railway Street
Hertford SG13 7BN
CIS:100331,1523

ISbiSTER International
1314 Cardigan Ave.
Garland TX 75040

Ideal Engineering Software
#29 - 8560 162nd Street
Surrey BC V4N 1B4
CANADA
604-572-8614
CIS:76625,2337

ImageFX
3021 Brighton-Henrietta
Rd.
Rochester, NY 14623
716-272-8030 800-229-
8030 F:272-1873
CIS:76327,251
imagefx@eznet.net

ImageSoft Inc.
2 Haven Avenue
Port Washington NY 11050
516-767-2233 800-245-
8840
Fax:516-767-9067

In Touch Software
27934 Redwood Glen Road
Valencia, CA 91354
CIS:75330,746

InData
c/o Dean Audirsch
P.O. Box 9786
College Station TX 77842
CIS:73553,462

Indigo Rose Corporation
P.O. Box 2281
Winnipeg, MB R3C 4A6
CANADA
800-665-9668
204-668-8180
Fax:204-661-6904
Support@IndigoRose.mb.ca

Indra Technology, Inc.
8380 Miramar Mall #222
San Diego CA 92121
800-735-7776
Fax:619-558-1760
CIS:74214,1576

**Influential Technologies,
Inc.**
P.O.Box 2847
Southfield MI 49037

InfoSoft
P.O. Box 782057
Wichita, KS 67278-2057
414-282-0535
Fax:414-282-3321
CIS:70403,3412

Infobase
Skiba-Information
Technologygy
Neuheim 17
48553 Mnnster
GERMANY
+49-251-3111-484
Fax:+49-251-381-611
CIS:100034,3527

Infocomm(UK) Ltd.
Southbank House
Black Prince Road
London SE1 7SJ
UNITED KINGDOM

Inlog
P.O. Box 62054
La Perade, Ste-Foy, Quebec
G1W 4Z2
CANADA
inlog@microtec.ca

Innovation West
2275 Huntington Drive,
Suite 265
San Marino CA 91108
818-309-6085
Fax:818-309-9972
innovwest@aol.com

Innovative Solutions &
Technology
904 Jefferson Avenue
Joplin, MO 64801
417-781-3282
Fax:417-781-3299
CIS:74777,2651

Inspired MultiMedia Inc.
6284 San Ignacio Ave. Ste. E
San Jose CA 95119
408-281-0996
CIS:73523,752

Instance Corporation
206-836-0111
800-494-0550

Integrated Data Systems,
Inc.
23875 Ventura Blvd. #102
Calabasas CA 91302
818-223-3344
Fax:818-223-3341
CIS:73700,1622

IntegrationWare, Inc.
2149 Kenton Lane
Green Oaks, IL 60048

InterGroup Technologies
206-643-8089
Fax:206-643-6977
Outreach@World.Std.com

International Technology
36 Rue Cule
B-1410 Waterloo
BELGIUM
+32-0-2-353-17-12
Fax:+32-0-2-353-17-12
CIS:100427,400

Internet Software
Engineering
1120 22nd Avenue
Clarkston, WA 99403

Intersolv/Q+E Software
5540 Centerview Drive
Suite 324
Raleigh NC 27606
919-859-2220
800-547-PVCS
800-876-3101
Fax:919-859-9334

IntuiTech Systems, Inc.
5125 Walnut Dr.
Pleasant Hill IA 50317

Ippolito, Ian
4187 Brentwood Park Circle
Tampa, FL 33624
ILuvPasta7@AOL.COM

Irwin, Gregg
CIS:72450,676

Ivory Tower Software
Att: Richard Wagner
4319 W. 180th St.
Torrance CA 90504
310-370-7045
CIS:76427,2611

Iyer, Sunil
18 Chantry Close
Huncote, Leicester
LE9 6AE
ENGLAND

J&J Software
CIS:73474,3000

J&K Software Productions
7657 South 41st Street
Bellevue NE 68147
402-231-1292 Orders:800-
484-5833x2002
CIS:75507,1437

JOSWare, Inc.
25 Voorhis Dr.
Old Bethpage NY 11804
516-293-8915
CIS:71222,3522

JSD Software
Neumattstr. 26
CH-3127 Muhlethurnen
SWITZERLAND
+41-0-31-804-35-26
CIS:100410,2257

JSH Scientific
Joseph Hancock
425 8th Street NW #527
Washington, DC 20004
CIS:722030,1073

Jackson, Jacob A.
3897 Moran Way, Apt. A
Norcross GA 30092-2287

Jacques, Robert R.
Otium Corporation
773 Woodbriar Pl. S.W.
Calgary Alberta T2W 5Z3
CANADA
CIS:71610,1255

Jantzi, Steve
10 Homewood Ave.
Tavistock, Ontario
N0B 2R0
CANADA
519-655-2242

Jarvis, Jeffrey L.
CIS:72640,1141
jjarvis@ems.tdh.texas.gov

271

Jaster, John
Lake Arrowhead CA
CIS:73770,2233

Jeffery, John
CIS:100237,300
Fax:+61-7-841-1977

Jeffrey S. Hargett Consulting
3071 Providence Church Road
Climax NC 27233
jshargett@aol.com

Jiang, Jeng Long
PO Box 51731
Palo Alto CA 94303-9991

Jniblack
jniblack@ix.netcom.com

John Galt Software
P.O. Box 4417
Chicago, IL 60680-4417

Johnson, Nathaniel
CIS:73707,1166

Johnston, Robert J.
2017 Murchison Drive #15
Burlingame, CA 94010
415-697-1945
CIS:71611,1370

Johnston, Scott
CIS:72677,1570

Jones, Graham
44 Baynton Road
New Invention, Willenhall
West Midlands WV12 5AR
ENGLAND
CIS:100010,2164

Jones, Michael
CIS:73404,2202

Jones, Peter D.
Zero-1 Software Ltd.
53 Prestons Rd.,
PO Box 4475
Christchurch
NEW ZEALAND
+64-3-352-6481
CIS:100032,40
jonesp@zero-1.co.nz

Jones, Ron C.
CIS:75050,2615

Joussellin, Henri
3, Place Roger Salengro
44000 Nantes
FRANCE
+33-2-40480174
Fax:40480187 henryj@club-internet.fr CIS:100437,112

Joyce, Ben
CIS:100101,36

Juden, Eddie V.
PO Box 940062
Plano TX 75074
ejuden@airmail.net

Juden, Eddie
CIS:72154,1324

Jurcik, Hal
7819 S. Vanport Ave.
Whittier, CA 90606
CIS:71042,1566

Jwpc, Inc.
Att: Jeff Wilcox
4221 Locust Lane
Jackson MI 49201
jwpcemail@aol.com

KWG Software
+49-531-72982
CIS:100010,204
Kwg@Assi.S-Link.De

Kaenel, Brad
PC HELP-LINE
35250 Silver Leaf
Circleucaipa CA 92399
CIS:72357,3523

Kahn, Theodore
510-562-9900
Fax:562-9919
CIS:70353,2603
tedkahn@netcom.com

Kallonen, Jari
Sallinkatu 2 B 48
00250 Helsinki
FINLAND
CIS:100020,2452

Kappel, Jay
14629 Bodger Avenue
Hawthorne CA 90250

Kapune, Albert
Brunnenstrasse 1
4777 Welver
GERMANY
CIS:100010,2067

Karkada, Sudarshan
skarada@aol.com

Kaufman, Brad
1912 Stepping Stone Trail
Edmond OK 73013
CIS:76330,1156

Kaye, Harvey J.
633 Bay St.
Suite 1701
Toronto, Ontario M5G 2G4
CANADA
Fax:416-361-2883

Kearney, Stephen
4215 Terrace Street, #2
Oakland CA 94511
510-547-3189
neff123@garnet.berkeley.edu

Kennedy, Ian 'Ken'
ken@drl.ox.ac.uk

Kiehl, Thomas
P.O. Box 693
Indian Rocks Beach FL
34635
CIS:73215,427

Kienemund, Wilfried
Am Ginsterberg 11
40627 Duesseldorf
GERMANY
+49-211-203490
CIS:100015,2550

Kilgore, Tim
2601 S. Providence #40
Columbia MO 65203
314-442-5776
CIS:72760,1022

Kinasevych, Orest
502 Chestnut St. #34
Roselle Park NJ 07204
Fax:908-245-5120
CIS:71151,1457

Kitsos, Costas
CIS:73667,1755

**Klasman Quality
Consulting**
13 Vespa Lane
Nashua NH 03060
CIS:70233,1476
klasman@kqc.mv.com

Kligman, Rick
Golden Gate Software
3825 Baker Street
San Diego CA 92117-5706
619-483-8496
Fax:619-483-4651
CIS:75300,2530

Knippennerg, Jim
BusyWizard@aol.com

Knowledge Works, Inc.
att: Mark S. Burgess
4456 Vanderver Ave. Suite 6
San Diego CA 92120
619-528-1026
CIS:72220,2466

KnowledgeWorks
620 Rosal Way
San Rafael CA 94903-2926
CIS:72310,2614

Koch, Peter
1005 Segovia Circle
Placentia CA 92670
714-666-8250
CIS:74007,2450

Kochaniak, Grzegorz
gregko@kagi.com

Koffley, Tim
16614 SW 93 Ct
Miami FL 33157
CIS:70334,16
TimServo@aol.com

Kohn, Joseph
4333 Larchwood Circle NW
Canton OH 44718-2117
CIS:74641,116
JoeMKohn@aol.com

Koot, Andre
Jan Nieuwenhuyzenstraat 54
4818 RK Breda
NETHERLANDS
CIS:100120,2360

Kornbluth, Aaron
PCSI
383 Nordhoff Place, Suite
100
Englewood NJ 07631

Kostelecky, Will
6265 Columbia Road
Columbia, MD 21044

Kosten, Michael
8319 Jones Ave. NW
Seattle WA 98117
CIS:71520,161

Kraft, Rob and Jeff Trader
RobKraft@aol.com

Krausse, Ralph
Kustom Magic Software
CIS:71043,2434
rkrausse@world.std.com

Krouse, Donald
PO Box 3441
Everett WA 98203-8441

Krumsee, Art
CIS:76702,1526
art.krumsee@osu.edu

Krystal Cat Software
56 Almon Ave.
Brockton MA 02401
KrysCat@aol.com

Kubelka, Bob
Chrome Computing
Vista, CA
619-941-2893

LAN Services
219-P Berlin Road,
Suite 261
Cherry Hill NJ 08034
609-428-3633

LCI
Att: Rich Levin
PO Box 14546
Philadelphia PA 19115
215-887-8281
Fax:215-887-5485
CIS:72407,243
rblevin@msn.com

LDR Systems
PO Box 501109
Malabar FL 32950
407-726-1924
Fax:407-722-9758
CIS:102417,351

LEAD Technologies
900 Baxter Street
Charlotte, NC 28204
704-332-5532
800-637-4699x1
Fax:704-548-8161
CIS:71333.2237

Lake Forest Software
7300 N. Mona Lisa
Tucson AZ 85741
CIS:74361,22

Lake St. Clair Publishing
5421 Peninsula Drive SE
Olympia WA 98512
206-456-7000
Fax:206-456-7100
CIS:76376,737

Lambrellis, Michael
CIS:100406,2064

Landgrave, Tim
KiZAN Technologies, Inc.
200 Whittington Pkwy
#100A
Louisville KY 40222
800-223-8720
CIS:71760,12

Langley, Brent K.
CIS:70312,2142

Lapides Software Development
3508 Brenner Dr. N.W.
Calgary, AB T2L 1X9
CANADA
CIS:105333,3412
lapides@cadvision.com

Larcom And Young
P.O. Box 66379
Roseville MI 48066-6379
CIS:70555,312

Larcombe, Andrew
21 Marlborough Road
Ashford Middlesex
TW18 4XE
ENGLAND

Lassalle, Patrick
2, Rue Gutenberg
92100 Boulogne
FRANCE
+33-1-46-034220
CIS:100325,725

Lathrop, Steve
152 Crossbow Lane
Gaithersburg, MD 20878
CIS:70540,370

Leaning Birch Computer Cons.
225 Day's Ferry Road
Woolrich ME 04579
207-443-1664
CIS:72617,1770

Leckkett, Blaine
CIS:73730,761

Ledbetter, Keith
4240 Ketcham Drive
Chesterfield VA 23832
804-674-0780
CIS:72240,1221
GEnie:ORION.MICRO

Lee, Joseph
CIS:74013,3316

Lee, Michael
CIS:100431,3026

Lee, Michaelx
CIS:75720,1221
michael.lee@execnet.com

Lee, Tony
P. O. Box 5152
Katy TX 77491-5152
713-395-0345
Fax:713-395-0345
70531,1066

Lehman, Jeff
Jwlehman@Coastalnet.com

Leigh Business Enterprises
2 Dorland Gardens, Totton
Hampshire S040 8WR
UK
lbe@compuserve.com

Leithauser Research
4649 Van Kleech Dr.
New Smyrna Beach FL
32169

Leong, Mabel
21 Meadowbank
Hitchin Herts
SG4 0HX
UK
+44-1462-454703
CIS:100332,3614

Levy, Ronald S., M.D.
110-21 73rd Rd.
Forest Hills NY 11375
CIS:102065,736

Lewellen, Kirk
107 Juliet Ave.
Murfreesboro TN 37130
BBS:615-890-8715

Lewis, Tony
CIS:73357,1730

Liblick, Dathan
CIS:74663,1364

Liebowitz, Jay
CIS:72733,1601

Liedtke, Brian
Phillip-Weber-Strasse 44A
D-63477 Maintal
GERMANY
+49-6181-47710
Fax:+49-6181-432252
CIS:100140,2534

Lifeboat Publishing
1163 Shrewsbury Ave.
Shrewsbury NJ 07702
908-389-0037
800-447-1955
Fax:908-389-9227
BBS:908-389-9783

Ling, Sui
Exile Software
2816 Shaye Lane
Ft. Worth TX 76112
CIS:100267,546

Little, Thomas
CIS:100016,2355

Lorenzini, Greg
CIS:76507,2166

Lorenzo, Anastasi
Via Etna, 82
95018 Riposto (CT)
ITALY
+39-95-7791538
unisystem@dns.omnia.it

Lose Your Mind Software
Att: Bryan Kinkel
506 Wilder Square
Norristown, PA 19401-2643
215-275-7034
CIS:70564,2372

Lowrey, Richard
40 Eagle Run
Irvine CA 92714

Ludwig, Bill
CIS:76516,1274

Luhring, Mark
MLuhring@aol.com

Lundberg, Thomas
CIS:74447,1267

Lyk, Edward
Edlyk@Delphi.com

Lynn F. Solon Foundation
PO Box 99
Edwardsville IL 62025

MC Security
CIS:100042,364

**MIS Resources
International**
570 Colonial Park Dr. #301
Roswell GA 30075
404-640-3400
Fax:404-587-1932
CIS:75350,205

MJ-Datatechnic GbR
41472 Neuss
GERMANY
Fax:+49-2131-859353
CIS:100442,644

MM Technology
Att: Chaim Herman
136 Pershing Ave.
Ridgewood NJ 07450
201-612-8222
Fax:201-309-1006
CIS:71155,1010

MMC Software
C/O David Warren
PO Box 23336
Pleasant Hill CA
94523-0336
510-609-7580
CIS:72500,1406
info@mmcsoftware.com

Mabry Software
Att: James Shields
P.O. Box 31926
Seattle WA 98103-1926
206-634-1443
Fax:206-632-0272
CIS:71231,2066
Mabry@Halcyon.com

Macdonald, Peter
PO Box 173
East Derry NH 03041
CIS:73577,1416
Pmacd@Cmc.Mv.com

Macedob, Antonio
CIS:75210,3332

Mack, Jim
Editing Services Co.
PO Box 599
Plymouth MI 48170
CIS:76630,2012

Macware
Att: Philip Bush
748 N. Hwy 67, Suite 163
Florissant MO 63031

Main, Mark
CIS:75462,3157
MarkMain@aol.com

MainSoft
C/O Patrick Philippot
15 Avenue Des Pres Pierre
91210 Draveil
FRANCE
+33-1-69-40-94-85
CIS:72561,3532

Mainat, Josep M.
Gestmusic S.A. (R&D)
Barcelona
SPAIN
Cis:100414,1026

Mainat, Joseph M.
CIS:100414,1026

275

Malik Information Services
Attn: Nick Malik
21134 N.E. 5th Place
Miami, FL 33179
CIS:76055,2722

Malluf, Ibrahaim
P.O. Box 251
Moriarty NM 87035-0251

Manfred Walmeyer
oPen Software
Systemberatung
Louise-Schroeder-Ring 42
W-2082 Tornesch-Esingen
GERMANY

Mangold, Oliver
Hagbucherweg 20
89150 Laichingen
GERMANY
+49-7333-6007
Fax:+49-7333-21266
CIS:100277,511

Manoogian, Paul J
496 West Germantown Pike
Plymouth Meeting PA
19462
CIS:76646,3542

Mantec Development Group
Willemoesgade 44 4. Tv
2100 Coopenhagen
DENMARK

Maplerow Brothers Software
2161 Fawnwood Drive SE
Kentwood MI 49508
CIS:72047,2134
Phila@Sgtec.com

Marasco Newton Group Ltd.
1600 Wilson Blvd.
Suite 1100
Arlington VA 22209
703-516-9100
Fax:703-516-9109

Margraff, Tom
11632 Mt. Waverly Ct.
Alta Loma CA 91737
909-980-7344
Fax:909-980-4636
CIS:71165,2623
tmargraf@ix.netcom.com

MarilynSoft
2703 E. Bessemer Ave.
Greensboro NC 27405

Marino, Lou
18 Champlain Way
Franklin Park, NJ 08823
609-243-4979

Marks, Paul
CIS:102057,1230
PMarks8501@aol.com

Marlow, James
Dallas TX
CIS:72732,407

Marquardt, Doug
CIS:72253,3113

Marquette Computer Consultants
Att: Barry Seymour
22 Surard Lane
San Rafael CA 94901-1066
415-459-0835
CIS:70413,3405

Marquis Computing, Inc.
P.O. Box 387
Pomfret Center CT 06259
203-963-7065
800-818-1611
Fax:203-928-7727
CIS:76120,2413

MarshallSoft Computing
P.O. Box 4543
Huntsville AL 35815
205-881-4630
Fax:205-881-4630
BBS:205-880-9748

Martin, Wayne
CIS:100347,461

Martin, Wendell
CIS:73737,1237

Martinez, Brad
BradDuder@aol.com

Mass, Martin
670, Sebastien
Charlesbourg, Quebec
G2L 2W4
CANADA
418-624-9596
CIS:75034,1755

Mathison, Rolf
CIS:76376,3224

Mattingley, Byron
PO Box 91170
Tucson AZ 85752-1170

Maurer Associates
7324 Native Oak Dr.
Irving TX 75063-8405
CIS:74017,2140

McClure, Jim
QED, Inc.
CIS:76666,1303

McCreary, Jeremy
Cliffshade Computing
CIS:72341,3716

McFall, Pete
1672 Lark Avenue
Redwood City CA 94061

McGillicuddy, Rich
mcgill@creative.net

McGregor, Rob
Screaming Tiki Software

McGuiness, Charles
CIS:76701,11

McIntosh, Rob
CIS:100413,1342

McKean Consulting
Robin W. McKean
1042 Braddock Circle
Woodstock, GA 30188
CIS:72622,1403

McLaughlin, Thomas
TIMMY12952@aol.com

McLean, Bruce
800 S. HW. 1417 #1214
Sherman, TX 75090
CIS:71413,2664

McMullen, Leigh C.
xmcmullen@dsm1.dsmnet.com

**McNeill Consulting
Services**
2323 S. Barcelona St.
Spring Valley CA 91977
CIS:71043,1226

McPhail, G. E.
Geodan Trading Company
6942 FM 1960 E-168
Humble, TX 77346
CIS:72610,10

Meadows, Al
Andrews Davis Law Firm
500 West Main
Oklahoma City, OK 73102

Mech, Robert W.
711 Bismark Ct.
Elk Grove Village IL 60007
CIS:76271,3507

Media Architects, Inc.
1075 N.W. Murray Rd.
#230
Portland, OR 97229-5501
503-297-5010
Fax:503-297-6744

Megabyte Services
PO Box 821524
Dallas TX 75382
CIS:73422,3565

Melanson, Leo M.
CIS:74130,2141

Merriman, Loren
CIS:76701,156

Mey & Westphal
RIPOSTE Software GbR
Schottweg 1
22087 Hamburg
GERMANY
+49-40-22-17-23
Fax:+49-40-22-17-72
CIS:100111,305

Meyer, David
Computer Concepts
Unlimited

Mezaros, Mike
CIS:75300,1642

Michael, Seelig
CIS:100331,2153

Michael
CIS:74237,151

Michna, Hans-Georg
Notingerweg 42
D-85521 Ottobrunn
GERMANY
+49-89-605063
CIS:74776,2361

Micro90
First Floor, Hamworthy
House
New Quay Road
Poole Dorset BH15 4AD
ENGLAND
CIS:100534,1100

MicroHelp, Inc.
4359 Shallowford Indus.
Pkwy.
Marietta GA 30066
800-922-3383
404-516-0898
Fax:404-516-1099

Microsoft Product Support
206-454-2030

Microsoft
One Microsoft Way
Redmond WA 98052-6399
206-882-8080
800-992-3675
800-277-4679
Fax:206-936-7329

Milbery, Jim
132 N. West St.
Allentown PA 18102

Milligan, Keith
100 Lee Road #605
Smiths AL 36877
205-291-9712
CIS:70645,520

MitranoSoft
c/o Ken Fitzpatrick
27203 Hidden Trail North
Boerne TX 78006-5591
CIS:73367,3470

Mitromar, Inc.
1102 Coconut Row
Delray Beach FL 33483
561-276-7828
Fax:561-276-2091
mitromar@iypn.com

Moccia, Lou A.
109 Apple Lane
Mt. Laurel NJ 08054

Mohler, David S.
CIS:76450,1642
stilwater@delphi.com

Monasterio, Jorge
CIS:72147,2674

Monro, Chris
CIS:74250,1327

Monte Carlo Software
Domaine De Boistell
83560 Rians
FRANCE
+33-9480-3940
Fax:+33-8480-3993
CIS:100116,2550

Moon, Brian
424 Daniel Dr.
Birmingham AL 35215

Morelli Systems, Inc.
1934 60th Ct.
Cicero IL 60650
CIS:75034,376

Morris & Steinwart
CIS:72447,1545
CIS:73647,1613

Morris, Jeffrey
CIS:70751,1565

Mosher, Sue
CIS:75140,543

Moss, Kevin
CIS:75310,3415

Moyle, Greg
BBS:702-329-5610

Muehlenweg, Ulli
Kempener Allee 5
47803 Krefeld
GERMANY
+49-0-2151-75049
CIS:100331,1413

Mulks, Charles
CIS:70612,1117
21667cfm@Msu.Edu

Mullin, Dan
20 Mountview Lane
Suite D
Colorado Springs CO 80907
719-599-7477
CIS:72644,2423

Mullins, Robert
Ballyknockane
Clonmel, Co. Tipperary
IRELAND

Mullins, Robert
Ballyknockane
Clonmel, Co. Tipperary
IRELAND
rmullins@iol.ie

Mundy, Ward
P.O. Box 1169
Atlanta, GA 30301
BBS:706-746-5109

Murdoch, Duncan
79 John St. W
Waterloo ON N2L 1B7
CANADA
CIS:71631,122
dmurdoch@watstat.waterloo.edu

Murdoch, John
Wind Gap PA
CIS:71507,1212

Murphy, Michael J.
1385 Majolica Road
Salisbury, NC 28147
704-633-0792
CIS:71160,1275

Murphy, Stephen
CIS:70661,2461

NTG
C/O Stefano Petrone
BBS:+39-425-361776

Nannini, Stephen F.
1327 Great Plain Avenue
Neeham MA 02192-1751
617-444-9061
CIS:75031,1262

Nanoware
P.O. Box 7468
Seminole FL 33775-7468

Naroditsky, Vadim
30 West 63rd St. Suite 31V
New York NY 10023
Fax:212-541-8437
CIS:72133,1175

Naumann, Christian
CIS:100552,1570

Neal, Randy
CIS:72315,16

Nelson, Eugene
955 E. Gorham
Madison WI 53703
CIS:70662,2501

Nelson, John R.
Cornerstone Logic
CIS:70641,3562

New Leaf Software
NewLeaf@aol.com

NicheWare
8430-D Summerdale Road
San Diego CA 92126-5415
CIS:74777,447
DPMCS@aol.com
DPMCS@Cts.com

NicheWare
8430-D Summerdale Road
San Diego CA 92126-5415
CIS:74777,447
DPMCS@aol.com
DPMCS@cts.com

Nickle, John
Nickle and Dime Software
431A Huntsville Cres. NW,
#201
Calgary AB T2K 4W3
CANADA
403-274-0362
CIS:75124,1267

Nisus Development &
Technology
PO Box 703, Station A
Toronto, Ontario M1K 5C4
CANADA
416-261-7866
Fax:416-261-6399
CIS:70751,1647
murrays@tor.hookup.net

Noonan, Timothy D.
6501 Oakwood Drive
Falls Church VA 22041
703-941-3032
CIS:75212,664

Nordan, Matthew M.
122 Overbrook Drive
Concord NC 28025
CIS:76535,1421 BBS:704-
782-8921

NorthStar Solutions
PO Box 25262
Columbia SC 29224
CIS: 71561.2751

Northeast Data Corp.
2117 Buffalo Rd. Suite 290
Rochester, NY 14624
716-247-5934

Northington, Otha L.
Digital Solutions
26 East 14th Street #505
Indianapolis, IN 46202

Novell Inc.
5918 West Courtyard Drive
Austin TX 78732
512-794-1488 800-733-
9673
Fax:512-345-7478

Numatic International Ltd.
C/O Matthew Gailes
Chard, Somerset TA20 2BB
ENGLAND
+44-1460-68480x314
Fax:+44-1460-68550

Numatic International Ltd.
C/O Matthew Gailes
Chard, Somerset TA20 2BB
ENGLAND
01460-68480x314
Fax:01460-68550

O'Neill Software
9 Williamson Lane
Stratton WA 6056
AUSTRALIA
CIS:100242,2203

OSoft Development
Corporation
2964 Peachtree Road
Suite 350
Atlanta, GA 30305
404-233-1392
Fax:404-237-0706

Oakley Data Services
3 Oakley Close
Sandbach, Cheshire
CW11 9RQ
England
UK
+44-0270-759359
Fax:+44-0270-765272
CIS:100024,1763

Obeda, Ed
39149 Guardino Dr. Ste 351
Fremont, CA 94538
510-713-0814
Fax:510-713-0814
CIS:72537,163

Objective Technologies Ltd.
P.O. Box 8
TRURO TR4 9YG
UK
develop@objectech.co.uk

Odom, Ronnie
ronodd@aol.com

Okapi (Pat Hayes)
PO Box 322
Castaic CA 91310-322
805-257-3377
CIS:74437,134

Oliphant, Joe
CIS:71742,1451
joe_oliphant@csufresno.edu

Olowofoyeku, Dr.
Abimbola
268 Horwood
Newcastle
Staffs ST5 5BQ
ENGLAND
Laa1@keele.ac.uk

Olson, Stephan
HWA For Windows
4 Anaru Place
Palmerston North
NEW ZEALAND
+64-6-359-1408
Fax:+64-6-355-2775
CIS:100352,1315

One Point Software
1709 Hidden Bluff Trail
#2922
Arlington TX 76006
CIS:74211,1403

Opalko, John
Johnopalko@aol.com

Opaque Software
Brett Liddicott
P.O. Box 2483
Napa CA 94558
CIS:70621,3034
CIS:74777,3227

Optimax Corporation
PO Box 25447
Chicago IL 60625-9998
312-561-6363
CIS:75020,3617

Osborne, Greg
4516 N. Ripley St.
Davenport IA 52806-4033
Gregozzy@aol.com

OutRider Systems
3701 Kirby Drive
Ste. 1196
Houston TX 77098
713-726-0386 800-845-0386
Fax:713-523-0386

Overstreet, Mark
CIS:102227,3510

Owens, Mike
8836 Channing Drive
Jonesboro GA 30236
404-472-9017
CIS:75037,2625
Blindmello@aol.com

Owyen, Scott
P.O. Box 1108
Gold Bar WA 98251

PC HELP-LINE
35250 Silver Leaf
Circleucaipa CA 92399
Voice/Fax:909-797-3091
CIS:72357,3523

PCG Associates, LLC.
65 Cottage Street, Suite 4B
Port Chester NY 10573
914-937-0554
Fax:914-939-8847
MJCarlucci@Msn.com

PCSWare (Paul Coombes)
CIS:100413,155

PCs With Ease
32 Old Mill Road
Laflin PA 18702

PD Consulting
2249 Elm Avenue, Ste. 202
Cleveland OH 44113

PDA, Inc.
CIS:71150,3407
MailPDA@aol.com

PDC
16307 - 197th Ave. NE
Woodinville WA 98072
prang@halcyon.com

PTAHSoft
P.O. Box 193
CH-1723 MARLY 1
SWITZERLAND
CIS:75240,664
firma.ptasoft@buemplitzer.ch

Page, Preston
Sleepness Nights Software
11878 Cynthia Drive
St. Louis, MO 63043
CIS:71712,1473

Pagett, Paul
61 Earlsway
Curzon Park
Cheshire CH4 8AZ
ENGLAND
CIS:100257,3010

Parachute Software
324 Debbie Drive
Waukesha WI 53186

Parr, James
CIS:73312,3615

Pastel Programming
ATtt: T. R. Halvorson
HC56, Box 6038
Sidney MT 59270
CIS:71477,352

Paul James Barrett
CIS:71020,2624

Pazur, Scott
11225 Quailbrook Chase
Duluth, GA 30136
CIS:74457,2772
spazur@alfo06.attmail.com

Pedersen, John
RR #2
Orangeville, ON L9W 2Y9
CANADA
CIS:76547,357

Peninsula Software
28510 Blythewood Drive
Palos Verdes CA 90274
CIS:72356,556

Pennington, Bill
P.O. Box 3812
Sarasota, FL 34320
CIS:72154,167

Peopleware
1253 Monticello Road
Napa CA 94558
800-959-2509
Fax:707-258-0813

Perkins, Brad
Intelligence Mfg. Company
3136 Redwood Ave.
West Sacremento CA 95691
916-372-6680
CIS:76670,1030

Perry, Stephen M.
13740 SE Grant Ct.
Portland OR 97233
CIS:75251,3026

Persky, Jonathan D.
5 Oak Lane
Weston, CT 06883
jonpersky@aol.com

Peschka, Steve
13120 SE 137th Drive
Clackamas OR 97015
CIS:71722,55

Peters, Constantine
14409 Briarwood Terrace
Rockville, MD 20853
CIS:70761,6373

Petersen, Karl E.
Regional Transportation
Counci
1351 Officer's Row
Vancouver, Washington
98661
CIS:72302,3707

Pewitt, Woody
Midstream Inc.
1801 N. Hampton Rd. Suite
315
DeSoto TX 75115-2399
214-283-8426
CIS:71670,3203

Phares, Wayne
Phares@Rsi.Prc.com

Phase II Software
620 Galer Street, Suite 133
Seattle WA 98109
206-216-0772

Pienaar, Marc
Box 998
Kelvin 2054
SOUTH AFRICA
CIS:70750,1776

Pinnacle Publishing
P.O. Box 888
Kent WA 98035
206-251-1900 800-231-
1293
Fax:206-251-5057

Pirie, Brian
1416 2201 Riverside Drive
Ottawa, ON K1H 8K9
CANADA
FIDO:1:243/8
brian@bpecomm.ocunix.on.ca

Pleas, Keith R.
CIS:72331,2150

Plieger, R.S.
Postbus 70230
9704 AE Gronigen
NETHERLANDS
Plieger@Bnc.Nl

Plowman, Graham
PO Box 1124
Manly 2095 NSW
AUSTRALIA
CIS:100105,536

Pocket Change Software
9546 Mountain View Rd.
North Wilkesboro, NC
28659
CIS:71441,1264

Poellinger, Paul F.
2019 Round Lake Drive
Houston TX 77077
CIS:70732,3576
Pfpelican@aol.com
Pelican@Onramp.Net

Point Systems, Inc.
C/O Livio Bestulic
PO Box 76255
St. Petersburg FL 33734
Fax:813-528-0217
CIS:102370,3655
PointSysIn@gnn.com

Porcaro, Jeff
357 E. 650 N.
Orem UT 84057

Porter, Todd
7595 Baymeadows Cir. W.
Suite #1616
Jacksonville FL 32256
CIS:102024,3256
Porter@Gate.Net

Poseidon Software, Ltd.
389 East Harvard Circle
South Elgin IL 60177
800-931-1221
CIS:74244,1616

Potomac Software
19918 Hamil
Montgomery Village MD
20879
301-216-0604
weblib@potsoft.com

PowerBASIC Inc.
316 Mid Valley Center
Carmel CA 93923
408-659-8000
Fax:408-659-8008
CIS:75300,1742
sales@powerbasic.com

PowerTools Software
5353 Gamble Drive,
Suite 300
Minneapolis MN 55416
612-860-2181
Fax:612-595-9743
CIS:70651,1421

Pozharov, Vitaliy
1738 East Woodside Dr, #7
Salt Lake City UT 84124
VitaliyP@aol.com

PractiSys
4767 Via Bensa
Agoura, CA 91301
818-706-8877
Fax:818-706-8877

**Praxis Software
Developments**
28 Wellfield Grove
Penistone Sheffield S30 6GP
UNITED KINGDOM
CIS:100265,1064

Presley, Jack
C/O Presley Computing
29322 Mandetta Drive
Boerne TX 78006-4529
CIS:70700,166

Press, Barry
1571 E. Locksley Circle
Sandy UT 84092-4336
CIS:72467,2353

Price, N.
CIS:100063,3363

Pride! Software Works
P.O. Box 11152
High Point NC 27265
CIS:73337,2472
pride@infi.net

Princeton Computer

Consulting
20 Lorrie Lane
PO Box 7345
Princeton NJ 08543-7345
bmurray@pluto.njcc.com

Pro-Data / EVB Magazine
7151 El Cajon Blvd. Ste. L
San Diego, CA 92115
BBS:602-942-9405

**Professional Software
Systems**
P.O. Box 10702
Glendale, CA 91209-3702
CIS:71554,357
dwneder@kbbs.com

Programmer's Warehouse
Att: Corey Schwartz
602-443-0580
CIS:73240,2734

Pronexus
112 John Cavanagh
RR2 Carp, Ontario K0A 1L0
CANADA
613-839-0033x511
Fax:613-839-0035
CIS:71054,3225

Prospero Software Products
41 Athols Street
Douglas
Isle Of Man IM1 1LA
UNITED KINGDOM
+44-1624-681090
Fax:+44-1624-681097
CIS:100332,1257

Purcell, Tim
Viinirinne 1 B 6
02630 Espoo
FINLAND
+358-0-5022542

Q&D Software

Development
10-B Sentinel Court
Chatham NJ 07928
800-242-4775 713-524-
6394 CIS:76636,3271
dversch@intac.com

Quinion, Brian
18 Pittville Close
Thornbury, Bristol BS12
1SE
UNITED KINGDOM
+44-1454-411128
sales@quinion.demon.co.uk

RA-Ware Technologies, Inc.
1125 Duke Street
Alexandria VA 22314
703-518-4480
CIS:72400,2345
andre@rawtech.com

RCCO Research Associates
P.O. Box 196
Gatlinburg, TN 37738

RDB Knowledge Systems
503 Ambleside Drive
London, Ontario N6G 4Z1
CANADA
CIS:102420,2671

RGS Software
Mortimer House
Holmer Road
Hereford HR6 9SQ
UNITED KINGDOM
Richard@Rgs.U-Net.com

RMJ Software
4033 Elwood Ave.
Palmdale CA 93552
805-267-0217
Fax:310-372-5791

RUW-Computer
Robchestrae 5
58540 Meinerzhagen
GERMANY
+049-2358-7760
Fax:+049-2358-8709
CIS:100116,1532

Radford, Andrew
CIS:74151,2317

Radium Software
Boise ID
208-322-9350

Raffel, Matthew P.
3101 Treelodge Parkway
Dunwoody, GA 30350
404-394-8373
CIS:73113,2625

Raike, William
66 Simpson Rd.
Swanson
Auckland 8SW
NEW ZEALAND
CIS:100236,1656

Randriambololona, Roland
CIS:100331,2516

Rapallo, Angel
300 NW 42 Ave. #607
Miami FL 33126
305-448-2362

Rataycza, Richard A.
CIS:76753,127
diskdesk@execpc.com

Rathwick, Zane / Addsoft
Indigo Software
6029 Machado Way
Sacremento CA 95822

Redei Enterprises Inc.
1424 Brett Pl. #359
San Pedro CA 90732
310-832-6984
Fax:310-832-6984
CIS:71744,3633

Reed, Michael A.
CIS:71730,573

Reinstein, Robert
20 Singlewood Drive
Holbrook, New York 11741
CIS:76702,2075

Reisewitz, U.
CIS:100042,47

Renard, Michael
Kagi Shareware
1442-A Walnut Street
#392-AI
Berkeley, CA 94709-1405
Fax:510-652-6589
CIS:100042,3646
shareware@kagi.com

Resolutions Now
Att: Philip Rodgers, Jr.
P.O. Box 443
Blue Island IL 60406-0443
312-994-6450
Fax:312-994-6450

Resource Partners North
Box 689, Meadow Street
Wakefield NH 03872
603-522-9500
Fax:603-522-9747
CIS:74347,164
rpnorth@wchat.on.ca

Reynaert, John
10 Arnold Sayeau Dr.
P.O. Box 212
Delhi Ontario N4B 2W9
CANADA
CIS:76570,2275

Reynolds, Paul
CIS:71011,2040
paul.reynolds@channel1.com

Rezuke, Joe
243 Boston Post Rd. #9
Marlboro MA 01752
CIS:73177,606

Rhind, Jeff
P.O. Box 5
Avon MA 02322-0005
jarhind@aol.com

**Richards Software &
Consulting**
441 Bowden Street
Brundidge, AL 36081
CIS:72262,1315

Riley, Barth
153 Benjamin St.
Romeo MI 48065
CIS:72677,3172

Riley, Ian
CIS:100445,2626

Risholm, Bob
CIS:76030,270

Robar, R.
P.O. Box 254
Franconia NH 03580
CIS:100030,10

Robichaux, Roy J.
P.O. Box 5352
Thibodaux LA 70302
CIS:74031,1652

Robust Software
2345 Janin Way
Solvang CA 93463
805-688-6312
Fax:805-688-6193

Rodriguez, M. John
CIS:100321,620

Rofail, Ash
306 Belmont Street
Marion OH 43302
vbandc@aol.com

Rogers, Kerry
CIS:71514,735

Rohn, Gary W.
CIS:76050,1012

Roland, Al
Roalnd Consulting
1000 Lee Road 20
Auburn AL 36830
Fax:334-887-2305
droland@roland.viper.net

Rose, Joel
185 Shelley Ave.
Elizabeth, NJ 07208

Rossow, Frank
CIS:100074,1756

Rutledge, Thomas
CIS:72223,1637

Rutt, Rick
rrutt@delphi.com

Ruzicka, John
1290 25th Avenue #301
San Francisco, CA 94122
415-566-9225
CIS:75160,2376

SDK Software
steve@kalika.demon.co.uk

SMI Enterprises Corp
P.O. Box 582221
Tulsa, OK 74158
918-560-9536

SNS Software
2860 Colgate Drive
Oceanside CA 92056
CIS:72640,1442

SOFTWISE
P.O. Box 3881
Everett WA 98203
206-513-0415
softwise@halcyon.com

SP Services
P.O. Box 456
Southampton SO9 7XG
GREAT BRITAIN
+44-703-550037
Fax:703-322416
CIS:100016,1625
ih@ecs.soton.ac.uk

SRC Enterprises
Att: Steven R. Clabaugh
550 N. Pantano Rd. #286
Tucson, AZ 85710
520-296-7570
Fax:520-296-7570

SYNERGY Software &
Services
46 Little Brook Rd.
Wilton CT 06897
203-761-0749
CIS:73467,3661

Sandell, David
CIS:75366,235

Sands, Richard R.
PO Box 3917
Portland OR 97208
CIS:70274,103

Saucedo, Rosary
2145 Ingrid Ave.
San Diego CA 92154

Sauve, Eric
724 Lahaie #2
Laval, Qc
H7G 3C4
CANADA
CIS:73304,3541

Sax Software
203 Bellevue Way
Bellevue WA 98004
Fax:503-344-2459
800-MIKE-SAX
CIS:75470,1403
CIS:74774,710

Scherer, Bob
Newport Beach, CA
CIS:76237,514

Schmitt, Hans-Jochen
Paul-Wagner Str. 28
64285 Darmstadt
GERMANY
hajo@bwl.bwl.th-
darmstadt.de

Schoeffel, Dave
dRs Engineering
1313 Riverton Drive
Mukwonago WI 53149

Schoonover, Mark
VBWin Programmer's
Magazine
3755 Avocado Blvd Ste 228
La Mesa CA 91941
Schoone@Cts.com

Schulze, Peter
CIS:72253,2602

Scofield, M.L. "Sco"
CIS:71063,157

Scott, Dennis
7711 Butler Road
Myrtle Beach SC 29575-
6628
803-650-7460
CIS:71360,3701

Serpoul, Jean Jacques
CD Soft
8 Rue Linne
44100 Nantes
FRANCE
19-33-40-69-26-46
Fax:19-33-40-69-28-01
CIS:100350,1340

Shaftel Software
C/O Tony Shaftel
PO Box 12485
La Crescenta CA
91224-5485
Fax:818-957-7992
CIS:72540,1562

Shanghai KingS Computer
Jin Ding Hua
Room 501, No.5, Alley 285
Xin Hu Road, Shanghai
200436
CHINA
+86-21-5605-4376
kingscompu@hotmail.com

Shaw, Kevin
LogiSoft Software
1112 Pepperidge Drive
Palm Harbor, FL 34683
CIS:74002,315

Sheridan Software Systems
35 Pinelawn Road
Suite 206E
Melville, NY 11747
516-753-0985 800-VB-
DIRECT
Fax:516-753-3661
BBS:516-753-5452

Shoptalk Systems
P.O. Box 1062
Framingham, MA 01701
508-872-5315

Sigler, John
CIS:71631,776

Significa Software
6964 South FireFox Ct.
West Jordan UT 84084
800-214-0504
significa@inconnect.com

SilverWare, Inc.
3010 LBJ Freeway #740
Dallas TX 75234
214-247-0131
Fax:214-406-9999
BBS:214-247-2177

Silverwing Systems
13040 Gopher Wood Trail
Tallahassee FL 32312
904-668-8530
CIS:70254,613
alvin@freenet.Tlh.Fl.Us

Simha, Andre E.
CIS:100024,1574

Simmons, Jason
82 Stonehurst Lane
Dix Hills NY 11746
CIS:70254,2017
jsimmons@cs.sunysb.edu

Simmons, Paul
2410 Woodland Hills Drive
Cumming GA 30130
3674057@Mcimail.com

Simms, Jeff
813 Hyde Rd.
Silver Spring MD 20902
301-593-6067
Fax:301-593-9875
CIS:72200,3173

Simon
40 Broomfield Road
Newport, Shropshire TF107
+44-1952-405669
Simon@Tmsnet.Co.Uk

Simple Software (Bigford)
Att: Walter Bigford
8750 Point Park Dr., #1007
Houston TX 77095
wbigford@aol.com

Simply Solutions
3337 South Bristol, Suite
143
Santa Ana CA 92704
800-355-2405 310-575-
5047 Simply@Netcom.com
CIS:74777,3221

Six, Raymond W.
CIS:70530,433

SkiSoft Shareware
Att: Mike Skibeness
3499 223rd St. SW
Brier WA 98036
CIS:73042,3371
skibby@aol.com

Skoog, Bengt-Arne
CIS:74362,1256

Skyline Tools
11956 Riverside Dr. #206
North Hollywood CA 91607
818-766-3900
800-404-3832
Fax:818-766-9027
CIS:72130,353

Slagman, Herman
Insert Information
Technology
Bastenakenstraat 110
1066 JE Amsterdam
NETHERLANDS
CIS:100101,131

Slickware
Slickware@aol.com

Slutter, Carl
17500 Princess Anne Drive
Olney MD 20832
hardwood@erols.com

Smaby, Marcus
CIS:72571,3126

Smart Typesetting
6835 E. Phelps Rd.
Scottsdale AZ 85254-1539

Smith, Derek
4136 Orchard Drive
Fairfax VA 22032
DSmith2434@aol.com

Smith, Gordon
341 RiverBend Road
Great Falls, VA 22066
703-759-4415

Smith, Les
6523 Basswood Drive
Concord, NC 28025
CIS:72123,121

**Smith, Wilson, And
C.Rogers**
CIS:70741,422

Smythe, Robert E.
CIS:71174,430
bob.smythe@channel1.com

Smythe, William
CIS:74640,637

Snider, Charles K.
jArGoN cOmPuTiNg
CIS:73730,1315

Snyder, James Wj
Shattered Rose Studio
San Francisco CA
CIS:75141,3544
JamesWJS@aol.com

Soft Solutions
125 Warfieldsburg, Suite
310
Westminister MD 21557

SoftBit Enterprises
Terry Bittner
109 N. Garfield Rd.
Sterling, VA 20164
703-421-0225

SoftCircuits Programming
Att: Jonathan Wood
P.O. Box 16262
Irvine CA 92713
CIS:72134,263

SoftLand Inc.
Att: Alex Spektor
610 Valley Stream Circle
Langhorne PA 19053
215-741-2030
CIS:73321,1525

Softcraft, Inc.
16 N. Carroll Street
Madison, WI 53703
608-257-3300 800-351-
0500
Fax:608-257-6733
CIS:76702,1304

Software FX Inc.
2200 Corporate Blvd.
Suite 309
Boca Raton, FL 33481-0893
407-998-2377
Fax:407-998-2383
CIS:74032,2412

Software Factory UK Ltd.
110 Peerless Drive
Harefield, Uxbridge,
Middlesex
UB9 6JQ
ENGLAND
CIS:100023,3177

Software Interphase
82 Cucumber Hill Rd. #243
Foster, RI 02825-1212
401-397-2340
800-54-BASIC
Fax:401-397-6814

Software Savants
P.O. Box 4108
Waukesha WI 53187-4108
CIS:70404,1563

Software Shop
1625 Beth
Pocatello ID 83201

Software Source
836 Blossom Hill Rd. #210
San Jose CA 95123-2703
408-3363-0985
Fax:408-363-0987
CIS:75443,134

Solid Software Inc.
Att: George Tatge
gat@csn.org

Solomon Software
1218 Commerce Parkway
P.O. Box 414
Findlay OH 45839
419-424-0422 800-879-
0444
Fax:419-424-3400

Solomon, Maareyes
1007 Benge Dr. #135
Arlington TX 76013
MSolo1111@aol.com

Solugistics Ltd.
Whytegates House,
Berries Road
Cookham
Berkshire SL6 9SD
UNITED KINGDOM
CIS:100074,533

Solution Studios Inc.
2215 W. Willow Knolls
#513
Peoria IL 61614
309-692-9162
CIS:74454,117

Solutionsoft
999 Evelyn Terrace West
Suite 86
Sunnyvale CA 94086
408-736-1431
Fax:408-736-4013
CIS:75210,2214

Sorrentino, Silvio
CIS:100265,1725

Sparks, Ron
Blockbuster Online Services
CIS:74351,404
BlockTec@aol.com

Spinoza Ltd.
11333 Iowa Avenue
Los Angeles CA 90025
310-231-9770 800-700-
2217
Fax:310-231-9773
CIS:71461,2021

Staffin, Ed
402 Porter Way West
Bridgewater, NJ 08807
908-253-0246

Staley, Marc
6401 S. Westshore Blvd.
#1120
Tampa FL 33616
800-282-9218
CIS:76513,1650

Stanczak, Thomas
R&T Software
CIS:100735,327

Stanley, Mike
25 Lansdowne Street
Manchester NH 03103
CIS:74632,2227
MikeStanly@aol.com

StarBase
18872 MacArthur Blvd.,
#400
Irvine CA 92715
714-442-4400
800-891-3262
Fax:714-253-6712
UK:+44-342-850930

Stedy Software
64 Greeley St.
Manchester NH 03102-
2307
CIS:71740,3121
www.stedy.com

Stefanik, Michael J.
CIS:72202,1427
mikes@pacsoft.com

Stefano, David
CIS:72202,3046

Steingraeber Fachverlag
Basic Professionell Magazine
Knooper Weg 126-128
Kiel D-24143
GERMANY
+49-431-563212
Fax: +49-431-563273
CIS:100111,3245

Stenklyft, Jason Lee
17719 Pacific Ave. South
#407
Spanaway WA 98387
jls@masterpiece.com

Stephen Cramp
C/Systems
13582 Kennedy Rd. N.
Inglewood, Ontario
L0N 1K0
CANADA

Stewart, David
738 Hathaway Drive
Auburn Hills, MI 48326
CIS:72122,3562

Stewart, Michael
539 Dutch Neck Road
East Windsor NJ 08520
CIS:76234,3314

Stewart, Robert W.
1092 Avenue Road
Toronto, Ontario
CANADA
CIS:72632,3004

Stillwater Systems
32248 N.E. 94th Street
Carnation WA 98014
CIS:72643,604

Stine, Brian D.
Sahalie Software
3320 Harris St.
Eugene OR 97405
CIS:73617,323

Stingsoft
SWEDEN
CIS:100662,3013

Strathman, Michael D.
MeV Technology, Inc.
5150 Shadow Estates
San Jose CA 95135
408-238-6351
Fax:408-238-3466
CIS:75663,520

Streu, Randy
16619 Gaelhom
Houston TX 77084
CIS:73512,273

Stuart, Chuck
CIS:76560,51
ChukStuart@aol.com
Cstuart@Metronet.com

Stubbs, Scott
CIS:73474,313
Sstubbs@Iadfw.Net

Summers, Judy
Intelligence Engineering
CIS:70771,1444

Sycomp Limited
1 Stonecross
St. Albans
Herts, AL1 4AA
ENGLAND
+44-727-47806
Fax:+44-727-834052

Sylvain Faust Inc.
880 Boul. De La Carriere
Suite 120
Hull, Quebec J8Y 6T5
CANADA
819-778-5045
Fax:819-778-7943 800-567-9127 BBS:819-778-8556

Syme, Brian
Gxlr07@Udcf.Gla.Ac.Uk

Syncom, Inc.
P.O. Box 1592
Morristown NJ 07960-1592
800-457-7884
Fax:201-267-6605
CIS:72632,345

Synergy Software Technologies
159 Pearl St.
Essex Junction, VT 05452
802-878-8514
Fax:802-878-4055

Synergystic Productions
1503 Nance St.
Houston TX 77002-1127
CIS:72322,765

Systems Software Technology
5727 Canoga Ave. #283
Woodland Hills CA 91367
818-346-2784
Fax:818-346-7070
CIS:70233,2504
Sstinc@Netcom.com

TAGs
P. O. Box 2423
Cridersville OH 45806
tagraham@alpha.wcoil.com

TANSTAAFL Software
P.O. Box 260075
Lakewood, CO 80226
303-989-7389
CIS:73700,3053
GEnie:Tanstaafl

TARDIS DP Consultants
Department 45
6 Sedley Ct.
Greensboro, NC 27455
CIS:73337,2472

Tabb, Marchan
3960 Roebling Lane
Virginia Beach, VA 23452

Takriti, Nick
Nicktak@Eskimo.com

Tanner, Ahto
ESTONIA
ahto.taig@online.ee

Tanner, Ron
4955 E. Preserve Court
Greenwood Village CO 80121
303-689-0720
Fax:303-689-0730
CIS:75170,176

Taylor, Ian
Moorgate East Farm
Broad Lane
Rochdale OL16 4QL
ENGLAND
+44-706-353-412
CIS:100025,557

Taylor, Jonathan B.
Taylored Software
8504 Van Pelt Dr.
Dallas TX 75228
214-328-4276

Taylor, Rick
7347 Lonsdale Dr.
Salt Lake City, UT 84121
CIS:70472,115

TechnoTrends
31 Roosevelt Road
Lexington MA 02173-7411

Teletech Systems
750 Birch Ridge Drive
Roswell, GA 30076
CIS:72260,2217
Fbunn@Netcom.com
Codemstr@Mindspring.com

Temple, Tom
Tomtemple@aol.com

Tenholder, Edward J.
CIS:76447,1030

Tesserax Information Systems
18022 Starmont Lane
Huntington Beach CA 92649-4849
714-840-8822
CIS:72247,1463

Teter, C. Mark, M.D.
Indian Territory Software
P.O. Box 52765
Tulsa, OK 74152-0765
CIS:72530,626

Teunis, William
CIS:72066,304

Theis, H. Eric., Jr.
849 Boston Port Rd. #5H
Marlborough MA 01752
CIS:76270,1533

Theobald Soft Design
Att: Patrick Theobald
Scheffelstr. 14
71522 Backnang
07191-87023
Fax:07191-83022
CIS:106371,1036

Thomas, Neville W.
Unicom Aviation Services
10 Lindley Ave.
Warradale 5046
SOUTH AUSTRALIA
+61-8-2967745
CIS:100026,1461

Thornton, Michael
4901 6th Ave.
Vienna WV 26105
Frogware@aol.com

Thorp, Rick
CIS:72077,1701

Thorp, Ron
Thorp Technology
CIS:72557,3632

Throm, Edward D.
CIS:71223,166

Thunder Island Software
P.O. Box 1034
Eau Claire WI 54702
CIS:74777,2544

Tilson, Steven W.
CIS:102022,1330
stilson@atk.com
steve.tilson@windmill.com

Tisoft S.A.
Att: Christophe Tricaud
68, Bld Edgar Quinet
75 014 Paris
FRANCE
+33-1-43205108
CIS:100412,2653

Tissington, Mike
CIS:100430,614

Torralba, George R.
8728 Phinney Ave. N #8
Seattle, WA 98103
206-781-7622
Grtorlba@Seattleu.Edu

Trahan, Jeff
CIS:72737,2154

TransSend Technology
30 White Dr. N.
Cedarhurst NY 11516
CIS:72457,2444

Tricaud, Christophe
68, Bld Edgar Quinet
75 014 Paris
FRANCE
33-1-43-20-51-08
CIS:100412,2653

Trimble Technologies
619-599-0733
CIS:76306,1115

Trova, Marco
Via U. Cagni, 24
20162 Milano
ITALY
CIS:100321,1037
mc5292@mclink.it

Troy, Hailaeos
2300 Rock Springs Drive
#1081
Las Vegas NV 89128
702-256-6447

Truesdale, Greg
Suite 308
633 North Road
Coquitlam BC V3J 1P3
CANADA
CIS:74131,2175

Trupin, Joshua
CIS:75120,657

Tucker, Barry G.
PowerPro Systems, Inc.
CIS:70324,2404

Turpin, Jerry
1120 Woodcrest Dr.
Bedford, VA 24523
800-456-7775
703-586-8067

Tyminski, James D.
25 Voorhis Dr.
Old Bethpage NY 11804
CIS:76376,2375

U-Turn Productions
11560 E. Ponderosa Lane
Franktown CO 80116
JasonT668@aol.com

Unger, Guinn
Unger Business Systems
11926 Barrett Brae
Houston, TX 77072-4004
713-498-8517
Fax:713-498-8518
CIS:71053,2332

Universal Dynamics Inc.
16890 Via Tazon #160
San Diego, CA 92127
800-466-3400
619-675-0146

User Friendly, Inc.
1718 M Street NW
Suite 291
Washington, DC 20036
202-387-1949
CIS:76702,1605

VB Tech Journal
Oakley Publishing Company
PO Box 70167
Eugene OR 97401
800-234-0386
503-747-0800
Fax:503-746-0071
CIS:76701,32

VBxtras
1901 Powers Ferry Road
Suite 250
Atlanta GA 30339
404-952-6356
800-788-4794
Fax:404-952-6388

VXBase Systems
488 9707 - 110 Street
Edmonton AB T5K 2L9
CANADA
403-488-8100
800-992-0616
Fax:403-486-8150
BBS:488-8365

Valley Programming
Att: James Robinson
P.O. Box 34085
San Antonio TX
78265-4085
210-650-9515

Van Der Sar, D.
CIS:100103,3121

VanBrocklin Technical Services
4491 W. Rockwood Dr.
Tucson AZ 85741-3929

Velazquez, Chris
Trailblazers Software
9419 Valley Moss
San Antonio TX 78250
210-647-3105
CIS:74073,1566

Venema, John E.
CIS:100033,1415

Venugopalan, Vivek
CIS:73512,3675

Vermont Peripherals
PO Box 2063
Colchester VT 05446-2063
CIS:74514,2615
verpex@ix.netcom.com

Versatile Control Systems
2655 North Ocean Drive
Singer Island FL 33404
407-881-9050
Fax:407-881-7345
CIS:75144,3111

Vi Qual Software
28 Hill Drive
Rochester, New York
14626-1810

VideoFax Ltd.
East Green Farm, Great
Bradley
Newmarket
Suffolk CB8 9LU
UNITED KINGDOM
+44-1440-783789
Fax:+44-1440-783791
daisy@cityscape.co.uk

VideoSoft
5900 Hollis St. Ste. T
Emeryville CA 94608
510-595-2400
800-547-7295
Fax:510-595-2424
CIS:71552,3052

Villalon, Craig
2074 Pleasant Hill Rd.
Sebastopol, CA 95472-4948
villalon@crl.com
FIDO:1:125/7

Vision Software Tools
2101 Webster St., 8th floor
Oakland CA 94612
510-238-4100
800-984-7638
Fax:510-238-4118
sales@vision-soft.com

Visual Basic Programmer's
Gary Wisniewski
280 Second Street Suite 200
Los Altos, CA 94022-3603
800-848-5523
415-917-7650
Fax:415-948-7332
CIS:71732,3233

Visual Bits
P.O. Box 243
Watertown MA 02272-0243
CIS:70402,3651

Visual Components, Inc.
15721 College Blvd.
Lenexa, KS 66219
800-884-8665 913-599-6500
Fax:913-599-6597
CIS:72204,3521

VisualSoft
Att: Harshad Bahirsheth
415-565-4491 668-0831
800-662-0831
Fax:415-221-8610
BBS:415-386-7946

WINDOWS Magazine
CMP Publications
600 Community Drive
Manhasset NY 11030

Wallace, Robert
CIS:74604,501

Wallette, Nick
21-742 Apt. D Fig Street
Elmendorf AFB AK 99506
907-753-9263
CIS:71756,1207

Wang, Wallace
348 Palm Ave.
Chula Vista CA 91911
CIS:70334,3672

WareWithAll, Inc.
3033 Ogden Ave.
Suite 303
Lisle IL 60532
800-689-0747

Warning, Mike
6015 202nd St. S.W. #14
Lynnwood, WA 98036

Warwick, M. J.
70 Derwent Road
Grantham Lincs.
NG31 7PD
UNITED KINGDOM

Washington, Winefred
1702 Lion Heart Drive
Cedar Park TX 78613
CIS:72070,3713

Waty, Thierry
Rue Juliette Wytsman, 91
1050 Bruxelles
BELGIUM
watty_thiery@jpmorgan.com

Weaver, Peter R.
6-286 Cushman Road
St. Catharines, Ontario
L2M 6Z2
CANADA

Weber, Phil
CIS:72451,3401

Webster, Eli
6106 N. Monticello
Chicago IL 60659

Wedergren, Kevin
PO Box 788
Shepherd TX 77371

Weidinger, Andreas
EDV Beratung Und
Entwicklung
Glashttenstrase 41
40627 Dusseldorf
GERMANY
+49-211-273-988
CIS:100416,2775

Weimar Software
18515 Annie Lane
San Jose, CA 95120-1006
408-268-6638
Fax:408-268-7655

Weiss, Thomas R.
CIS:75000,327

Wells, Terre
1901 Winners Circle
Lawrenceville GA 30243

Wessex Systems
108 Ensbury Park Rd.
Bournemouth, Dorset
BH9 2SL
UNITED KINGDOM
CIS:100112,2164
+44-0202-546466
Fax:+44-0202-535557

Westacott, Andrew
4 Crest Avenue
Pitsea, Basildon
Essex SS13 2EF
UK
CIS:100023,702
andywest@sound.demon.co.uk

Whiplash Software
2312 N. Marybrrok Drive #2
Plainfield IL 60544
CIS:74364,3406

WhippleWare
Att: Ben Whipple
20 Cedar St.
Charlestown MA
02129-2502
617-241-2992
800-241-8727
Fax:617-241-8496
CIS:72321,362

White, George M.
CIS:71511,1072

White, Wayne
AdvantEdge Computer
Consultant
2719 Pine Grove Court
Austell GA 30001
404-948-0711
CIS:70242,2742
waynew29@aol.com

Whittaker, Ross
CIS:100275,317

Whittlesley, Scott
96 Faneuil St.
Windsor CT 06095-4522

Wild Rose Software
Ralph, James Q.
2187 University Street
Eugene OR 97403-1543
541-342-6152
CIS:70713,2660
wild_rose@msn.com

Wildcat Software
1511 S. Pennsylvania St.
Denver CO 80210
303-733-3924

Wilkinson, Robert
Technocratix
2350 E. North Lane
Phoenix, AZ 85028
602-493-0196
Fax:602-992-2743
CIS:72730,3433

Williams, Charles
WIST Consulting
CIS:100334,677

Williams, Cris
8694 Debbie Kay Lane
Cordova TN 38018
Crisw@aol.com

Williams, Jeff
Microsoft Premier
Applications
jeffwill@microsoft.com

Williamson, Gary
CIS:70600,1751

Willits, Don
Withheld by request

Willy, C. Scott
AA-Software International
12 Ter Domaine Du Bois
Joli
06330 Roquefort-Les-Pins
FRANCE
33-93-77-50-47
Fax:33-93-77-19-78
CIS:100343,2570
cswilly@acm.org

Wilson, Michael
CIS:71261,63

Wiltbank, Lee
869 South 930 West
Payson UT 84651
CIS:71776,1274

**WinCorp Consulting
Company**
5211 Sapphire Street
Alta Loma CA 91701
909-900-7344
800-663-9775
CIS:71165,2426

WinWare
P.O.Box 2923
Mission Viejo, CA 92690
CIS:70272,1656
BBS:714-363-9802

WinWay Corporation
Attn:Erez Carmel
916-332-2671
CIS:70523,2574

Winchester Soft srl
Via del Duomo
3/C 67010
Coppito AQ
ITALY
Fax:1-39-862-314823

Windley, Jay
jaywindley@aol.com

WingedAxe Software, Inc.
829 Ninth Avenue Suite 3C
New York NY 10019
CIS:73764,3540

Winkelbach, Dirk
Reuenthalerstrabe 25 A
63937 Weilbach
GERMANY
Fax:+49-9373-99911
CIS:100270,3245

Winter, G. M.
44 Southfield Road
Pocklingtonork YO4 2XE
ENGLAND
CIS:100025,1056

Winworks Software Corp.
P.O. Box 859
El Dorado CA 95623-0859
CIS:74211,2503
querydef@winworks.com

Wogan, David
122 Chadwin Road
London E13 8NF
ENGLAND
CIS:100535,3235

Wolfebyte Ltd.
4925 Beverly Blvd. Suite 11
Los Angeles CA 90004
CIS:76742,1422

**Wonderful Computer
Services**
Melbourne
AUSTRALIA
CIS:100026,506

Wood, Raymond
UNITED KINGDOM
CIS:100037,37

Woodhouse, Mike
CIS:100023,604
CIS:73503,2522

Woodruff, Ben
158 Milstead Road
Newport News VA 23606
804-930-2039
CoHanDew@aol.com

Woodward, Kirk
People Centered Programs
PO Box 610171
Dallas, TX 75261-0171
800-553-5883
Fax:800-841-3137
CIS:70146,51

Woolfe, Jeremy
CIS:73663,3666

World Wide Development
7904 East Chapparel Road
Suite A110-222
Scottsdale AZ 85250
tomt@wwwdev.com

Wright Futures, Inc.
17781 NE 90th
Suite K-358
Redmond WA 98052

Wykes, Harry
CIS:100014,2573

XDev Inc.
+41-41-280-93-33
Fax:+41-41-280-05-33
CIS:74014,3204

XFrench
CIS:102251,3060
xfrench@aol.com

Xceed Software
345A De Gentilly Est
Longueuil QC J4H 1Y7
CANADA
514-442-2626
800-865-2626

Young, Ted
CIS:76703,4343

Yukish, Gary
c/o Microsoft
One Microsoft Way
Redmond WA 98052
CIS:72662,1616

Zanna, A.
Hauptstr. 41
71263 Merklingen
Weil derStadt
GERMANY
+49-7033-33800
zanna@multimedia.it

Zeitlin, Eli And Dani
Yeuda Ha-Nasi 6
93269 Jerusalem
ISRAEL
972-2-793-895
CIS:100274,1321
sts@datasrv.co.il

Zieglar, Adam
CIS:72147,2221

Zimmer Informatik
Postfach 14 05 40
D-40075 Duesseldorf
GERMANY
CIS:100276,3020

INDEX

J

Author

John Robert Onda - Program selection, collection and description. John Robert Onda is an independent computer and graphics specialist who has worked with all versions of Microsoft Basic Compiler, QuickBasic, Visual Basic, and Microsoft Access. He was one of the original designers of portions of America Online and its forerunner PC-Link. He has contributed articles to Computer Shopper, The Transactor, and MAD Magazine. He can be reached at 73765.1444@compuserve.com. Dedication: Because of A., B., C., H., K., L., M., P., V., and R. Thank you, JRO

Eric Engelmann - Database and HTML preparation. Eric Engelmann is the series editor, and has been architecting and compiling similar distributions for many years. Eric consults on a variety of Internet, CD-ROM, and publishing projects, for both small/local and large/international clients. Besides this Visual Basic Toolkit, Eric produces a number of other collections of programmer's software on CD-ROMs. He can be reached at eengelmann@advice.com.

Colophon

Our mission at ADVICE Press is to provide convenient value-added tools for craftsmen of a new age of human achievement — the programmers, software engineers and other technology professionals whose current work will have lasting impact for the years, decades and possibly even centuries to come. The Developer's Toolkit series is intended to ease the task of staying up to date allowing professionals to concentrate on creative implementation.

In keeping with this mission, the photo featured on the cover of *Visual Basic Developer's Toolkit* captures a moment in the four year construction of the Golden Gate Bridge in San Francisco. Since its construction, the bridge has become the single most identifiable feature of San Francisco. Designed by Joseph B. Strauss (1870 - 1938) to carry 160 million pounds on an open span of 4,260 feet, the bridge features an almost ideal balance of function and beauty.

The cover of this book was created by Sherrie Stinson of the Printed Image based on a design by Jerry Jager of Jager Communications.